"Mr. Hart has written a much-needed corrective to current dogma. He demonstrates that our freedoms, and the morality that sustains them, grew out of religious faith, and makes a strong case for the proposition that democracy without religion is not enough to guarantee liberty. I found *Faith and Freedom* a powerful and thought-provoking book."

ROBERT H. BORK
John M. Olin Scholar in Legal Studies,
American Enterprise Institute

"Ben Hart has written a rich book, systematically argued in a way that is sustained to the final page. *Faith and Freedom* makes an irrefutable case that the American political order cannot be explained apart from our original religious commitment as a people."

M.E. BRADFORD
Professor of American Studies, University of Dallas
Author, *A Better Guide Than Reason* and *A Worthy Company*

"Religious freedom is, in largest part, a religious achievement. Mr. Hart underscores that truth with lively narrative and forceful argument. In recent decades many Americans have been miseducated to believe that religious freedom, and most other freedoms, were historically secured against the forces of religion. Hart does not merely right the balance, he puts things back into their proper order, reminding us that, without 'unalienable rights' bestowed prior to the State, all rights are imperiled by the State."

RICHARD JOHN NEUHAUS
Director, The Center on Religion and Society
Author, *The Naked Public Square*

"WHERE THE SPIRIT OF THE LORD IS, THERE IS LIBERTY"
(2 Corinthians 3:17)

FAITH &
FREEDOM

THE CHRISTIAN ROOTS
OF AMERICAN LIBERTY

BENJAMIN HART

A publication of the
Christian Defense Fund

Library of Congress Cataloging-in-Publication Data
Hart, Benjamin.
Faith and Freedom

Bibliography: p.
Includes index.
1. United States-Caurch history-Colonial period, ca. 1600-1775.2. Puritans-United
States-History. 8. United States-History-Revolution, 1775-1783-Religious aspects.
4. liberty-Religious aspects-Christianity-History of doctrines-l8th century. 5.
Freedom (Theology)-History of doctrines - 18th century.
I. Title.

BR520.H334	1988	277.3'07	88-8258	
ISBN	0-929510-00-3		Cloth	
ISBN	0-929510-04-6		Paper	
ISBN	0-89840-239-5		Here's Life Publishers	

For my wife Betsy,
whose love, faith, and unwavering commitment
to individual liberty enabled me to complete this book.

A NOTE OF ACKNOWLEDGEMENT

I thank Stan Oakes of Christian Leadership Ministries, without whose encouragement and support this book would not have been written; American historians Forrest McDonald and M. E. Bradford, who provided wise counsel; my father Jeffrey Hart, mother-in-law Eloise Canileld, *and* editors Harry Crocker, Patti Culver, *and* Rebecca S. Cotton, who all meticulously combed the manuscript; Pamela Hallett, who managed the project, and Judy Chalmers and Donna Metcalf, who assisted with many of the details of production; my colleagues Ed Feulner, Phil Truluck, and Burt Pines of The Heritage Foundation, whose efforts have done so much to bring back freedom as an intellectually and morally defensible principle; and, most of all, my beloved wife Betsy, whose boundless enthusiasm for this project spurred me to begin writing every morning at 6 a.m. until the book was finished.

CONTENTS

CHAPTER ONE

WE HOLD THESE TRUTHS

When George Washington announced in the autumn of 1796 that he was stepping down as President, all of America was stunned. "How can you retreat?" an alarmed Alexander Hamilton asked the grey-haired legend. "How will our new nation survive without its leader?" cried editorials in newspapers across the countryside. Americans looked to the future with fear and trembling. The young nation was traveling into uncharted waters now. All were aware that the free and democratic society they had created was unique in world history.

Washington achieved legendary status early in life with his heroic exploits during the French and Indian War. He never sought fame however; in fact he spent all his adult years trying to shun the public life. But destiny always seemed to demand that he serve his country one more time. He had no desire to lead the Continental forces against the British in America's War of Independence, but Congress pleaded with him, saying there was no one else. So Washington sacrificed the private life he so cherished and accepted the daunting task-for which he refused financial compensation. He endured with his troops the winter at Valley Forge. After six years of war, and with the aid of the French fleet, he finally forced the surrender of the British General Charles Cornwallis at the Battle of Yorktown. Again, Washington hoped to retire; and again Congress informed him that only he could raise this new nation from its infancy.

Washington was the Electoral Colleges unanimous choice for President of the United States. He expected to serve only one term, but was told that if he did not serve a second this new republic would likely collapse. After eight years as President, Washington decided to retire for good, and no one could persuade him otherwise. For almost 40 years this American legend had been trying to return to the peace and privacy of Mount Vernon and his wife Martha. At age 64 he was getting old. His bones were weary. He may have sensed that he had only three more years remaining in this life. America would either have to stand on its own, or perish. He knew the pitfalls that awaited a nation without a strong leader. But he saw an even greater threat in a people becoming dependent on one man, a dependency that would tend to undermine the very principles of liberty for which they had struggled so long.

If this experiment in constitutional democracy were to succeed, Washington concluded, it would have to succeed without him. To run for a third term would be to turn the clock back and reestablish over the American nation a *de facto* monarchy, a prospect no one loathed more than Washington. He always placed principle above personal aggrandizement, which is a rarity in the annals of man. Because of this, the legacy he would leave would not be the usual one of tyranny and human misery-but one of political, economic, and religious liberty.

The United States of America is the freest, strongest, and most prosperous nation in human history. We owe this miraculous development in large part to the life of one man - his bravery in battle, his perseverance through hardships, his patience with those who opposed him, his wisdom while in power. What was astonishing about this gallant Virginian, who rode a white horse, was that he actually lived by the ideals of which he spoke. There were not many dry eyes in America when George Washington on September 17, 1796, announced his final farewell from public life. From this moment on, he said, the survival of freedom on American soil would have nothing to do with him, and everything to do with the character of its people and the government they would elect:

"Of all the dispositions and habits which lead to political prosperity, religion and morality are indispensable supports," he said. "In vain would that man claim the tribute of patriotism who should labor to subvert these great pillars of human happiness, these firmest props of the duties of men and citizens. The mere politician, equally with pious man, ought to respect and cherish them. A volume could not trace all the connections with private and public felicity. Let it simply be asked where is the security for property, for reputation, for life, if the sense of religious obligation desert the oaths, which are the instruments of investigation in Courts of Justice? And let us with caution indulge the supposition that morality can be maintained without religion. Whatever may be conceded to the influence of refined education on minds of peculiar structure, reason and experience both forbid us to expect that national morality can prevail in exclusion of religious principle." Washington knew well that a nation's laws spring from its morals and that its morals spring from its religion. And the religion of which Washington spoke was clear to all who knew him: "It is impossible to govern rightly without God and the Bible," he said.

In his essay "What I Saw in America," the great English writer G. K. Chesterton observed that "America is the only nation in the world that is founded on a creed. That creed is set forth with dogmatic and even theological lucidity in the Declaration of Independence." Chesterton was referring to the second paragraph of America's founding document which states: "We hold these truths to be self-evident, that all men are *created* equal, that they are endowed by their *Creator* with certain unalienable rights, that among these are life, liberty and the pursuit of happiness" (emphasis added). The starting point of the Declaration's argument was faith in man's "Creator," and is very similar to the Apostle Paul's initial proposition in his letter to the Romans:

"Because that which is known about God is evident within them; for God made it evident to them. For since the creation of the world His invisible attributes, His eternal power and divine nature, have been clearly seen, being understood through what has been made, so that they are without excuse" (Romans 1:19-20).

Thomas Jefferson was the primary author of the Declaration, and believed it was sufficient to assert certain transcendent truths as self-evident. To him God's existence was manifest in creation. Jefferson was not here talking about the God of Islam, faith in whom laid the foundation for a different kind of social order altogether. He meant the God of the Old and New Testaments. Whether Jefferson was himself a Christian is in dispute. But he understood the society in which he lived and who his audience was when he made the case for severing ties with Britain on the grounds that England had "violated the laws of nature and of nature's God."

There were no Moslems, Buddhists, Confucianists, or Hindus present at either the signing of the Declaration, or eleven years hence at the Constitutional Convention in Philadelphia. Jefferson was addressing Christians. His entire argument about people having "unalienable rights" is contingent on the existence of God, and One who cares deeply about each and every individual. As Jefferson asked rhetorically on another occasion: "Can the liberties of a nation be thought secure when we have removed their only firm basis, a conviction in the minds of the people that their liberties are the gift of God?"

With no higher lawgiver, the state becomes the highest moral authority, in which case rights are no longer "unalienable," but become subject to the whim of the monarch, dictator, assembly, or the vicissitudes of human fashion. Therefore, warns Paul in his letter to the Romans: "Let every person be in subjection to the governing authorities. For there is no authority except from God .. ." (Romans 13:1). "Unalienable" is another word for eternal, not subject to change under any circumstance. It implies that there are moral absolutes.

If the life of an individual amounts to no more than a brief flicker in history, then the perpetuation of the state, society, or empire becomes the overriding political concern. This was Hitler's philosophy, and it is the driving ideological force behind communism. Inherent in collectivist political systems is the idea that the interests of the individual must be subordinate to the supposed (and I stress the word "supposed") interests of the whole. We begin to hear phrases like "national purpose," "world government," and "social theory"-ideas completely at odds with what America's founding fathers had in mind.

But if, on the other hand, the span of civilizations amounts to less than a blink of an eye in comparison to the eternal life of a person, then the protection of God's most valued creation, the individual, becomes the primary function of government. Indeed, this was the fervent belief not only of Jefferson (who is often portrayed by historians, erroneously, as an agnostic) but also of all the major figures involved in the creation of the American Republic. George Washington was so eager to leave public life precisely because he did not believe in the final claim of the state. He believed in freedom. He had a Christian view of the sanctity of man and the immortality of the soul. Under the American political system, soul, mind, and body are to be free from human constraints to fulfill their destinies in this life and the next.

Even if one does not accept the truth of the Christian faith, prudence argues for the promulgation of its moral code in every area of public life, because history has demonstrated that Christian morality is indispensable to the preservation of a free society. Alexis de Tocqueville in the early part of the 19th century was commissioned by the French government to travel throughout the United States in order to discover the secret of the astounding success of this experiment in democracy. The French were puzzled at the conditions of unparalleled freedom and social tranquility that prevailed in America. Previously, it was thought that where there was liberty, anarchy would inevitably follow because of the inability of people to govern themselves. But in America people were free - and also well-behaved. In fact, nowhere on earth was there so little social discord. How could this be? This is what Tocqueville reported.

"I do not know whether all Americans have a sincere faith in their religion - for who can know the human heart? - but I am certain that they hold it to be indispensable for the maintenance of republican institutions. This opinion is not peculiar to a class of citizens or to a party, but it belongs to the whole rank of society." America, Tocqueville added, is "the place where the Christian religion has kept the greatest power over men's souls; and nothing better demonstrates how useful and natural it is to man, since the country where it now has the widest sway is both the most enlightened and the freest." John Quincy Adams, America's sixth President, acknowledged that from the begin-fling Americans "connected in one indissoluble band the principles of civil government with the principles of Christianity."

Unless law is anchored in moral absolutes, Supreme Court Justice John Marshall's statement that the government of the United States is a "government of laws and not men" makes no sense. If there is no consensus as to what constitutes the law, often called the "Higher Law," and where it can be found, then we are governed by men and not laws. The colonists believed that this "Higher Law" was a definite thing and could be found in a particular place, namely the Bible, under whose commandments all would be equally subjected: "The right of freedom being a gift of God Almighty, ... the rights of the colonists as Christians ... may be best understood by reading and carefully studying the institutes of the Great Law Giver ... which are to be found clearly written and promulgated in the New Testament," wrote Samuel Adams, the great revolutionary organizer, in his 1772 classic of political history, *The Rights of the Colonists*.

The notion of the "Higher Law" goes all the way back to Moses, when Yahweh[1] handed down His commandments to the people of Israel for their protection. God, through Moses, taught the Israelites how to live with each other, how to order their moral

---

1. The Hebrew name for God in the Old Testament.

lives and their community, and how to please Him. Mosaic Law taught restraint, and conveyed Yahweh's wishes on how His children were to treat their fellow human beings, whether in person or through the instrument of the state. Jesus broadened the covenant to include Gentiles as well. The new covenant is spelled out in very clear terms in the New Testament. The word "covenant" refers, in the Bible, to an unbreakable contract between God and man; it is an eternal and cosmic constitution that governs our relationship with the Creator.

As writer and constitutional scholar John Whitehead points out, the idea of the "Higher Law" is closely connected to "common law," a legal term referring to Christian principles adapted to the legal structure of civil life. The phrase first entered the vocabulary of English lawyers of the 12th century, after King John at Runnymede was forced by Pope Innocent III, English landowners, and the "Army of God" to sign England's first written constitution, designed mainly to protect property rights. *Magna Carta,* or the Great Charter, is filled with such phrases as: "The King himself ought not to be under a man but under God and under the law, because the law makes the king for there is no king where will governs and not law." And: "Know ye that we, in the presence of God, and for the salvation of our souls, and the souls of all our ancestors and heirs, and unto the honor of God and the advancement of Holy Church... have in the first place granted to God, and by this our present charter confirmed for us and our heirs forever."

The Continental Congress of the United States on October 14, 1774, issued its Declaration of Rights stating that the colonists of the several states were entitled to the protections of the common law of England. Everyone understood this as a reference to a legal tradition beginning five centuries earlier with *Magna Carta,* whose moral authority was firmly grounded in Christianity. Whitehead points out in *The Second American Revolution* that the phrase "common law" comes from jus *cornmune,* which was the canon law of the Catholic Church. "The usages of God's people

and the institutes of our forefathers are to be held for the law,"
wrote Augustine (354-430); and William Blackstone, the great
English legal theorist, rephrased the idea in 1765: "Upon these
two foundations, the law of nature and the law of Revelation[2],
depend all human laws," he wrote, articulating the common law
principle, which has been with us since Moses brought the tablets
down from Mount Sinai. Judges throughout English and
American history, following the common law tradition, have often
handed down decisions with explicit references to the Ten
Commandments. James Madison, known as the father of the
U.S. Constitution, put it this way: "We have staked the whole
future of the American civilization, not upon the power of government, far from it. We have staked the future... upon the
capacity of each and all of us to govern ourselves, to control ourselves, to sustain ourselves according to the Ten Commandments
of God."

Perhaps with some of this history in mind, the Kentucky
Legislature in 1978 thought it important that students understand the source of America's common law tradition and to make
the point that the preservation of freedom is a direct consequence
of our adherence to the "institutes of the Great Law Giver," as
Samuel Adams had said. Thus Kentucky required that the Ten
Commandments be posted in the public schools along with the
following statement: "The secular application of the Ten
Commandments is clearly seen in its adoption as the fundamental
legal code of Western civilization and the common law of the
United States."

But in 1980, the Supreme Court ruled that Kentucky's
decision to post the Ten Commandments in the public schools
was a violation of the First Amendment's clause forbidding the
establishment of religion. Thus, for public schools to teach the
true origin of America's common law heritage, which undergirds
the U.S. Constitution and which is specifically referred to in the
Seventh Amendment, is now deemed "unconstitutional." This
ruling followed the equally astounding decision in 1962 and 1963

2. The Bible.

banning all religious expression from the public schools. Already, many public schools, in order to follow the spirit of recent Supreme Court rulings, have replaced traditional Christmas programs with "Winter" festivals, and have stopped the singing of such traditional Christmas songs as "Silent Night" and "Joy to the World." This state of affairs bears no resemblance to what James Madison and Fisher Ames had in mind when they introduced the First Amendment, which was intended to guarantee "the free exercise" of religion, not obliterate religion.

The history of America's laws, its constitutional system, the reason for the American Revolution, or the basis of its guiding political philosophy cannot accurately be discussed without reference to its biblical roots. Every President, from George Washington to George Bush, has placed his hand on a Bible and asked for the protection of God upon taking office. Both Houses of Congress open each daily session with a prayer. The phrase "In God We Trust" is emblazoned on all U.S. currency. Witnesses are expected to swear on a Bible before testifying in a court of law. The Christian Sabbath is a national day of rest; many states restrict the sale of liquor and the operation of restaurants on the Lord's Day in order to encourage religious worship and time spent at home. A government official opens each day's session of the Supreme Court with the plea, "God save the United States and the Honorable Court." The Ten Commandments appear on the wall above the head of the Chief Justice in the Supreme Court; which is ironic when one considers that it is this very judicial body that declared it unconstitutional for states to do the same in the public schools. These laws and customs all have their origins in America's Christian past and provide a clue as to the assumptions guiding the creation of America's form of government, assumptions the founding fathers had about man's nature, his place in eternity, and the character of the God to whom he is accountable. It is these ultimate concerns that determine the shape of society.

Man can never escape his religious nature. Everyone holds a certain world-view. Atheists, such as Madalyn Murray O'Hair and Bertrand Russell, are every bit as religious as Francis of Assisi, John Wesley, and Mother Teresa of Calcutta. The atheist believes passionately, and hopes dearly, that God does not exist, that there is no life on the other side of the grave. The theist, specifically the Christian, believes with equal passion that God does exist and that one's choices here on earth have a bearing on one's eternal destiny. Neither faith can be proven definitively in the sense that a mathematical equation can be proven. But is is clear to anyone who has met Madalyn Murray O'Hair and Mother Teresa of Calcutta (I have met both of them) that their religious faiths have a direct effect on their behavior, their views of their fellow man, and their attitude toward life. Moreover, I would venture to guess that a government established under the direction of Mother Teresa would be far more pleasant and humane than one set up according to the prescriptions of Madalyn Murray O'Hair, and that even the atheist would prefer to live in a society governed by Mother Teresa.

Agnosticism is no less of a faith than Christianity or atheism. The agnostic does not know if God exists, but he is firmly convinced that if God exists, it makes no difference in his life. The agnostic's world-view is every bit as self-contained and closed as that of any other religion or ideology, and has a direct impact on the way he chooses to live and the kind of society he would establish.

In the minds of many Americans, to say that one is an agnostic is to suggest that one is tolerant, a moral relativist. Agnostics generally like to present themselves as relaxed and easygoing. America has become politically and culturally agnostic, and the Christian faith in the minds of many has come to represent intolerance. Cited as evidence is the Christian conviction that there are moral absolutes - a notion that sounds authoritarian and dogmatic, even to some Christians. The principle we are offered as a substitute is a fuzzy agnostic "pluralism."

Now pluralism in theory sounds appealing to almost anyone. The word connotes a non-confrontational, humane, alive

and-let-live attitude. But under the agnostic pluralistic regime in
practice we have seen quite the opposite. The Supreme Court's
abortion ruling, for example, with a stroke of the pen overturned
laws in all 50 states and millions of unborn babies have since
gone to the slaughter. The decision states explicitly that religious
belief can have no bearing on how we determine when human
life begins. But, in the name of pluralism and tolerance, why
not? Even William O. Douglas, one of the most liberal Supreme
Court justices in history, admitted that "we are a religious people
whose institutions presuppose a supreme being." Since man,
left to his own devices, has not provided a satisfactory refutation
of the biblical position that life begins at conception,[3] why shouldn't
our laws also adopt that position rather than run the risk that
as a society we are condoning mass murder? Should we not err
on the side of caution and protect life until it is proven definitively that there is no life in the womb?

The answer is that agnostic pluralism logically excludes
moral absolutes. Such assertions as "thou shalt not steal," "thou
shalt not commit adultery," and even "thou shalt not murder" are
open to debate and are adjusted to suit the "needs of the times."
Agnostic pluralism releases man from the constraints placed on
him by God, and absolutizes "man as the measure of all things,"
as Protagoras put it. Thus, it becomes up to the in dividuai or a
court to determine when life begins and whether or not it deserves
protection. Proponents of so-called pluralism feel compelled to
ban religious considerations from public discourse because they
know, instinctively if not intellectually, that their faith is in direct
conflict with the God of the Bible, and that in the end the two
positions are irreconcilable.

All gods require submission: either we will submit to the
God of Scripture, immutable and unchanging, or we will submit
to the ever-shifting god of human convenience. Agnostic pluralism, too, is a jealous god. It is a militant philosophy, a closed
system that in the end cannot tolerate other creeds. Thus, when
a minister or a clergyman takes seriously unfashionable Christian

---

3. "For Thous didst form my inward parts; Thou didst weave me in my mother's
womd" (Psalm 139:13). No distinction is made in Scripture between babies in
the womb and those already born. See Luke 1:41,44 and Luke 18:15-17 for
comparison.

doctrines which condemn sex outside marriage, homosexuality, abortion, and feminism, and injects his views into the political debate, he is immediately denounced as a "reactionary." Indeed, he can count on being the victim of a character smear campaign by Planned Parenthood, the American Civil Liberties Union, People for the American Way, and various abortion rights and gay groups, whose complaints are given ample air time in the national media. Their attacks on religion are often hysterical, and their approach bears no resemblance to the tolerant, pluralistic society they purport to promote.

The problem with the word *pluralism* is that it is misleading. There really is no such thing. Our society, for example, does not accept polygamy as a legitimate way to live because it is anti-biblical and, therefore, counter to the American tradition.[4] Moreover, there are many things our culture tolerates, but does not condone. We tolerate homosexuality, but do not condone it. We don't live that way here, and the fact that we don't is a reflection of our understanding of right and wrong. We tolerate promiscuous lifestyles, but don't condone them. There are those crusading under the banner of pluralism, however, who are not satisfied that we put up with adultery; we must endorse it, promote it as liberating. And not only is abortion a constitutional right, but it must also be financed by the taxpayers, even by taxpayers who believe doctors who perform abortions are the moral equivalent of Joseph Mengele. Georgetown University, a Catholic school, lost a lawsuit to a group of homosexual militants because it refused to subsidize a gay student organization. Thus we get the feeling that something more than "pluralism" is being foisted upon us.

Pluralism is a loaded word, intended to tip the scales against a certain kind of absolute it does not like, specifically that embodied in the Judeo-Christian moral code. In place of the old morality, we will get the new morality-one that's more relevant-namely that "nothing is real except our world of desires and passions," as Friedrich Nietzsche phrased it in his book *Beyond Good*

---

5. Jesus claims to be God: John 8:58, 10:27-30; 14:9.

and Evil. Formally, this philosophy is not called pluralism, but secular humanism. The problem Christians have with secular humanism is not that it is truly pluralistic, but that it subjects man to the sentimentality and enthusiasms of the moment. Indeed, history has shown that secular humanism - the view that man is the sole judge of the world, including morality, the shape of society, and the value of the individual - is very bad for humanity.

In the American context, the secular humanist philosophy was illustrated well in statements by two senior Supreme Court justices, Thurgood Marshall and William Brennan. "A too literal quest for the advice of the founding fathers seems to me futile and misdirected," said Brennan in 1963. "I do not believe that the meaning of the Constitution was forever fixed at the Philadelphia convention," added Marshall in May 1987. "Nor do I find the wisdom, foresight and sense of justice exhibited by the framers particularly profound. To the contrary, the government they devised was defective from the start." As a consequence of this judicial philosophy, a Supreme Court ruling in recent decades has become like a lottery. Says Justice Antonin Scalia, the Court is "in a state of utter chaos and confusion."

Under the Marshall and Brennan view of the law, political power rather than "nature's God" (Jefferson's phrase) becomes the sole arbiter of the law of the land, and this conforms precisely to the framers' definition of tyranny. The First Amendment, established for the purpose of protecting free expression and the free exercise of religion, can be turned on its head to make the utterance of a prayer and the posting of the Ten Commandments in a public school a criminal offense. What at another time would be thought unthinkable can quickly become the governing philosophy of a nation. The progressive income tax, for example, now taken for granted, would have been considered in George Washington's day an egregious violation of the constitutional guarantee of "equal protection under the laws." What was once illegal can in an instant become a constitutional right, which can

in turn be reversed overnight. Under such a regime, political disputes rapidly become more violent, as we saw in the ferocious
and dishonest attacks launched by Senator Edward Kennedy
against conservative Supreme Court nominee Robert Bork.
Secular humanism at its core is materialistic, situational, and a
matter of individual and social convenience. The law under the
secular humanist approach becomes pliable, like "Silly Putty," to
be molded by the impulses of those in power, whether this power
happens to be a dictator in the mold of Joseph Stalin, or the nine
people in black robes who preside over America's highest court.

At present, secular humanism in America is still held in
check by a Christian tradition, though much faded. We have
heard often the assertion that Jesus was a good moral teacher,
but nothing more. (How reliable a moral teacher can He be if He
lied about who He was?)[5] Even the most trendy secular humanist
in America wants to preserve some aspects of the moral code
handed down from Mount Sinai and the Sermon on the Mount.
But as the string connecting public policy with America's Christian
past becomes longer and longer, and eventually snaps altogether,
the New Testament God will not be replaced by nothing. Man is
a spiritual being; when one faith is eliminated, a new god will
rush in to fill the spiritual void. Throughout history, this has
been a man-made god called the state.

In just a few short years the public sector has ballooned
so that it now consumes about one-third of the entire U.S.
economy-and most of this has occurred since the ban on prayer
in public schools in 1962-63. It's not surprising that a people who
would permit the government to outlaw God from a major part
of life would simultaneously acquiesce in the submerging of other
rights, once thought "unalienable." For if God becomes irrelevant to the public life of a nation, then no freedoms are truly
sacred. "Where the Spirit of the Lord is, there is liberty," the
Apostle Paul says in his second *letter* to the Corinthians (3:17).
"We must obey God rather than men!" the Apostle Peter warns
emphatically in the Book of Acts (5:29).

Alexis de Tocqueville foresaw the likely consequences of permitting the erosion of America's moral foundations, and predicted that if this occurred, we would see the rise of a new form of despotism, unique to democratic societies; over its people, he wrote, will stand "an immense, protective power which is alone responsible for securing their enjoyment and watching over their fate ... it gladly works for their happiness but wants to be the sole agent and judge of it. It provides for their security, foresees and supplies their necessities, facilitates their pleasures, manages their principal concerns, directs their industry, makes rules for their testaments, and divides their inheritances... Thus it daily makes the exercise of free choice less useful and more rare, restricts the activity of free will within a more narrow compass, and little by little robs each citizen of the proper use of his own faculties."

Responsibility for one's actions and the ability to choose one's destiny is an essential component of both the American dream and the Christian faith. There is no virtue in being forced by other men, who are all equal in God's eyes, to make sacrifices. The virtue is in freely choosing the right course of action. But as Americans increasingly permit the state to make decisions on their behalf-to be the sole judge of "compassion" (a buzz word for a new government program) - it is not surprising that Americans also begin to lose their moral bearings, culminating in complete confusion over what constitutes right and wrong.

There is a myth aggressively promoted in modern American society that to be released from "the chains of religious obligation" is to achieve liberation for the individual, sometimes called "self-realization" or "self-fulfillment." As writer Joseph Sobran notes, we are continuously reminded in history classes of the sins of Christianity-the Crusades, the Spanish Inquisition, the Salem witch trials - as if these episodes represent the essence of Christianity. In fact, they only prove the reality of original sin and the corruption of human nature, which is a central doctrine of both the Old and New Testaments. The lesson we are supposed to learn from focusing on the worst moments in Christian history is that as faith faded more and more into the background, man was able to free himself from bondage. But the opposite is, in fact, the case. As a substitute for religious obligation, we have found our fates increasingly sealed by the decisions of faceless bureaucrats, Internal Revenue Service tax auditors, and unelected Supreme Court justices. Government has crept its way into almost every aspect of human existence, making decisions for individuals and consuming resources in ways not at all envisioned by the framers of our constitution.

Tocqueville warned of the threat to liberty posed by this ever-expanding paternalistic power, covering "the whole range of social life with a network of petty, complicated rules. . . through which even men of the greatest originality and most vigorous temperament cannot force their heads above the crowd. It does not break man's will, but softens, bends and guides it; it seldom enjoins, but often inhibits action; it does not destroy anything, but prevents much from being born."

If unchecked, the state will inexorably set itself up as the absolute authority in all areas of life, beyond which there can be no appeal. The law becomes whatever suits those who hold the levers of power, who proceed unrestricted even by their own consciences. Expedience becomes the final standard by which all is judged. If we continue down this path, we will have only ourselves to blame. By behaving like goats, we have started thinking like goats; and by abdicating responsibilities, Americans have gone a long way towards surrendering their freedoms. "No private rights are of such little importance," warned Tocqueville, "that they can safely be left subject to arbitrary decisions." The erosion of our constitutional protections, he wrote, "deeply corrupts the mores of a nation and puts the whole society in danger, because the very idea of right tends constantly among us to become impaired and lost."

America's founding fathers understood very well the principle that faith and freedom go together, and that one cannot survive long without the other. Daniel Webster, the great statesman, lawyer, and orator of the early days of the Republic, in a speech delivered on December 22, 1820, at Plymouth, Massachusetts, in celebration of the Pilgrim landing at Plymouth Rock, underscored this point: "Finally, let us not forget the religious character of our origin," said Webster. "Our fathers were brought hither by their high veneration for the Christian religion. They journeyed by its light and labored in its hope. They sought to incorporate its principles with the elements of their society and to diffuse its influence through all their institutions, civil, political, or literary. Let us cherish these sentiments, and extend this influence still more widely, in the full conviction that that is the happiest society which partakes in the highest degree of the mild and peaceful spirit of Christianity."

It is not surprising, therefore, that the enemies of liberty very often first attack the religious institutions of a nation. The Romans brutally persecuted the early Christians because they were seen as a political threat. It being counter to Christian teaching to worship false gods, Christians refused to acknowledge Caesar as god-man, and proclaimed instead Christ to be the God-Man who ruled even Caesar. When the Pharisees attempted to trap Jesus into denying Caesar's authority, Jesus answered: "Then render to Caesar the things that are Caesar's; and to God the things that are God's" (Matt. 22:21). What Jesus meant here was that Caesar's authority was negligible when measured against God's. He was de-sanctifying the state, a point that was certainly not lost on Caesar.

In communist countries today, Christians and Jews are the first to feel the wrath of the state. The Bible is viewed as subversive and, therefore, outlawed reading by the Marxist god of dialectical materialism. Priests, ministers, and rabbis are routinely jailed as inherently threatening to the underlying premise of the totalitarian state. Secular ideologies take many forms: Marxism, Nazism, Socialism, and various forms of collectivism. All are incompatible with the God of the Bible because all end in the rule of man over man, with the aid of an enormous governing apparatus attempting to squeeze human nature into unnatural shapes. That those in America who are always promoting a larger state role in the lives of the people tend to be the same ones who shriek about Christian involvement in politics is no accident; for they have placed their faith in a different god.

Liberty is under attack in all quarters of existence; in brutal fashion by totalitarian powers abroad, and in more subtle ways by an ever-expanding bureaucratic welfare state here at home. Our situation in fact is similar to that of the colonists when they decided to stand firm on first principles and declare their independence from British rule. What is needed today is less of a revolution than a reformation in American thinking, a sweeping away of the intellectual debris that now hides America's past.

There has been a concentrated attempt in American academic circles to recast the Christian-based American Revolution in the image of the virulently anti-Christian French Revolution, which predictably ended in tyranny. Liberation of the individual was not an idea of the *philosophes;* it was a Christian idea, and specifically a Reformation idea, as America was settled overwhelmingly by fundamentalist Protestants. The Mayflower Compact, signed by the Pilgrims in 1620, is proof that the "social compact" was a blueprint for government enacted by Christians long before thinkers of the Enlightenment claimed to have arrived at the notion through human "reason." Separation of church and state was not a reaction against religion, but a reaction against the state; and it was not introduced by skeptics, but by Protestants largely for religious reasons. The revisionist pens of such 20th-century historians as Charles Beard, Henry Steele Commager, Gary Wills, and the standard textbook writers have gone a long way toward altering America's heritage to conform to an agnostic, secular humanist creed. "To destroy a people you must first sever their roots," wrote Alexander Solzhenitsyn. The plan of this book is to correct the many popular misconceptions about America's past, repair the damage inflicted on our nation's heritage by the liberal history lesson, and to tell the true story of the unfolding of an idea we often take for granted - the idea of liberty. Our mission as citizens is to rediscover exactly how it is we came to be Americans so that we will understand exactly what is required to remain Americans.

CHAPTER TWO

STATECRAFT IS NOT SOULCRAFT

For Christians to ever hope for the establishment of Christianity as the official state religion is a very serious mistake. Men like Thomas Jefferson and James Madison understood this point well, which is why they worked so hard for the disestablishment of the Anglican Church in Virginia. Christians should not look back with nostalgia on the age of Christendom, when church and state were a unified whole. I would strongly disagree with the thesis of George Will; statecraft is not "soulcraft." The role of the state, in essence, is to curb violent behavior, not pry into people's hearts. In one's zeal to convert, one is sometimes tempted to use the coercive arm of government to compel the unconvinced. This is easier than painstakingly taking a skeptic through the Scriptures and arguments. But Jesus and the Apostles sought converts through persuasion, not force. Indeed, history has demonstrated repeatedly that whenever the state involves itself in church business and, conversely, whenever the church has behaved as an arm of government, Christianity- or "soulcraft" - has suffered grievously.

To correctly put in perspective the contribution of Christianity to the emergence of free and democratic institutions in America, we must look briefly at the classical world. In important respects, America's federalist political order was patterned after the loose confederation of self-governing local churches of the first century. Indeed, apostolic Christianity planted the seeds of separation of church and state, so essential to a free society. But the conversion of the emperor Constantine, with his marriage of church and state, began very early the corruption of the original Christian spirit. When the Pilgrims landed on Plymouth Rock in 1620, the primary mission was to escape Constantine's legacy (as it played itself out through the Middle Ages and Renaissance) and return to the pristine Christianity of the Book of Acts, free of the concerns of power politics and other worldly mixtures. In fact, this was a major aim of the great majority of early American colonists, especially the New England settlers, who saw the New World as an opportunity to fulfill the aspirations of the Protestant Reformation.

Christianity spread most rapidly not when it was allied with the state, but when it was pitted against the state, indeed when society was officially pagan. Christ and the Apostles did not rely on human institutions to spread their message, but put their trust in the message itself. At its beginning, Christianity was pure gospel; voluntary, informal congregations of believers provided its only institutional support. Affection, commonality of purpose, and above all, the power of Christ's message of salvation-not coercion-were the forces that drew them together.

The churches of the first two centuries were distinct communities of their own that existed either within or apart from Roman society, depending on political conditions. Early Christianity was federalist in structure and was therefore flexible. It could survive brutal persecution and it could penetrate, almost unnoticed, every segment of society, and won converts from the ranks of slaves on up through the ruling class and intellectual community. During the first and second centuries we read about "the rage of the heathen," the severed heads of Christians displayed on the road sides, and the famous scenes in the Colosseum where Christians were torn apart by wild beasts. Historian Paul Johnson recounts an incident in which one Christian lady, Blandina, was "tortured from dawn till evening, till her torturers were exhausted and... marvelled that the breath was still in her body." She was whipped, roasted in a frying pan, and then thrown in with wild bulls which tore her to pieces. But Christianity was

incredibly resilient, and converted the empire, in part by display-
ing courage rarely seen.

    Jesus told his disciples that the meek shall inherit the
earth, and Christianity continued to spread. While it seemed to
be losing politically, it was winning hearts and minds. Indeed,
the fact that it was so institutionally loose made it impossible for
the pagan state to control. The society of believers in Christ was
a little republic within an empire - similar in many respects to
the Sons of Liberty, an underground organization that was thriving
apart from official control on the eve of the American Revolution.
The Christian influence seemed to be everywhere, but could not
be confronted by the Roman army at any particular location.

    The Christianity of Scripture is decidedly anti-institu-
tional. We read in the Book of Acts, for example, that the society
of believers continued "breaking bread from house to house" and
"taking their meals together with gladness and sincerity of heart,"
and that "the Lord was adding to their number day by day those
who were being saved" (Acts 2:46-47). Nowhere in the New
Testament were the Apostles called to establish the institution
of the papacy - or any central church authority whatsoever. "Pope,"
which means father, was used as a term of affection in the third
century in reference to bishops of the various cities, but was not
applied exclusively to the Bishop of Rome until the fifth century.
While Jesus clearly accords Peter special significance, and his
name is at the top of lists of the Apostles throughout the Gospels,
there is no Scriptural evidence that he was to be the sole head of
the church, no indication that he was to have papal successors,
and it is certainly never suggested that such successors were to
have specially ordained spiritual powers. After Jesus, Paul was
actually the dominant figure in the New Testament. Peter's name
fades from Luke's Acts of the Apostles halfway through. In his
two letters, addressed "to those who reside as aliens, scattered
throughout Pontus, Galatia, Cappadocia, Asia, and Bithynia,"
Peter calls himself merely "an Apostle of Jesus Christ" and "bond-
servant." In the New Testament we read about the saints of

Philippi, the "seven churches of Asia," the Thessalonian churches, the churches of Galatia, and what appear to be an unorganized brotherhood of believers in Rome. The Colossians seem to have the seeds of a church structure, but it is not connected to any other overarching institutional authority.

We are told throughout the New Testament that Christians are to evangelize and bring the message of eternal life to the world. The church is a place for fellowship, refuge, and communion. Nowhere is it suggested that we are to organize churches under episcopates and dioceses, and nowhere is it indicated that a bishop is to preside over the affairs of all the churches, or even a number of them. The New Testament gives us some guidelines, but no formula for organizing houses of religious worship. The term "Church Militant," seen in much medieval literature portraying the Christian role of punishing non-believers and compelling religious conformity, is clearly counter to the Christian spirit seen in Scripture. That Christ intended to establish a formal universal church structure seems at best doubtful; that He intended it to be a militant organization is most definitely not the case. Obviously, Christ, as God, had the power to compel belief if He had so desired. The fact that He chose preaching as the means of spreading faith, and implored His followers to do the same, suggests the nature of the church He had in mind.

Throughout the Old Testament, God often treats the Israelites, those within the covenant, with severity; the same holds true in the New Testament, with Jesus and Paul directing some of their most virulent language toward Christians. But we are constantly exhorted to treat non-believers with kindness: "The Lord's bond-servant must not be quarrelsome, but be kind to all, able to teach, patient when wronged, with gentleness correcting those who are in opposition" (2 Tim. 2:24-25); "Endure hardship, do the work of an evangelist, fulfill your ministry" (2 Tim. 4:5). And throughout the Old Testament, the Israelites are commanded to take special care to recognize the freedom of those outside God's covenant, the unchosen. In Exodus, for ex-ample, we are told that "the same law shall apply to the native as to the stranger who sojourns among you" (v.12:49). In Numbers, the Jews are warned: "You shall have one statute, both for the alien and for the native of the land" (v.9:14). And Christ is even more emphatic on this point: "Blessed are the merciful, for they shall receive mercy" (Matt. 5:7).

There are many passages in the New Testament which tell us how God wants us to treat our neighbors. The following is a partial list of such passages which contain the phrase "one another":

Romans 12:10	Be devoted to one another.
Romans 13:8	Be devoted to one another.
Romans 14:13	Let us not judge one another
Romans 15:7	Accept one another.
Ephesians 4:2	Show forbearance to one another.
Colossians 8:12	Bear with one another.
Hebrews 8:13	Encourage one another.
James 4:11	Do not speak against one another.
1 Peter4:9	Be hospitable to one another.
1 John 3:11	Love one another.
1 John 3:23	Love one another.
1 John4:7	Love one another.
1 John 4:11	Love one another.
1 John 4:12	Love one another.
2 John 5	Love one another.

Christianity has been the most successful creed in human history at fostering a sense of civility, without which a free society cannot stand. The community suggested here is not geographical, but is held together by a sense of Christian love and respect for "one another," whether or not they are part of the faithful. Nowhere in the New Testament is it remotely suggested that Christians employ the resources of the state to compel belief or force religious conformity. To do so, in fact, makes no sense, since the New Testament aims not at changing behavior, but at changing hearts. Jesus promises that "whoever drinks of the water that I shall give him shall never thirst" (John 4:14). But it is up to the individual person to drink. Jesus compels no one to do so.

The Roman empire in many ways was the archetype of the pluralistic society. It tolerated, and indeed sanctioned, hundreds of religious cults. There were sun worshippers, and the cult of Attis and Cybele with their eunuch priests and ritual fasting and bloodletting. The Hilaria resurrection feast on March 25 of every year was very popular. All faiths were tolerated, including those that involved idol worship and orgies. Religion, no matter how peculiar, was considered good for society in that it provided cohesion and purpose in the lives of the people. At first, the Romans considered Christianity just another cult. The attacks on Christians were usually confined to local regions during the first century and a half. But at the end of the second century the persecution of Christians achieved imperial proportions. In the year 200 A.D. the great Christian apologist Tertullian described their cruel deaths in the circus, the beheading of the Bishop Cyprian, and the drenching of the soil with Christian blood. Tertullian wrote with stunned amazement that Christians-who were among the most law-abiding citizens, who paid their taxes, and who made the best soldiers - were suddenly being treated as dangerous criminals:

> We respect in the emperors the ordinance of God, who has set them over the nations. We know that there is that in them which God has willed; and to what God has willed we desire all safety, and we count an oath by it a great oath . . . On valid grounds, I might say Caesar is more ours than yours, for our God has appointed him.

Thus, not only was Tertullian willing to live under pagan government, he acknowledged Caesar as a legitimate ruler, even over Christians: "We are forever making intercession for the emperors. We pray for them a long life, a secure rule, a safe home, brave armies, a faithful senate, an honest people, a quiet world, and everything for which man and Caesar might pray," wrote Tertullian. "We know that the great force which threatens the whole world, the end of the age itself with its menace of hideous sufferings is delayed by the respite which the Roman empire means for us." What more could Caesar ask for?

A clue can be found by examining the coins during the time of Caesar Augustus which proclaim him divine savior and king, and Rome as eternal. Augustus often made the assertion that the foundations "I have laid will be permanent." The Roman college of priests, as part of a purification ritual, distributed incense to the people, and citizens ceremoniously made offerings to the emperor-god. But to Tertullian, Caesar was just a man whom Christians *chose* to obey. Moreover, Tertullian wrote, "If he is but a man, it is in his interest as man to give God His higher place. Let him think it enough to bear the name of emperor. That, too, is a great name of God's giving. To call him god is to rob him of his title. If he is not a man, emperor he could not be."

With these kinds of statements, Christianity declared war on the pagan idea of the state, not a war over territory but for the soul of the empire. And by the turn of the second century it had become clear that paganism was losing. Tertullian points out how quickly an unarmed Christian faith was able to overwhelm Caesar: "We are but of yesterday, and we fill everything you have - cities, tenements, forts, towns, exchanges, yes! and camps, tribes, palace, senate, forum. All we leave you with are the temples!" Tertullian was saying, in effect, that we will give Caesar his due, but not divine status.

In an environment of religious toleration, paganism was doomed - which is why in the end it could not afford to be truly pluralistic. Some parallels can be drawn here with modern secular education's hostile attitude toward Christians, who tend to be the best students, the most orderly and well-behaved. Disrespectful and anti-social behavior is tolerated on school grounds, but not prayers or religious expression, especially if the content is Christian. The state education establishment knows very well that to acknowledge that the Ten Commandments have validity-that they are in fact commandments and not suggestions - is to annihilate the ever-shifting foundations upon which civil humanist society stands. Similarly, paganism saw quite clearly that its only hope for survival was brutal repression. Under the doctrine of religious toleration, all religions were to be absorbed into the Roman state; instead, the Roman state was being absorbed into Christianity. It did not matter that Christians were law-abiding and peaceful, because they were destroying a weak civil religion intellectually, spiritually, and culturally with a living faith that defied human institutional constraints. The influence of Christianity appealed first to the poor and uneducated, but then moved up through the social classes. Often slaves converted their masters; a stream of apologetics by the Christian theologian Origen, who wrote some 6,000 tracts, won over large segments of the intellectual community.

By the beginning of the fourth century, the last obstacle to total Christian victory was Caesar himself. Galerius was crowned emperor in 305. He was motivated by a straightforward hatred of Christianity. As Paul Johnson recounts in his *History of Christianity,* edicts came forward requiring the burning of all churches and the arresting of all church leaders: priests and dea-cons, along with their dependents, were condemned to prison or death without any proof or confession. Certificates were required of all citizens proving they had paid homage to the pagan gods, and those who refused were tortured until they did so. Christianity, however, seemed to spread more rapidly as the persecution inten-sified. Suddenly Galerius had a change of heart. Perhaps he had made a shrewd calculation that imperial Rome, even with all its armies, had little hope of success against this unarmed faith. According to the pagan convert Lactanius, in his book *On the Deaths of the Persecutors,* Galerius greatly admired the fortitude of the martyrs, many of whom went to their deaths singing praises to God. There is evidence that suggests he may have converted. But whatever the precise reason, Galerius decided to call off the persecution, and permitted the Christians to restore their churches and to worship their own God. He asked only that they also pray for the safety and well-being of the empire. Christianity could not be eradicated; so it was accepted - and in fact became the new civil religion.

Constantine was crowned emperor on October 28, 312 A.D., and that event would change dramatically the character of Christianity. His Edict of Milan, in 313, granted "both to Christians and to all men freedom to follow whatever religion each one wishes, in order that whatever divinity there is in the seat of heaven may be appeased and made propitious towards us and towards all who have been set under our power." In some ways, this was landmark for the cause of religious liberty. But the pervasive nature of the Roman state made true religious liberty impossible. The old civil religion, paganism, had proved inadequate as a means of social control, and so the state gradually tilted in the direction of Christianity.

Constantine made very public his conversion to Christianity, though it is unclear whether his conversion was genuine or just pragmatic. There is little evidence, for example, that his faith changed his behavior in any way. After his conversion he committed several murders, including the killing of his wife and son. He also had his sister's son flogged to death and his sister's husband strangled. It seems that Constantine merely saw the value of Christianity in achieving his chief political aim, which was imperial unity.

Christianity, to Constantine, was a more effective social glue than paganism. Moreover, bishops proved exceedingly valuable as political aides; and many bishops, enticed by the splendor of the court, returned Constantine's favors by lauding him as an angel of God and a sacred being. This theme was reinforced by embellishments, on the part of both the emperor and the church, of Constantine's vision of the Cross prior to his victory at the

Battle of Milvian Bridge, when, according to legend, he was commanded by God, "In this sigu conquer." That the God of the New Testament would issue such a command seems remote. The Catholic Church of today admits that the episode is probably fiction. What is clear is that the story served the purposes of both the state and the institutional church; it helped to re-divinize the Roman emperor along Christian lines, thus enhancing the grandeur of Constantine as well as elevating the status of the Catholic Church. Constantine began subsidizing the Christian churches lavishly out of the treasury and became involved in the appointment of bishops. He was never much interested in theology. But he presided over Church councils anyway, and agreed to suppress any opinions the majority thought divisive.

Constantine is the first person on record to speak of the clergy as a distinct class of people with special spiritual powers. Bishops and priests also acquired secular duties, and anticlericalism soon became a major movement within Christianity. The historian Arminius in 366 wrote that the bishops of Rome had become "enriched by offerings from married women, riding in carriages, dressing splendidly, feasting luxuriantly - their banquets are better than imperial ones." And a council, held at Sardica in the Balkans, expressed alarm at how the Church, now favored by the state, was attracting the politically ambitious rather than men of God: "All are aflame with the fires of greed, and are slaves of ambition," the council lamented.

Most alarming was Constantine's tendency to try and mix what he thought was the best of paganism with the best of Christianity. In the dedication of Constantinople, for example, a ceremony that was part pagan and part Christian was used. Coins minted by Constantine featured the Cross, but also the pagan gods, Mars and Apollo. He continued to cali on the pagan gods to cure disease and ensure a good crop. Doctrinal purity was less important to the emperor than having a religion that was inclusive, accepting the widest range of religious practice possible. The result was a perversion of the Christian teachings of the

Bible.

Many Christians saw a grave danger in Christianity achieving official status and becoming the legally favored creed. The Church was unrecognizable from the days prior to Constantine's edict, when it was impoverished-as Christians were not protected by the law, or permitted to own property. But at least the faith was pure. Seeing the new Church as nothing more than a corrupt human institution of ambitious men, Christians by the thousands followed the example of Anthony and went into the Egyptian desert to live lives of radical poverty and chastity. A number of Christian writers denounced the new splendor of their religious establishments: "Our walls glitter with gold," wrote Jerome, "and the gold gleams upon our ceilings and the capitals of our pillars; yet Christ is dying at our doors in the person of His poor, naked and hungry." Jerome recognized that as the Church had become increasingly enmeshed in the affairs of state and high society, it had lost its moral authority. Christianity under Constantine had become hierarchical, full of pomp, pageantry, and ritual. No longer was the priesthood made up of "all believers"; instead the clergy had become an elite corps, distinct from the laity, with special spiritual powers of its own. In 380, the emperor Theodosius repealed Constantine's statement of religious freedom, and established Christianity as the official church of the empire. All who dissented, Theodosius announced, would be punished "in accordance with the celestial will." The martyrs had become the Inquisitors, a development that was clearly anti-Scriptural and which turned out to be a catastrophe for both Christianity and progress toward civil liberty.

The church-state marriage necessarily perverted both church and state. Man on his own is both corrupt and violent by nature, which is why the centralization of power also compounds the human tendency toward brutality and perversion. Lord Acton's dictum, "Power corrupts and absolute power corrupts absolutely," applies equally to church and state. Whether one talks about a priest or a king makes little difference, since both are equally human and subject to original sin. The corruption inherent in man's nature is magnified when it is transferred to human institutions. A man with a gang is far more dangerous than a man without a gang. With this view of man in mind, America's founders sought to decentralize political authority, through the separation of powers, states' rights, executive veto, judicial review of legislation, specifically enumerated governmental responsibilities, and all the various checks and balances that were instituted to prevent government from dominating all of human life.

Another problem with centralization is that it creates rigidity and institutionalizes its mistakes. For this reason, a society administered by a central government is a weak society. The tendency of those in authority is always to unify, simplify, and universalize. This is what happened to Rome and, as a result, Rome disappeared. The Roman empire was at its healthiest when - mostly because it did not have the resources to manage all its territories - it permitted a certain amount of autonomy, and ideas were able to flow relatively freely. Tribal customs and barriers of speech were overcome, not chiefly by force, but because Roman civilization had something attractive to offer people; most importantly the protection of Roman laws.

Rome grew weak, however, not by allowing freedom and local autonomy, but when it tightened administrative controls, imposed uniform standards, and became rigid in structure. Rome was never a representative government; it was always administered by prefects and generals from Rome, figures such as Pontius Pilate. But there was still a healthy local political life. As community decisions were increasingly made from Rome, the internal strength of the empire evaporated. Despots increased their personal authority at the expense of local leaders. The empire became a hollow shell eventually falling to pieces, collapsing under its own weight. As Rome grew more tyrannical, it became more fragile. Freedom, self-government, and local rule is the lifeblood of civilization, as James Madison pointed out repeatedly in *The Federalist*. Federalism - meaning a loose confederation of many small governments and communities-permits civilization to extend indefinitely over territory, which is exactly the principle behind the establishment of America's federalist republic.

Central authority, by contrast, can work only over a limited area, since its power becomes diluted the farther one travels from its source. Indeed, Mao Tse-Tung once remarked that he had little control over events more than about 20 miles outside Peking. Although Mao was able to kill 60 million of his own people, his influence on China's destiny will be less than was George Washington's on the future of America. The same idea holds true for the influence of Christianity. The Church, after Constantine, adopted Roman methods of rule, and began to see the state as an ally. Instead of proselytizing to make converts, it began an attempt to force belief.

CHAPTER THREE

AUGUSTINE'S MISTAKE

Constantine laid the institutional foundation for unifying church and state, while Augustine, Bishop of Hippo in North Africa provided the philosophical justification. Augustine was a great man and a great Christian. He was the father of Christian theology and the father of the monastic movement. His precise and relentless intellect enabled orthodox Christianity to withstand formidable and savage assaults by the Manichaean, Arian, and Pelagian heresies. His classic Confessions is one of the most moving accounts ever written of a sinner dedicating his life to Christ.

Strangely, however, it was this great saint whose thought paved the way for the medieval church compelling the unconverted to believe. Seeing the awful destruction wrought by dangerous heresy and heathen practices in the waning days of the Roman empire, Augustine became obsessed with preserving church unity. He saw the church as the last bulwark against the savagery of the encroaching barbaric hordes. The political apparatus of the state during his day was in disarray, divided, almost non-existent, with one despot succeeding another. The only hope for civilization, in Augustine's mind, as he peered over the abyss around the year 429 into the long night of the Dark Ages, was to bring administrative conformity to a universal church. To survive the onslaught of the barbarians and heresy, he thought, the church could not be defined as merely the body of believers, but had to be a specific all-encompassing institutional structure.

At this juncture, it is worth making a brief digression into the background of this brilliant but tortured church father because he is such a pivotal figure in the history of the West, and because the story of his conversion provides insight into his thinking on matters of church and state. As detailed in his Confessions, Augustine's youth was a tale of debauchery. His mother Monica tried to raise him as a Christian. But Augustine, his mental agility obvious from childhood, scoffed at the Scriptures and took delight in pointing out apparent contradictions. He recounts his exploits in the brothels of that infamous city of sin, Carthage, with his friend Licentius. He took part in the orgiastic feasts of Bacchus in which no depravity was considered too perverse. He took delight in the bloody spectacles of the circus. He had mistresses and an illegitimate son named Adeodatus. His mother Monica wept and prayed for her lost son.

But young Augustine was troubled. He found the temporary pleasures of the senses unsatisfying. He longed for true joy, but did not know where to find it. He was a consumer of pagan philosophy, and he sought frantically to find an answer to the problem of evil. He rejected Christianity at first because he did not see how a good and compassionate God could preside over a creation where there was so much obvious pain and suffering. For nine years, Augustine took refuge in Manichaeism, a philosophy of dualism.

According to the Manichaeans, the material world was under the dominion of evil; the spiritual world, including the soul, was under the dominion of good. The evil material world and the good spiritual world were in constant war with each other. Evil, according to the Manichaean view, would continue to triumph over the material body until the soul was liberated from the flesh by death. Manichaeism permitted Augustine to continue in his licentious ways because, according to this doctrine, man was powerless to overcome evil so long as he was held captive by the evil body. To Augustine, it seemed to explain why he was incapable of controlling his sexual appetites. Manichaeism contradicted the

Book of Genesis, in which God pronounces that his creation is good.

But Augustine eventually rejected Manichaeism because the Manichaean intellectuals could not answer Augustine's main objection. To him, there appeared to be too much beauty in the material world for it really to be inherently evil. The world seemed good, yet tainted. He turned to the writings of Plato and Plotinus (a neoplatonist) for answers. He thought there was some truth in Plato's notion that the material world is an imperfect representation of the true reality which is spiritual, but which we can perceive through our minds. According to Plato, abstract ideas are superior to physical objects. Thus, our conception of a table is the perfect table, while the material table, though good, is flawed; moreover, the idea, according to Plato, actually exists in some spiritual sphere. Though these notions would later strike Augustine as absurd, Plato induced him to begin thinking more about the transcendent, and helped shed light on the mysterious passage at the beginning of the Book of John. Augustine wrote:

> I read, not indeed, in these words but much the same thought, enforced by many varied arguments, that in the beginning was the Word, and the Word was with God, and the Word was God. The same was in the beginning with God. All things were made by Him, and without Him nothing was made.

To Augustine, it became obvious that Plato was inadequate, that he had taken man as far as unaided human reason could go. Meanwhile, Augustine had started taking an interest in the preaching of the great Ambrose, Bishop of Milan. He admired Ambrose's intellect, abandoned his bias against Christianity as a religion for the ignorant, and began studying the Scriptures. The problem of evil, though, continued to bother Augustine. What makes us sin? Why can't we make ourselves stop?

Over time, Augustine came to the conclusion that it was

not argument that prevented him from believing. It was sin. "Oh Lord," he once exclaimed, "make me chaste, but not yet." He wanted to turn his back on the pleasures of the flesh, but every time he tried, he heard the same tyrannical voice of ephemeral joy: "Do not cast us off" - "you cannot live without us." For many years he believed what those ephemeral joys continued to tell him.

But then one day, late in the summer of the year 386, the troubled Augustine was strolling through a garden in Milan. As recounted in the eighth book of the Confessions, suddenly he collapsed under a fig tree, wept, and began to pray: "And you, O Lord, how long? Will you be angry forever? Remember not our past iniquities. How long, how long? 'Tomorrow and tomorrow?' Why not now? Why not this very hour an end to my uncleanness?"

He then heard the voice of a little girl singing wistfully in the distance: "Tolle, lege. Tolle, lege [Take up and read. Take up and read]," she seemed to say with her melodious voice. Augustine reached for the New Testament, opened the book to Paul's letter to the Romans, and read the first lines upon which his eyes fixed: "Let us behave properly as in the day, not in carousing and drunkenness, not in sexual promiscuity and sensuality, not in strife and jealousy. But put on the Lord Jesus Christ, and make no provision for the flesh in regard to its lusts" (Romans 13:13-14).

At that moment Augustine renounced everything-worldly ambition, sensual delights, intellectual pride - and he "put on the Lord Jesus Christ." He had been born again. He would subject his life to rigorous discipline and prayer. He threw off his ornate african garb, and put on a black robe, a leather belt and sandals, a uniform that for him would never change. All his life, however, Augustine would take precautions against his major weakness-promiscuity. He would never permit a woman in his residence, not even his sister; when he spoke with a member of the opposite sex, he made sure a witness was present; and, when he went to bed at night, he always kept the door open. He had known evil first-hand; he knew that if extreme precautions were not taken in regulating his personal life, sin would swallow him again.

In the light of this background, we can see the source of Augustine's bias in favor of compulsion. The human will was extremely weak, in his experience, and subject to all sorts of temptation. Without external support the individual seemed almost helpless in his battle against Satan. Moreover, he saw that orthodox Christianity was on the brink of extinction. He lashed out furiously at the Arian heresy, which said Jesus was not divine but only an instrument of God; and the Pelagian error, which said that we are not condemned by original sin, but that each individual has the opportunity to live without the stain of Adam's fall from grace. Augustine said no, Jesus is divine, and He came to earth to pay for our sins with His death, because "all have sinned and fall short of the glory of God" (Romans 3:23).

Meanwhile, the state had completely abdicated its responsibility to protect the people from disorder. Christian-hating bands of robbers, often marching under the banner of Arius, constantly burned and pillaged farms owned by Catholics. Christians were routinely kidnapped and tortured, and their bodies desecrated in the most foul ways. Augustine saw priests' eyes burned out with chalk and vinegar, married women and nuns being violated, and blood flowing daily in the gutters of the streets. He himself was beaten severely by a rampaging band of fanatical heretics. At first, he believed that to force people to become Catholics would only lead non-believers to lie about their conversion. But the horrors he witnessed around him suggested that compulsory measures on behalf of Christian ideals were called for: "Why should not earthly kings who serve Christ," he wrote, "not make laws in favor of Christ?"

Alaric's hordes sacked Rome on August 24, 410, raping, slaying, and burning. Fortunes were lost, priceless art destroyed. There was massacre and carnage as the Goths reveled in their rampage. after news of this event reached frica, Augustine sat down at his table in Hippo and wrote at the top of a blank page the title of his greatest book: *Concerning the City of God Against the*

Pagans.

Augustine would have liked nothing more than to write in isolation and meditate on God. He envied the solitary life of Anthony in the desert. But circumstances demanded that he become an administrator, that he take a part in saving civilization. The world, as he saw it, was in crisis, and stern measures were called for, a view that was reinforced by the fact that he was a convert, a man who knew darkness, as he himself recognized: "Within the soul of a convert who has been an unbeliever and a sinner there develops a sort of fanatical anxiety. Remembrance of past errors exasperates him," he wrote.

Augustine's darkest moment as a Christian was in his treatment of the Donatists in Northern Africa. The Donatists rejected the Roman political order, and lambasted the official church for its corrupt and ungodly alliance with the state: "What has the emperor to do with the church?" they often asked. They attacked idols, the special powers of the priesthood, held church services in the vernacular, and may have even possessed copies of Scripture translated into their native tongues. They also denounced the institution of slavery, and many slaves abandoned their masters and became influential in the Donatist church. In a sense, the Donatist's were the first Separatist Protestants, similar to those who fled Europe on the Mayflower in 1620 to establish in the New World Christian communities undefiled by a worldly lust for power. Donatist-style dissent against worldly church power and extravagance would become a major force within Christianity: St. Francis of Assisi, John Wycliffe, William Tyndale, and Martin Luther are examples of men leading movements agitating for a return to the pure Christianity of the Apostle's. Donatists outnumbered the Catholics in many North african region's. The center of their movement was Hippo. Augustine, according to a letter he wrote to a friend, was commissioned by the emperor Honorius to help bring the Donatists "over to the Catholic unity by fear of the imperial edicts."

In 411, a church tribunal was held at Carthage and

presided over by Marcellinus, a functionary of the emperor. Two hundred seventy-eight Donatist bishops arrived to make the case that they represented the true Catholic Church. Augustine did not like the role into which he was thrust. But he also saw the unity of both church and empire as crucial: "The eyes of the Christian world," he said, "are fixed on this assemblage in Carthage. The people have forgotten the origin of the schism. We have seen the contemptible chicanery of individual's substituted for the great issue of Christian solidarity. When the barbarians are in Rome, when all mankind is eager to learn of the things of God, we are here engaged in miserable litigation."

The Donatist schism was then condemned by the emperor's man Marcellinus. In reality, the decision had been made before the tribunal had assembled. Augustine wrote the minutes of what had transpired. The emperor Honorius levied heavy fines on all members of the Donatist church, ordered them to return to the Catholic fold, and had their places of worship turned over to the Catholic authorities. Those who refused were either executed or imprisoned; some fled to the desert; others committed suicide rather than submit to the imperial decision.

Augustine did not enjoy his role as inquisitor, but all Catholics looked to him as a lighthouse in the midst of a turbulent sea. He took it upon himself to repair the cracks in the foundation of civilization and guide disabled Christian ships into tranquil waters. If persuasion did not work, force might be necessary. "Compel them to come in," he sometimes said during these years of distress. Always looking at his own experience, he recalled: "I was treated as I deserved, since instead of being given the bread of instruction, I was made to feel the lash of the whip." "Ah, how quickly you will be disabused of these ideas if you will but seek out in the Catholic Church those best instructed in sacred doctrine." For the Catholic Church "knows how to form men by instructions and exercises proportioned to the strength and age of each one, which in its salutary teachings has foreseen and understood everything."

Augustine did not want to use force. But his extremely dark (probably correct) view of human nature drove him to do so. "What else is the message of the evils of humanity?" he asked. ". . . quarrels, disputes, wars, treacheries, hatreds, enmities, deceits, flattery, fraud, theft, rapine, perfidy, pride, ambition, envy, murder, patricide, cruelty, savagery, villainy, lust, promiscuity, indecency, fornication, adultery, incest, unnatural vice in men and women (disgusting acts too filthy to be named), sacrilege, collusion, false witness, unjust judgment, violence, robbery, and all other such evils which do not immediately come to mind, although they never cease to beset this life of man ..." Leave people to their own devices and "men's brazen capacity to do harm, their urge to self-indulgence, would rage to the full. No king in his kingdom, no general with his troops, no husband with his wife, no father with his son, could attempt to put a stop, by any threats or punishments, to the freedom and sheer, sweet taste of sinning."

But Augustine failed to transfer this bleak view of the human heart to human institutions. His City of God Against the Pagans portrays Rome as a holy citadel, as having made possible the rise of Christianity, and as a mighty fortress that protected civilization from the savagery that awaited man without the protection of Caesar's armies. In his view, the state played an important role in man's 'salvation; a position that would dominate Christian thinking until the 17th century. Though he opposed the death penalty for heresy, he provided the rationale for the Spanish Inquisition of the 13th century, as historian Paul Johnson has pointed out. Near the end of his life, we find this great saint corresponding with the fanatical Spanish heretic hunter Paul Orosius.

It is easy, of course, to sympathize with Augustine, given the age in which he lived. For in his last days a Vandal army, estimated at 80,000 men who were following the doctrines of Arius, moved from Spain into africa, everywhere destroying churches and monasteries. Catholic priests and virgins were disemboweled; bishops burned alive. There was desolation from

Tangier to Tripoli. "Who could have believed such a thing!" Augustine wrote. "They ravage and pillage, change into a desert this prosperous and populous land. Not even a single fruit tree remains standing." Errors were not merely errors, as Augustine saw them, but often led to the most brutal butchery. In this light, we can understand Augustine's reasons for allying the kingdom of God with the kingdom of Caesar. For mankind was about to enter into the long night of barbarism.

Nevertheless, Augustine's marriage of church and state was counter to the entire spirit of the New Testament, and ultimately failed. It led to a savagery of its own. Augustine cited the parable of the great banquet, which contains the line "compel them to come in" (Luke 14:23), to justify using force to bring the unconverted into the church. In this parable people were giving weak excuses for why they could not attend the great feast planned by the householder. Try harder, the host told his servants; "compel them to come in." This was certainly strong language, but it was not a mandate to employ the coercive powers of the state. The host, who represents God, was invoking His servants (Christians) to make their arguments for coming to the feast (Heaven) more compelling. People failed to respond to God's invitation to the banquet because the case made by His evangelists was so feeble that many did not think the offer worthwhile. Augustine's misuse of the parable is a good illustration of the danger of pulling an isolated phrase out of the context of the Scriptural whole. The true meaning of that parable is this: if presented properly, and with urgency, by evangelists, Christ's message should "compel them to come in." This was by no means a call for yoking church and 'state together.

Augustine's "unity" was a political unity, dependent upon human structures - whereas the unity of which Paul speaks is a spiritual fellowship: "[Be] diligent to preserve the unity of the Spirit in the bond of peace" (Eph. 4:3). Jesus explicitly commands his followers not to use force in the conversion process: "[The] rulers of the Gentiles lord it over them; and their great men exercise authority over them. But it is *not* so among you . . . " (Mark 10:42-43, italics mine). Peter, the Apostle, in his letter, exhorts the elders of the church to "shepherd the flock of God among you, not under compulsion, but voluntarily, according the will of God" (1 Peter 5:2). And Paul's call to universalism is not an invocation to the church to conquer more territory: "There is . . . one Lord, one faith, one baptism, one God and Father of all who is over all and through all and in all" (Eph. 4:4-6). The Christian unity suggested here is spiritual, not material. God is not tied down by an alliance with a particular government, geographical location or race of people; nor does Caesar have anything to say about man's salvation: "No one comes to the Father, but through Me," Jesus says (John 14:6). The Augustinian vertical church structure, and its integration with Caesar's political reach, in fact, made the universal church impossible, a's the political realm will always be limited. Augustine's fatal twist on Christ's view of Christian unity would later lead to the Protestant Reformation, and fuel the dissenting spirit that brought the Mayflower Pilgrims from the Old World to the New.

CHAPTER FOUR

JOHN WYCLIFFE, FATHER OF AMERICAN DISSENT

Following the disintegration of the Roman Empire we see in many ways a rebirth of the apostolic Christian spirit. Even though the Church still held to Augustine's "City of God" ideal of the total Christian society, there was no state to speak of with which the Church could unite. Nomadic tribes settled the areas once patrolled by Caesar's armies. There was no coherent body of law and no system of police protection. The survival of Christianity hinged not on making an alliance with a powerful ruler, but on its ability to convince the various barbaric tribes of the merits of its case. The world was, once again, decentralized, without any unifying political agent, and with no single institution setting down standards to which everyone had to conform. There was no military at the disposal of the Church, and so it needed to return to evangelism as practiced by Christians of the first three centuries prior to the conversion of Constantine. The result was the stunning spread of Christianity throughout Europe during the period that has come to be called the Dark Ages. Christianity during these centuries stood for progress, learning, and civilization. It discouraged slavery, elevated the status of women, tended to the suffering, and organized poor-houses. The Church handed down laws to the barbarian kingdoms and was a tremendous defender of the dignity of the individual.

But the Church, even though it had recaptured the missionary spirit of the New Testament, retained Augustine's vision of imperial Christianity. In the late seventh century, we see the emergence of the regal pontiff with the tall, white headpiece. And during the eighth century, the papacy began to promote itself as the sole head of the Church and successor to Peter. We also see paintings of Pope John VII receiving papal symbols from the Virgin Mary. But it was the Frankish emperor Charlemagne who in 800 formally reunited church and state, and began the age of the medieval church.

Charlemagne was an extremely religious man and Pope Leo III was eager for him to look with favor on the Church. Most of all, Leo wanted the protection of Charlemagne's armies; and Charlemagne wanted to become the "Lord's anointed" leader of a reconstructed Roman empire. This new empire, however, was to be Christian rather than pagan. Charlemagne saw a clear connection between building civilization and spreading Christianity, and so expanded enormously the ranks of the clergy, who represented the most learned class of people. He subsidized churches, monasteries, abbeys, and universities, and became involved in the appointment of bishops. Church councils became his legislative assemblies, and priests, abbotts, and monks his royal administrators. The Church once again had become a political arm of the secular monarch. The advantages to both church and state were clear. The Church received government protection and favors, and vastly increased its wealth, while the king or emperor received divine sanction for his activities. Indeed, at the end of the ninth century, Pope John VIII praised the Carolingian emperor Charles II as the savior of the world and "Vicar of Christ," thus beginning the medieval tradition of the divine right of kings.

Charlemagne was a great ruler in many ways, and fully intended to use the Church for the benefit of the people. But the contrast between the simple Christianity that was brought to the Franks and the version that emerged after Charlemagne was stark. Not only did the Church provide spiritual answers, it provided all the political answers. Every aspect of human and social relations was regulated to the minutest detail, all forms of deviation were crushed, and the clergy became a disciplined army serving at the behest of the secular power. Under Charlemagne, bishops were royal functionaries. They sat as judges, collected taxes, served as ambassadors, and wrote legislation. For their services, they were given large tracts of land. More than half of Carolingian legislation dealt with church matters. The monarch was in every sense a priest, which was the meaning of his coronation. The only spiritual power he did not have was the disposal of the sacraments. By the time of the Renaissance, the Church was an enormously rich and cynical center of political ambition, with the papacy largely subservient to secular tyrants. A good illustration of how the church-state alliance worked was the Spanish Inquisition, which had its formal beginning in 1233. The Inquisition in Spain and Italy was a national tool for crushing political dissent. The Church would investigate alleged heresy and the state would exact punishment.

More often than not, genuine Christians within the church have been a restraining influence on the state. Almost by necessity, however, the official church establishment has frequently behaved as just another player in the struggle for political power, often subordinating itself to the authority of the secular ruler. The case of John Hus is a good example. Hus at tacked the legitimacy of Pope John XXIII (1410-15). Pope John was one of three men, including Benedict XIII and Gregory XII, who claimed to be the true pope.

John XXIII was a man who had purchased the office of Cardinal, denied the resurrection, reportedly seduced and violated some 300 nuns, and poisoned his predecessor, Pope Alexander V. He was later accused by 37 witnesses (mostly priests) of sodomy, theft, murder, and other crimes. Hus denounced as un-Christian and blasphemous John's authorization of the sale of indulgences "for the remission of sins" to finance a military crusade against Pope Gregory XII. Hus's views were upheld by Inquisitor Nicholas, Bishop of Nazareth, who exonerated Hus and gave him a certificate of orthodoxy.

But Pope John had the support of the Emperor Sigismund, who saw Hus as a threat to the unity of church and empire. Sigismund presided over the Council of Constance (1414-1418), which was dominated by civil officials and academicians. Sigismund preferred John XXIII over his rival popes because John was subservient to the emperor. Sigismund and the council declared their authority as supreme over that of the church, including the three popes.

Sigismund tricked Hus into attending the council in order to defend his views, including his attacks on John. Sigismund promised Hus safe conduct to and from the council regardless of the verdict. When Hus arrived, however, he was arrested, put on trial, and charged with 62 counts of heresy - none of which correctly stated Hus's views. "You have heard of many and heavy crimes which are not only proved against Hus by reliable witnesses but also confessed by him. I deem that each one of them is worthy of death," declared Sigismund.

Hus said he would humbly and gladly recant if he could be proven wrong from Scripture. The emperor and the council refused Hus's plea, and on July 6, 1415, consigned his soul to the devil. That same day, the secular authorities burned Hus at the stake. He committed his soul to the Lord and prayed loudly until the smoke choked his voice.

The sentiment of the council, including Sigismund, ultimately turned against all three popes: Gregory resigned, while John and Benedict were deposed. Martin V, who had become the consensus choice among the reigning secular heads of state, was then pronounced pope. The Church later proclaimed Gregory, whom Hus had supported against John, as the canonical pope.

Throughout history, the state performed the chief function of Inquisitor, and dominated the church. There have been only brief periods when the pope held the upper hand. Often the church gained in power and wealth by entering into alliances with the secular authorities - but it did so to the detriment of religious faith.

Anti-papal literature began circulating during the 12th century. The Franciscans were but one of the many reform movements taking place under the surface of official society. Their dedication to poverty and chastity, their denunciation of worldly ambition, aversion to violence, and their determination to live the pure and simple Christian life gained followers by the tens of thousands. Not surprisingly, the land was soon ablaze with Franciscan friars who were often condemned (almost always by the state) for their non-conformist behavior and their rejection of the pomp and ritual that characterized the so-called orthodox church. The great Italian poet Dante, once a Franciscan himself, writing in the early 14th century, described the Vatican as a "sewer of corruption" and placed Popes Boniface VIII, Nicolas II, and Clement V in the lower regions of his *Inferno* (Hell). Dante lamented the alliance the Church had made with the emperor Constantine:

> Ah Constantine! What ills were gendered there
> No, not from thy conversion, but the dower
> The first rich Pope received from thee as heir.

Dante himself got into serious difficulty, not only for portraying local church and political figures in unflattering terms, but for writing about Christianity in the vernacular, so that the average person could understand him. Transmitting the Bible's teachings in vulgar Italian, rather than high Latin, threatened the position of the clergy by taking the mystery out of Christianity, which was to be apprehended only by an elite core of theologians. Dante spent much of his life in exile from his native city of Florence, dying an outlaw in 1321. His poetry was considered politically dangerous and blasphemous - even though its purpose was to win converts to Christ.

Into this world John Wycliffe was born, around the year 1330, in North Riding of Yorkshire, England. He was the father of Protestant dissent in the English-speaking world, which is important for us because British Protestantism would later be transplanted to the colonies of North America. Wycliffe, a doctor of divinity, was a towering intellectual force at Oxford, writing some 200 books during the course of his career. For most of his life he was a staunch and orthodox Catholic. There were, however, two events that sowed the seeds of his discontent with the papacy. The first was the total submission of the pope to the demands of the French, historically loathed by the English. The second was the spectacle of rival popes excommunicating each other during the Great Schism. These two episodes seemed to call into question both the pope's political authority and his infallibility.

Wycliffe began criticizing papal extravagance, noting that the primacy of Peter in the New Testament was not in worldly grandeur and might, but in faith and humility. Christ Himself had no political power: "It is the plain fact," Wycliffe pointed out in his book *De Potestate Papae,* "that no man should be pope unless he is the son of Christ and of Peter, imitating them in deeds." For his arguments, Wycliffe relied on Scripture, constantly contrasting the example of Peter, who Catholics say was the first pope, with the regal pontiff of the Middle Ages. Peter wore no tall hat, no expensive robes, and carried no golden staff. Moreover, the Bible, thought Wycliffe, was a far more trustworthy authority than papal pronouncements or church tradition:

"All law, all philosophy, all logic and all ethics are in Holy Scripture," he said. The Bible is "one perfect word, proceeding from the mouth of God," and is "the basis for every Catholic opinion." Wycliffe's thinking broke sharply from medieval scholasticism, which considered church tradition as co-equal in authority with Scripture; many saw the Church as the primary authority, a view articulated by Guido Terreni, when he said that "the whole authority of Scripture depends upon the church." Wycliffe said this was wrong, and that in fact the opposite was the case: "In Holy Scripture is all truth."

Needless to say, church authorities were not amused. Pope

Gregory XI issued five bulls against Wycliffe in 1377 and denounced him as "the master of errors." Gregory ordered the English church to arrest Wycliffe and try him for heresy. The English authorities, however, were cautious because of Wycliffe's enormous popularity, and Oxford was not eager to condemn so outstanding a scholar. He was placed quietly under house arrest, and continued to write.

By the end of the 14th century, church ritual had become so elaborate that Chrishanity was inaccessible to all but the most learned. The Mass was said in Latin. "There are many thousands of people who could not imagine in their hearts how Christ was crucified unless they had learned it from the sight of images and paintings," Wycliffe wrote, noting that "Christ and his Apostles taught to people in that tongue that was best known to them." Wycliffe, like Dante, sought to make God's message available to anyone who wanted to hear it. While still at Oxford, he embarked on his historic enterprise to translate the Bible into English, something that had never been done: "Every Christian," he thought, "ought to study this book because it is the whole truth."

But translations of the New Testament would be expensive to buy, and the poor - most of whom could not read - would still have no direct access to God's words. Essential to Wycliffe was a revival of the evangelistic spirit of the Apostles, a spirit that was discouraged and often repressed in the medieval church. As Martin Luther would observe later, "the whole world is full of priests, bishops, cardinals and clergy, not one of whom, as far as his official responsibilities go, is a preacher."

Wycliffe believed that praying was certainly important, but did not approve of monastic orders, pointing again to Scripture: "Among all duties of the pastor after justice of life, holy preaching is most to be praised." For it was the only possible way to bring the message of salvation to the poor and illiterate. Thus, in addition to his translation, he began to train a core of evangelists at Oxford, whom he called the "Poor Preachers." Their task was to bring the Bible verbally to England's under-class, indeed to anyone who would listen. His earliest followers at Oxford included the famous preacher John Aston, the enthusiastic layman William Smith, and William Swinderby, whose performances drew large crowds. The more scholarly Nicholas Hereford and John Purvey assisted Wycliffe in his translation. These men were the pioneers of what came to be called the Lollard movement.

The Archbishop of Canterbury, William Courtenay, was a staunch defender of the traditional church structure and grew alarmed by the implications of what was happening at Oxford. He decided that it was time to move against Wycliffe. On May 17, 1382, Courtenay summoned to Blackfriars a special committee to examine 24 conclusions from Wycliffe's works. Ten were deemed heretical, and the other 14 erroneous. Upon the completion of the council's investigation there was an earthquake, which contributed to the apocalyptic atmosphere. Wycliffe's writings were banned and he was expelled from the university. He had many influential friends in the government, which is probably why he was permitted to retire unmolested to his parish at Lutterworth.

He would live for only two more years. But during that time he continued to write furiously and translate Scripture. And while many of Wycliffe's earlier views pointed in the direction of his final conclusions, his vision of Christianity took on its most radical form late in life. He wrote scathingly of the papal practice of selling indulgences, calling this "an open blasphemy that men should horror for to hear." God does not sell righteousness, nor had He "left in His law this power to the pope." In his earlier days, Wycliffe had criticized papal extravagance, but still believed church unity was important and saw the Great Schism as a catastrophe for the faith. In his final years, however, he concluded that it was in fact healthy that schism had exposed the spiritual bankruptcy of the papal office: "Many noble Catholic truths are made plain by this happy division."

He also attacked the "Caesarian clergy," and articulated the principles of separation of church and state in even more radical terms than our own First Amendment: "No man is honorable who joins together the peculiar value and authority of the clerical office with the authority and value of the lay office." Such a union, as he saw it, was "inexcusable" and "blasphemous." He assaulted starkly and systematically the sacramental powers of the clergy. The forgiveness of sin, he said, had nothing to do with priests, sacraments, or external ceremony, but rested solely upon a change in heart and the individual's response to God's call. His Bible replaced the pope as the infallible guide to the Christian life; the pulpit, instead of the Eucharist, became the channel through which God's grace was to be transmitted. He believed passionately that the church should give away all its earthly possessions and operate in a state of poverty, and that its ministers should carry with them nothing but a Bible and a sermon. He preferred to call houses of religious worship "conventicles," as the term church seemed too pretentious. Church, for him, was the mystical body of believers, not a building or human structure, and existed wherever two or three gathered together in Christ's name.

Wycliffe died of a stroke in his parish at Lutterworth in 1384, in nominal communion with the Roman Church. He was convicted posthumously of heresy by the Council of Constance. And in 1482, Richard Flemming, Bishop of Lincoln, exhumed Wycliffe's bones from consecrated ground, burned them, and scattered the ashes into the River Swift. Though Wycliffe himself probably did not fully understand the momentous implications of his own work, he had put into motion a spiritual, intellectual, and political force that would shatter the medieval church-state world. His brand of Protestantism - more than a century before the actual Protestant Reformation - was far more radical than either Luther's or Calvin's. Both Luther and Calvin believed in a state church -just a different kind of state church than what existed during their day. Wycliffe opposed all official religious establishments, and his ideas would continue to express themselves in the Lollard movement.

The tendency of Lollardry and its children was to constantly tear away at authoritarian structures, to undermine hierarchy, and to decentralize. The descendants of Wycliffe shunned human authority in favor of Scripture. The Bible was their manifesto of dissent, a revolutionary document that could topple popes and monarchs. The Bible was brandished by Oliver Cromwell against King Charles I; by the supporters of William of Orange against King James II; and by Samuel Adams and the New England Patriots against King George III. In Wycliffe's teaching we find the source of all the demands for a free church and a free state. Thus, it hardly can be said that separation of church and state was a victory for secular ideas over religious intolerance, because it was clearly a victory for the Bible over human authority. Indeed, the ideas of Wycliffe and his Protestant descendants placed all men, including popes and monarchs, under the same law, as written in Scripture, which far from promoting tyranny, turned out to be a great equalizer.

We see the same phenomenon at work in the Lollard movement that we saw in apostolic Christianity. The influence of the "Poor Preachers," with no property to defend, no visible organization and no apparent leadership, permeated every rank of English society. When Henry IV came to the throne in 1399, he began a systematic campaign to suppress Lollardry. In 1401, Wilijam Sawtry, John Badby, and John Reseby were burned at the stake. Wycliffe's works were incinerated in 1410, and John Oldcastle, a close friend and advisor to the King, was hanged and roasted for his Lollard convictions in 1417. We see long lists of martyrs from 1430 to 1466. Despite all this, complaints were rampant in ruling circles that the Lollard heresy was spreading. Everywhere the heresy seemed to be the same: the Bible is the sole authority, everyone is their own priest, and preaching goes on unlicensed in the secrecy of private homes. When the persecution was especially fierce, the Lollard movement went underground where "only God knew its members," and the ranks of the Lollards continued to grow. "The Lollards are as numerous as ever," lamented Archbishop Chichele in 1416 at the end of a vigilant period of suppression. Historians estimate that by the middle of the 15th century, half the English population was Lollard.

In all sorts of ways, Protestantism appealed to in dividualism and contributed to the development of a middle class. The notion that the individual could speak directly to God and did not need a saint or a priest to mediate on his behalf tended to break down aristocracy and church hierarchy. It was up to the individual to ask for his own salvation, not an enclave of monks praying for an entire community or a bishop granting absolution. Households began saying their own prayers tailored to their specific needs. The emergence of Protestantism was tied to the development of printing, which permitted the mass distribution of Bibles translated into the vernacular, making it possible for the *individual* to read and interpret Scripture. The phrase "the individual" first appears in its modern sense in the late 16th century. All these developments had their origins in the Lollard movement.

When we think of Protestant England most people think of Anglicanism, forgetting that the official English Church has never called itself Protestant. Henry VIII based his decision to break from Rome solely on power politics and his desire to divorce his wife Katharine of Aragon - hardly the Protestant ideals for which Wycliffe, Luther, and Calvin struggled. In fact, when Henry died he believed he was still a Catholic. A case can easily be made that to place the king at the head of the church was a far more oppressive and corrupting influence on Christianity than the pope in far-off Italy. The bishops, formerly responsible to the Roman authority, often served as an effective check on royal power. Now they were little more than a political arm of the state, used to stamp out religious dissent, which was seen as a threat to social order. William Tyndale, for example, carried on the Wycliffe tradition of translating the Bible into modern English. But he did so in hiding, relentlessly pursued by the King's henchman Cardinal Thomas Wolsey and his agents. One of Tyndale's offenses was to write a tract criticizing Henry VIII's divorce. Betrayed by people he thought he could trust, Tyndale was apprehended in 1536 in Antwerp, condemned for heresy, and put to death. His New Testament translation was burned in St. Paul's Cathedral. In many important respects, placing the English Church under secular rule was actually a setback for religious freedom and grievously compromised the purity of the Christian faith in England.

Anti-papal feeling was so strong that Henry had the full support of the Lollard-type Protestants in severing ties with Rome. After the break the Anglican Church service underwent a few modifications, but still looked virtually identical to the Catholic Mass. What had occurred in England was a schism, not a reformation. The church-state relationship was still intact, in fact more firmly than before. Soon it was obvious that Lollardry was incompatible with the monarchical Anglican religious structure. To the children of Wycliffe, the cathedrals, vestments, crucifixes, sacraments, and stained glass windows, even if they fell under the jurisdiction of the Crown rather than papal authority, still represented "Roman popery."

When religious orthodoxy, political orthodoxy, or orthodoxy of any type, is determined by whoever happens to hold the levers of power, whatever is orthodox one day can suddenly become unorthodox the next. This is exactly what happened continuously in England, where a bishop, appointed by a previous monarch, could suddenly find himself burning at the stake under the new regime. Thus, when Mary Stuart ascended the throne in 1553 and subsequently sought to bring England back to the Roman fold, Bishops Latimer, Ridley, Hooper, and Cranmer were burned at the stake. Even though these men held official church positions, their incredible bravery in the face of death indicates that radical Protestant notions had penetrated even the ruling classes, and fueled anti-Roman sentiments. Cranmer recanted his Lollard views under torture, but then retracted his recantation as he went up in flames. And Latimer's last words to his fellow martyr are worth repeating: "Be of good comfort Master Ridley, and play the man. We shall this day light such a candle, by God's grace, in

England, as I trust shall never be put out." These are not the sentiments of a cynical position-seeker, but of someone who took the Reformation seriously. These men were forerunners of a powerful reform movement called Puritanism.

Protestant dissent in England began as a counterculture movement, achieved critical mass by the end of the 15th century, and penetrated even the ruling establishment. The reign of Mary, her executions of dissenters, and her collusion with Catholic Spain, tended to radicalize the population and turned many in the English Church against Roman ideas. Mary was herself a sincere Catholic who thought it important to reunify Christendom, a goal that was unattainable, so pervasive had Protestant opinion become in England. She died a very unpopular monarch on November 17, 1558. Her views did not represent England's, a fact that was obvious to her successor, Elizabeth I.

Elizabeth attempted a new approach. Instead of a rigid religious orthodoxy, she instituted a "broad church," which was to put England on an even keel by accommodating as many Christian perspectives as was politically possible. In other words, she attempted "pluralism"-within certain limits. This came to be known as the Elizabethan settlement, which aimed not for purity of religious doctrine, but for political stability. Elizabeth's preference was for a relaxed form of Christianity that did not make rigorous demands on the people. But a moderate, compromising church was not what the descendants of Wycliffe and Tyndale, or the followers of Luther and Calvin, wanted either. Truth and compromise are not, in the end, compatible ideas. An official civil religion, no matter how broad, could not accommodate those who took their Christianity seriously.

Within the Elizabethan Church there emerged a more moderate movement that sought to reform Anglicanism. Its ranks were not Lollard Separatists, completely opposed to the state church structure. Rather, they wanted the official church to be more Protestant. Their inspiration was John Calvin more than John Wycliffe, and they went by the name of Puritan. Generally they sought a presbyterian rather than episcopal church rule. But even though they were willing to work within the official church, emotionally they were far closer to Separatism than High Church Anglicanism. They were interested in "godly, preaching ministers," not clerics who spent their energy amassing titles and offices. They considered the official church vestments to be "rags of popery," and most Puritans, such as Laurence Humphrey and Thomas Sampson, refused to wear the "obnoxious garments." They objected to the sign of the cross, the use of wedding rings in marriage, kneeling, and the term "priest" in the *Book of Common Prayer.* In short, they became a major source of irritation to Queen Elizabeth. Preaching before the Queen, Edward Dering, for example, scolded her: "I need not seek far for offenses whereat God's people are grieved, even 'round about this chapel I see many," he said. Everywhere "all these whoredoms are committed," and yet, he added, "you sit still and are careless." Many Puritans, unconcerned about the consequences to themselves, were outspoken against Elizabeth's Church. And they proved far more dangerous to the Crown because they were political and highly organized, forming a distinct political party. Peter Wentworth typified the Puritan spirit when in 1576 he told his colleagues in Parliament that it was useless to wait for the Queen to begin reforming the Church, and proposed that Parliament take the initiative. Wentworth spent the rest of the Parliamentary session in the Queen's dungeon.

While the Puritans and Separatists disagreed on the desirability of the church-state relationship, both wanted an end to the state-enforced monopoly of the High Anglican Church. Both agreed on the primacy of the Bible, with the Puritans giving some weight to doctrine as formulated by the fathers of the Church. The Lollard-style Separatists rejected any teaching that was not explicitly stated in Scripture, and relied on the Holy Spirit, rather than church organization or tradition, to make clear Christ's message and to steer the sincere believer away from grave errors. As Wycliffe put it: "The Holy Ghost teaches us the meaning of

Scripture, as Christ opened the Scriptures to the Apostles."

The children of Calvin were not as radical in their Protestantism as the descendants of Wycliffe, but they had much in common, and in practice were allies against the official church of the Elizabethan settlement. Nevertheless, it is important to make a distinction between the Presbyterianism of the Puritans and the total hostility to a state religion on the part of the Separatists, because while the Puritans spent much energy and shed much blood fighting for control of a spiritually bankrupt official church in the 1640s, Separatism would prevail in the United States of America. Today, these radical Protestants would be considered fanatics, as they were indeed considered fanatics by the defenders of the church-state alliance. But, as it turns out, these Lollard-style Separatists, who insisted on adhering to the bare letter of Scripture, could not justify a state-enforced religion, no matter how mild and inoffensive that religion might be. It was Protestants of the most radical stripe, most zealous in their religious convictions (those whom the American Civil Liberties Union would like to see outlawed from the public discourse) who were in fact the greatest proponents of religious liberty as codified in America's governing charter 200 years later.

Elizabeth's civil religion was pluralistic and easygoing by the standards of her day. But to force those who did not believe in it to support it and to participate in it, still conforms to the American understanding of tyranny. Obvious parallels can be drawn here between Elizabeth's attempt to use the Anglican Church to promote a national civil religion and the American public school system's attempt to promote its morally bankrupt world-view. The state is a secular, not a spiritual, entity; and as such is incapable of drafting a uniform religious creed that can suit everyone's spiritual needs. According to the Christian faith, salvation is contingent on a personal commitment to Jesus. The corporate body of believers in the New Testament plays a vital role in administering baptism and communion, providing fellowship among believers, reinforcing faith, and spreading the Gospel.

But, in the end, the Christian's relationship to his Creator is intensely individualistic, and cannot be mediated by an overarching government apparatus no matter how broad and accommodating its apparatus might be. In fact, civil religion's lack of rigor, intellectual carelessness, and the obvious moral degeneracy of so many of its proponents, often leads to social unrest - as was the case with Oliver Cromwell's Puritan Revolution of the 1640s, the Glorious Revolution of 1688, and finally the American Revolution of 1776.

CHAPTER FIVE

PILGRIM'S PROGRESS

When Queen Elizabeth died in 1603, hopes for Protestant reform in England went from bad to worse. She was succeeded by James I, who enjoyed saturating young ladies with liquor and then watching them collapse and vomit at his feet. James was openly homosexual, and once justified his sodomy with blasphemy, remarking that "Jesus Christ did the same, and therefore I cannot be blamed. Christ had his John, and I have my George." Ironically, James also commissioned the famous Bible translation that bears his name, a fact that seemed, to many, to underscore the perverse nature of his position as head of the Anglican Church. At one point, he ordered that the "Book of Sports" be read from every pulpit for the purpose of encouraging recreation on Sundays. This was an open insult directed at the Puritan ministers, who were trying to exist within the English Church; it also confirmed the view of the independent Christians that their decision to separate themselves from state-sponsored Christianity had been a correct one. The Sabbath for both the Puritans and the Separatists was to be reserved for God, not amusements. A church headed by a man such as James was not what serious reformers had in mind in supporting England's break from Rome.

In this context, John Robinson's congregation in Scrooby (formed in 1602) began to attract members. They met in the privacy of the home of Postmaster William Brewster. Robinson, Brewster and their followers merely wanted to be left alone, to worship Christ in their own way, undefiled by James's perversions and Anglican extravagance. Robinson was a peaceful man, did not seek a confrontation with the government, and made it clear to the King's men that he certainly had no intention of causing trouble for the official church. He was even willing to call himself an Anglican: "It is not we which refuse them, but they us," he said. But he also made quite clear his dissatisfaction with the King's version of Christianity. "There is but one body, the church, but one Lord, or head of that body, Christ: and whoever separates from the body, the church, separates from the head, Christ," said Robinson. In his view, it was the English Church, not his congregation, which had separated from the body of Christ.

The body of believers in Scrooby were often called "Brownists" - a derisive term in the minds of state and church officials. Robert Browne, like Robinson, was a graduate of Cambridge University, which became the intellectual center for Protestant dissent in England. Browne founded a Congregational church at Norwich, and in 1582 fled under pressure to Middelburg in Zeeland. There he published his famous *Treatise of Reformation Without Tarying for Anie,* in which he outlined a view of the church as follows: "The church planted or gathered is a company or number of Christians or believers, which by willing covenant made with their God, are under the government of God and Christ1 and keep His laws in one holy communion." Robinson's view of the church was similar, and can be found in his *Justification of Separation from the Church of England,* published in 1610: "A company of faithful people thus covenanting together are a church, though they may be without any officers among them, contrary to your popish opinion."

The royal authorities saw groups, such as the one in Scrooby, as far more threatening than the Puritans, who at least theoretically professed to support the state church. Puritans could be located if they became too demanding and unruly-and defrocked, fined, or imprisoned if necessary to maintain social harmony. But the Separatists, who had no church buildings, were highly mobile and could easily disappear into the countryside.

King James I, much exasperated by the disrespect they continually demonstrated for his authority, ordered that the police hunt down this "private sect, lurking within the bowels of this nation." He saw them as dangerous religious "fanatics" being "ever-discontented with the present government and impatient to suffer any superiority, which maketh their sect unable to be suffered in any well-governed commonwealth." Either "conform yourselves," he declared, "or I will harry you out of the land!"

The Separatists were hunted with zeal. Spies and informers watched the roads and reported any clues to the appropriate authorities as to Brownist whereabouts. Even though the Congregationalists were usually able to elude James's wrath, Robinson and Brewster were concerned about the safety of their women and children. Reluctantly, they decided, after consulting with the congregation, that it was necessary to flee England. "They were both scoffed and scorned by the profane multitude ... and the poor people were so vexed with apparitors, and pursuants and commissarie courts, as truly their affliction was not small," wrote William Bradford, the future governor of Plymouth colony. His famous and moving diary, a *History of Plymouth Plantation,* one of the great works of New England literature, will be drawn on heavily here. Bradford was not only a gifted writer, he would also become one of the heroic pioneers of Western history, laying the cornerstones that made possible the building of the American Republic. In Scrooby, however, he was just one member of Robinson's and Brewster's congregation and had no grand human ambitions.

In his *journal,* Bradford wrote poignantly of how dificult it was to leave friends and acquaintances behind for "an adventure almost desperate." But, he said, "these things did not dismay them (though they did at times trouble them) for their desires were set on the ways of God, and to enjoy His ordinances. They rested on His providence, and knew who they believed."

In order to launch their voyage, explained Bradford, they needed to commission a ship. "But the ports were shut against them." Unfortunately, they were forced to rely on people they did not know to provide safe passage, and were betrayed by an unscrupulous shipper on the docks of Lincolnshire. He seemed cheerful and eager to help, accepted their money, and made arrangements for them to leave on a particular day. "After long waiting, and large expenses he [the shipper] came at length and took them in... But when he had them and their goods aboard, he betrayed them, having beforehand plotted with searchers and other officers . . . who took them, and put them in open boats, and rifled and ransacked them, searching their shirts for money." Of most concern to Bradford, was that the women were handled without "modesty." The police then "carried them back to town and made them a spectacle and wonder to the multitude." Most of the men were able to escape, thus avoiding almost certain execution. But the women and children were thrown into dungeons. People were not expected to survive long in a 17th-century English prison. "Pitiful it was to see" these "poor women in this distress," wrote Bradford. "What weeping and crying on every side, some for their husbands . . . others not knowing what should become of them, and their little ones; others again melted in tears, seeing their poor little ones hanging about them, crying for fear, and quaking with cold."

But then, said Bradford, "their cause became famous, and occasioned many to look into . . . their godly carriage and Christian behavior," which "left a deep impression in the minds of many." Because of their courageous example as martyrs for their faith, "many more came with fresh courage and greatly animated others." The imprisonment of so many Brownist women and children became a source of political embarrassment to King James, who reluctantly released the pilgrims on the condition that they conform themselves to the Anglican Church, or leave the country. The decision for them was obvious. They joined their husbands who had made it to the Netherlands under much duress and spent a year in Amsterdam, before finally taking up residence in the university town of Leyden.

Many of Robinson's Brownists were, at one time, well-to-do Englishmen, with good educations from Cambridge University, and had bright futures ahead of them if they had merely conformed themselves to the English Church. Instead, they lost their homes and all their possessions to tax collectors, officers of the state, and unscrupulous shippers. They were unwelcome in their native country because they believed that the Bible, not the king of England, should be the final authority, not only on matters of faith, but in all areas of life. In their view, James came under the rule of Christ, Christ did not come under the rule of James. Their insistence on this one point caused them many personal hardships - but in the end would make possible the emergence of the freest, richest, and most fervently Christian (in the Brownist sense) society in the history of man.

But all this would come later. First, they would have to carry the cross. As immigrants in Holland, they were permitted only to engage in menial labor and were paid barely subsistence wages. They lived this way in Leyden for 11 years, often working from dawn until well into the night. Because of "the hardness of the place," they aged quickly and a number of them "were taken away by death." But the abject poverty did not discourage the Brownists. "The people generally bore all these difficulties very cheerfully and with resolute courage." Far more pernicious, wrote Bradford, was the "manifold temptations of the place." The children were being drawn away from their parents by the "evil examples" of the Dutch. Many in the Leyden congregation thought it preferable to endure the prisons of England rather than risk falling away from the Gospel by continuing to live in "licentious" Holland.

The Leydenites elected to travel to the New World, to become "Pilgrims," a name coined by Bradford. "It was answered that all great and honorable actions are accompanied with great difficulties, and must be enterprised and overcome with answerable courages," he wrote. "It was granted that the dangers were great, but not desperate, and the difficulties were many, but not

invincible... and all of them, through the help of God, by fortitude and patience, might either be borne or overcome."

Their pastor John Robinson perceived that God beckoned
his people to go to this new land to build a new Jerusalem. As
he saw it, the Leydenites, like "the people of God in old time, were
called out of Babylon, the place of their bodily bondage, and were
to come to Jerusalem, and there build the Lord's temple."

Robinson and Brewster first approached, in a letter, a
wealthy businessman, Sir Edwin Sandys, for financial backing:
"We verily believe and trust the Lord is with us, unto Whom and
Whose Service we have given ourselves in many trials, and that
He will graciously prosper our endeavors according to the simplicity of our hearts therein," they wrote. Sandys was a staunch
Puritan, and sympathetic to the more radical Brownists. But he
was recovering from recent financial setbacks, including an investment in an unfruitful expedition to Virginia, and was forced to
turn them down. Subsequently, they were approached by a conniving London merchant named Thomas Weston, who sought to
take advantage of their plight.

Weston agreed to finance their journey in exchange for a
seven-year period of indentured servitude. Each settler would
be given one share of the company at the outset, and an additional share if they equipped themselves. At the end of seven
years, the profits of the company would be divided in proportion
to the number of shares. This struck the Pilgrims as fair. So
Weston, along with a group of merchants, worked out arrangements to provide them with ships, the *Speedwell* and the
Mayflower. The *Speedwell* proved completely unseaworthy, and
so the Pilgrims were forced to crowd themselves onto the
Mayflower. The 40 Brownists were actually a minority among
those on the 102-passenger ship. The others were adventurers
looking for excitement and people of low social rank hoping to
find a better life. Most of the Leyden congregation could not go on
the journey because there was not enough room. And John
Robinson, the man who most wanted to go, felt obligated to stay

with the bulk of his flock, and so remained in Holland. Brewster was made acting pastor.

In addition to providing the Pilgrims with shoddy vessels, Weston, at the last possible moment, presented them with a revised contract. The major change was that all property, including the land they cleared and the homes they built in New England, would remain the property of the company after the seven years of service were concluded. The Pilgrims refused, not because they would not have agreed to this condition had it been clearly stated at the beginning, but because in their minds an agreement was an agreement. Weston, shocked and enraged that they would not immediately accede to his demands, in desperation informed them he would not settle their final debts. Undeterred, the Pilgrims sold off all food and supplies not absolutely required for the voyage to meet their financial obligations. They then sent off a letter to the London merchants informing them that if the settlement was not profitable after seven years, they would continue to labor until every cent was repaid in addition to yielding a healthy return on the company's investment. This was, in fact, a better deal for the London group than the arrangement Weston had tried to force the Pilgrims to sign.

Prior to boarding the ship, Brewster assembled the congregation to read a letter by John Robinson:

> Loving Christian friends, I do heartily and in the Lord salute you all, as being they with whom I am present in my best affection, and most earnest longings after you, though I be constrained for a while to be bodily absent from you. . . We are daily to renew our repentance with our God, especially for our own sins known, and generally for our unknown trespasses, so does the Lord call us in a singular manner upon occasions of such difficulty and danger as lies before you.

Anticipating conflict with their non-Christian brethren on

the ship, Robinson's particular concern was that the Pilgrims exercise patience: "Your intended course of civil community will minister continual occasion of offense, and will be as fuel for that fire, except you diligently quench it with brotherly forbearance . . . Store up therefore patience against that evil day, without which we take offense at the Lord Himself in His holy and just works."

Finally, Robinson advised, the form of government established should be democratic (congregational), that is, officers reporting to the people and serving at their pleasure: "Whereas you are to become a civil body politic, using amongst yourselves civil government, and are not furnished with any persons of special eminence above the rest, to be chosen by you into office of government, let your wisdom and godliness appear, not only in choosing such persons as do entirely love and promote the common good, but also in yielding unto them all due honor and obedience in their lawful administrations."

Thus, we see in Robinson's letter to the Pilgrims many qualities unique to the American character and form of government still evident today. His concern was for tolerance of those who did not share their world-view; democratic rule in which even those outside their church would have a voice; and government according to the rule of law. Above all, from Robinson's perspective, their survival as a "civil community" was contingent on staying true to God's wishes and in being a model of Christian charity to the others: "Though it be necessary (considering the malice of Satan and man's corruption) that offenses come... [this] doth require at your hands much wisdom and charity for the covering and preventing of incident offenses."

On August 5, 1620, they set sail, encountering, according to Bradford, "many fierce storms in which the ship was soundly shaken." Amazingly, only two died on the voyage, one of a mysterious illness and the other of scurvy. After seven weeks, and "a long beating at sea," the ship arrived on November 9, 1620, at Cape Cod. They had been blown by a severe storm 300 miles north of their intended destination, which was Virginia. They sailed up and down the rocky coast for two days, finally returning to the Cape as the most suitable place to drop anchor.

But the *Mayflower's* passengers were faced with a new problem: by choosing to settle outside the Virginia boundary, their patent was no longer valid. Thus, as one passenger pointed out, the ship was under no one's jurisdiction. They were without a sovereign, and were therefore subject to no formal legal or social arrangements whatsoever. Without a government, to use John Locke's term, they were in "a state of nature." And a number of the non-Pilgrim men began behaving as one might expect men to behave in a state of nature. Rebellion stirred in the bowels of the ship, and the Pilgrim leadership had to act quickly in order to avoid mutiny, which quite clearly would doom the expedition. As Bradford described it, the Pilgrims huddled together amongst themselves and drew up an agreement, a sacred "covenant," making them a "civil body politic" and promising "just and equal laws."

That the decision to form such a compact was so instinctive for the Pilgrims is noteworthy. It was a natural outgrowth of the covenantal nature of their Scrooby congregation, which was formed by people coming together voluntarily for a common purpose, which in England and Holland had been to live in strict adherence to the letter of Scripture. But on the *Mayflower,* an additional covenant was needed to form a legitimate government, necessary for their individual protection, as well as to make possible the emergence on virgin territory of civilized society.

The Mayflower Compact

Having undertaken, for the Glory of God and the advancement of the Christian Faith and the honor of our King and country, a voyage to plant the first colony in the northern parts of Virginia, do by the presents solemnly and mutually in the presence of God and one of another, covenant and combine ourselves together into a civil body

politic, for our better ordering and preservation and fur-
therance of the ends aforesaid, and by virtue hereof to
enact, constitute and frame such just and equal laws,
ordinances, acts, constitutions and offices from time to
time, as shall be thought most meet and convenient for
the general good of the colony...

This became known as the Mayflower Compact, and is a
pivotal document in the development of constitutional government in America. John Carver, who Bradford said was "a man
godly and well approved amongst them," was elected governor
"for that year."

The signing of the Mayflower Compact by almost all of the
adult men on the voyage disproves the impression left by many
historians that the "social compact" was an idea of the Enlightenment, invented by John Locke at the time of the Glorious
Revolution in England 68 years hence. Now Locke is perhaps
the single most important thinker in the codification of American constitutional philosophy; Thomas Jefferson and the founders relied heavily on him for their views on the proper role of the
state. But it is very important to understand the correct sequence
of events-if for no other reason than to understand Locke.

Locke himself, as we will see in more detail later, was a
pious man, educated in fact by Protestant dissenters in England
(very similar in outlook to Robinson and Brewster). Locke developed his ardent spirit for liberty largely from his admiration of
Protestant sects founded on the "right of private judgment," and
was firmly committed not only to their political cause of religious
liberty, but also to their religious convictions. His "social compact" theory was not really a theory at all, but was derived mainly
from Scripture and his experience with the Congregational church,
or "conventicle," which was patterned after the example of the
apostolic churches.

The concept of "equal laws" is also very much part of the
Hebrew tradition, as the Jews of the Old Testament were people

of the covenant that is, they had a compact with God. The Ten Commandments apply equally to everyone within the covenant. Similarly, the Pilgrims, with the Bible in hand, had no difficulty beginning a new society from scratch, just as the early Christians established autonomous societies that were set apart from the Roman empire.[1]

The non-Pilgrims, by contrast, were confused and anarchic, apparently helpless without a human authority handing down orders. Absent the strong influence of men such as Brewster, Carver, and Bradford, the *Mayflower* adventurers and thrill-seekers, less firm in their biblical convictions, would have been on the road to very rapid demise. The Virginia settlement of 1607 failed largely because the spiritual bond between the people was weak; there was little sense of mission in Jamestown drawing the people together, in contrast to the Plymouth expedition. That a social covenant, such as the one drawn up by the Pilgrims, could have worked if they had not been an intensely religious people is doubtful. For without God as overseer, always tugging at the strings of conscience, the Mayflower Compact would have been nothing more than a scrap of paper. There was, after all, no real legal redress available against those who decided to violate the agreement.

Similarly, the U.S. Constitution has worked because there has been a sacred aura surrounding the document; it has been something more than a legal contract; it was a covenant, an oath before God, very much related to the covenant the Pilgrims signed. Indeed, when the President takes his oath of office he places his hand on a Bible and swears before Almighty God to uphold the Constitution of the United States. He makes a sacred promise; and the same holds true for Supreme Court justices who take an oath to follow the letter of the written Constitution. The moment America's leaders begin treating the Constitution as though it were a mere sheet of paper is the moment the American Republic-or *American Covenant-ends.* The American people are bound together by an oath; an oath between the people to form a gov-

---

1. They abided, though, by pagan laws that did not contradict
   Scripture.

ernment of "just and equal laws" under God. When that oath is violated, the bond, too, is dis solved - which is the grave danger our nation faces today.

A sacred bond, both spiritual and actual (as written on paper), enabled the Plymouth settlement to survive the first winter, for which, having arrived in November, they had little time to prepare. The task before them when they first set foot on that "wild and savage hue" was frightening to the sojourners, and the obstacles must have appeared almost insurmountable. As Bradford described their lonely situation, the Pilgrims had "no friends to welcome them, no inns to entertain or refresh their weather-beaten bodies, no houses . . . to repair to." And as he turned to look whence they came he saw only "the mighty ocean which they had passed," which "was now a main bar and gulf to separate them from all the civil parts of the world . .

What could now sustain them but the Spirit of God and His Grace?" But, said Bradford in a more cheerful tone, they also had much to be thankful for: "Being thus arrived in good harbor, they fell upon their knees and blessed the God of heaven who had brought them over this vast and furious ocean, and delivered them from all the perik and miseries thereof, again to set their feet on the firm and stable earth."

What comes through in these lines by Bradford is the human qualities and emotions these Pilgrims had. They were not supermen. Bradford's diary is an account of very ordinary people who, without their unflinching faith that God was looking after them, could never have accompbshed such a feat. Often they doubted their own abilities. But not once does Bradford allude to any instance in which the Pilgrims doubted, even for a moment, God's commitment to them, His covenant, His promise to make certain their work would bear fruit, and to see their enterprise through the terrible tribulations that awaited. They often read aloud to each other passages in Scripture such as the Prophet Isaiah's promise to "the offspring of Abraham":

You whom I have taken from the ends of the earth,
And called from its remotest parts,
And said to you, 'You are My servant,
I have chosen you and not rejected you.
Do not fear, for I am with you;
Do not anxiously look about you, for I am your God.
I will strengthen you, surely I will help you,
Surely I will uphold you with My righteous right band.'
(vv. 41:9-10)

The Pilgrims were absolutely certain that God would not abandon them, and that all hardships and all disasters they would have to confront somehow fit His divine plan. They were there on a mission - on God's errand into the wilderness. They were the new children of Israel, spiritual descendants of Abraham, sent by the winds of Providence into a desolate wasteland, just as Moses and the Jews were sent for 40 years into the desert. But the faith of Brewster, Carver, Bradford, and their Pilgrim brethren, that indeed their ordeal would serve a purpose, was very definitely the source of their power to begin the awesome task of building the United States of America - a fact that should cause even the atheist to marvel.

But the trials of the journey, of which Bradford wrote, were small in comparison to the deadly miseries of the winter months to follow: "That which was most sad and lamentable was that in two or three months time half of their company died, especially in January and February, being the depth of winter, and wanting houses and other comforts; being infected with scurvy and other diseases, which this long voyage and their unaccommodate condition had brought upon them. They died, sometimes two or three on a day.. . and of the times of most distress six or seven sound persons," one of which was Bradford's wife. Her death must have grieved him terribly, though he never mentioned it in his journal. But this would be in keeping with Bradford's character which was to never discuss his own suffering. The word he used was always "they," never "I" or even "we"; it was a precaution he took against engaging in self-pity as well as protection from the ever-present threat to the soul posed by the ego.

But with spring came a thaw, and when the cold left so did the "starving time." The colonists met two Indians, one named Samoset and the other Squanto. Squanto knew English, as he had spent time in England, traveling there with a previous expedition sponsored by the Virginia Company. They exchanged gifts, according to Bradford, and then they went back to their tribe to the "great Sachem, called Massasoit, who, about four or five days after," arrived with a cadre of braves. To Bradford's great relief, the tribe proved hospitable. Chief Massasoit provided entertainment and ordered that the settlers be given back their tools, which the Indians had stolen that winter.

The Pilgrims were craftsmen and townspeople in England, with virtually no experience as farmers or hunters. In four months time they had caught only one codfish. Squanto taught the Pilgrims how to provide for the necessities of life, including how to plant corn and fish for cod. The English-speaking Indian seemed to Bradford a gift delivered from Heaven. The settlers and Indians agreed to sign a treaty of peace and mutual assistance, which read as follows:

1. That neither he nor any of his, should injure or hurt any of their people.
2. That if any of his did hurt any of theirs, he should send the offender, that they might punish him.
3. That if anything were taken away from any of theirs, he should cause it to be restored; and they should do like to his.
4. If any did unjustly war against him, they would aid him; if any did war against them, he should aid them...

This compact, really an expansion of the covenant the

Pilgrims had signed on the *Mayflower,* would last inviolated for 50 years. Squanto continued to assist the settlers, teaching them how to stalk deer, plant pumpkins, and skin beavers. Governor Carver, however, while working in the fields, died suddenly of an unknown cause, perhaps of a heart attack. This was a sad moment in the midst of so much encouragement. But our eloquent historian, William Bradford, was elected unanimously as governor, and would win re-election 30 consecutive times.

Even with the coming of spring, friendly relations with the Indians, and Squanto's assistance, the colony was still a long way from prospering. Weston's contract imposed a socialist system on the settlement, in which all property was owned by the company. In addition, all produce had to go into a common store, from which each individual would receive an equal ration, regardless of how much he had contributed. Any excess produce belonged to the investors. Also, the Pilgrims' homes, which they had built, and all land, which they had cleared, was company property - terms the Pilgrims wanted to abide by, despite Weston's shenanigans.

Under this essentially communist economic system the people received no reward for individual effort and the colony was unable to produce enough food. "No supply was heard of, neither knew they when they might expect any," wrote Bradford, who went on to reflect on the folly of coliectivist economics:

"The experience that was had in this common course and condition, tried sundry years, and that amongst godly and sober men, may well evince the vanity of that conceit of Plato and other ancients, applauded by some of later times, that by taking away of property, and bringing community into a common wealth, would make them happy and flourishing-as if they were wiser than God. For this community (so far as it was) was found to breed much confusion and discontent, and retard much employment that would have been to their benefit and comfort. For young men that were most able and fit for labor and service did repine that they should spend their time and strength to work for other men's wives and children without any recompense... This was thought injustice."

Not only did socialism fail to provide for the basic needs of the people, in Bradford's estimation, it was counter to God's plan for man. "If it did not cut relations God established among men, it did at least diminish and take mutual respect that should be preserved among them," he observed. "Seeing all men have corruption in them, God in His wisdom saw another course fitter for them." Because of man's fallen state, man cannot be expected to labor for no reward, which, in Bradford's view, is why the God of Scripture rewards man for his good works. The Pilgrim leadership - after much discussion about whether it was right to ignore their company charter - abolished the socialist system, and "assigned every family a parcel of land," observing that: "This had very good success, for it made all hands very industrious, so as much more corn was planted than otherwise would have been by any means the governor or any other could use, and saved him a great deal of trouble, and gave far better content."

The elimination of communal, or corporate, property in favor of private ownership created prosperity. In fact, the Pilgrims soon found themselves with more food than they could use. They set themselves up as a trading post, exchanging their surplus corn to the Indians for beaver skins, which they in turn shipped back to England to the enormous delight of the investors. When news of the colony's success began circulating, more ships arrived with more settlers, mostly separatist Protestants. At first, Bradford worried that they would not be able to feed them all, but Plymouth's free enterprise system easily absorbed all who wanted to settle there: "Instead of famine, now God gave them plenty, and the face of things was changed to rejoicing in the hearts of many, for which they blessed God." Bradford's decision to conform to the dictates of the profit motive inherent in human nature - rather than adhere to the letter of their corporate charter - enabled the Pilgrims to purchase their land outright from the company, thus more than adequately fulfilling their part of the bargain.

In addition, Bradford added a seven-member governor's council, also elected annually, the purpose of which was to give as many people as possible an opportunity to take on the responsibilities of government. In his view, government was not a privilege to be enjoyed by a special ruling aristocracy at the expense of the citizenry; government was a burden which ought to be shared by everyone. American constitutional democracy and free enterprise, quite clearly then, did not stand in opposition to the supposed "theocracy" of Plymouth (which was not a theocracy at all, as many historians would have us believe). Nor were such ideas first developed during the European Enlightenment (so-called) of the 18th century. What Abraham Lincoln described as government "of the people, by the people, and for the people," was inherited from a tradition beginning with the Congregationalist Protestant settlement in Plymouth, Massachusetts, in the 1620s.

CHAPTER SIX

JOHN WINTHROP'S SHINING CITY

The story of religion in America is the story of Puritanism. About three-quarters of the North American colonists at the time of the American Revolution were of Puritan extraction. Puritanism[1] was the dominant political and intellectual force throughout the 17th and the 18th centuries. Given all we owe to the Puritan legacy, then, it is a curious fact that the term Puritan carries with it such negative connotations today. The Puritans gave us our first written constitutions, regular elections, the secret ballot, the federalist principle, and separation of church and state. The Puritans, with their work ethic and their stress on equality under the law, made it possible for the capitalist spirit to triumph over hereditary privilege.

Many historians have made the point that Puritanism failed, and cite as evidence that there are no more Puritans to be found. But Puritanism was never a formal Christian sect. In fact, it was considered a term of derision, first used, as far as we know, by Queen Elizabeth. She had branded those who refused to conform to the *"Liturgie, Ceremonies and Discipline of the Church"* with the "invidious" name of "Puritane." No Puritan would have called himself a Puritan, and actually would have regarded the label an insult. The Puritans thought of themselves merely as Christians.

A Puritan might have been Congregationalist, Presbyterian, Anabaptist, or even Anglican. St. Francis of Assisi and

---

1. Including the various offshoots of Puritanism.

John Wycliffe could be considered forerunners of Puritanism, though formally they were Roman Catholics. Puritan described a tendency, not a particular denomination. What the English Puritans had in common was a feeling that the official church was not a true Christian church in the sense of resembling the church established by Jesus and his Apostles. While the Puritans had differences with regard to the zeal with which they should press their points - whether they should be Separatists, or Non-Separatists working for reform within the system - they agreed that the Anglican Church was an abomination. To many, a church under the authority of a monarch was scarcely different from a church under the rule of a pope.

Puritanism always found itself in the position of defying human authority. This was not a conscious decision, but was the result of measuring the conduct of public officials by Scriptural standards. The Puritans attacked anything resembling "popish" ritual in the English Church. In the mind of Queen Elizabeth, they were "over bold with God Almighty, making too many subtle scannings of His Blessed Will." And Thomas Hobbes, writing in the 1630s, expressed well the sentiments of the ruling class when he said that such people were poor security risks. Oliver Cromwell described the essence of Puritanism to be getting to "the root of the matter," the peeling away of the layers of human intermediaries until the individual stands alone, face-to-face with the Lord. Puritanism has always been associated with rebellion. Rebellion was an act they engaged in reluctantly, but when their government forced them, as it often did, to choose between their monarch's will and what they believed to be Christ's will, there was no doubt whom they would obey.

The Apostle Paul said that government is a divinely ordained institution, established by God for man's protection. In the Puritan mind, even a corrupt and unjust regime was better than no government at all-up to a point. Determining just where that point was remained a question to be answered by the individual conscience, after applying principles set forth in the Bible.

The point at which the individual Protestant in England decided to separate from, or rebel against, the established church varied, and thus had a bearing on the type of Protestants with whom he associated. The Episcopalian rejected the pope, but accepted bishops; the Presbyterian said no to bishops in favor of presbyters; Congregationalists shunned all ecclesiastical jurisdiction outside of the particular parish; Anabaptists were similar to Congregationalists, but were more radical in their separatist views. Perhaps more than any Christian sect, Anabaptists rejected human pronouncements and accepted as authoritative only the unadorned word of God. The branch of Protestantism one associated with usually had a bearing on one's politics. Episcopalians identified more readily with aristocracy and Toryism; Presbyterianism with republican government; Congregationalism with democracy; while Anabaptist Separatists tended to be hostile to all man-made constructions, and might be considered libertarian (though certainly not libertine). It was these kinds of people, mainly Congregationalist and Separatist Protestants, who, prodded by the royal and church bureaucracy, decided in the 1630s to leave Old England for New England. It was a mass exodus. They emigrated, in fact, in such numbers that it must have appeared as though all of England was leaving. They included men of wealth, education, and position: lawyers, doctors, merchants, college professors, and some of the most famous evangelists and theologians.

They decided to go to the New World because the Protestant cause in England appeared dead. Under Queen Elizabeth, and even under James, there was hope that someday the English Church might abandon its hierarchical Romanized structure. But with the ascent of Charles I, all hope for reform seemed vain. In addition, the French Calvinists (Huguenots) were crushed by the French Catholic forces at La Rochelle in October 1628. The Spanish armies overran the Calvinists in Bohemia and the Rhineland. The Protestant forces in Germany had endured a 10-year string of uninterrupted defeats.

In his own way, Charles was as fervent about Anglicanism as Oliver Cromwell and John Milton were about Puritanism. Charles was no irreverent dandy like James. Charles believed that reform was needed, but reform in an Episcopal direction, not toward Presbyterianism and certainly not toward Congregationalism. Charles commissioned Archbishop William Laud to purge from England all those who attacked the stately grandeur of his royal church. Branding and life imprisonment were the usual penalties for criticizing church policy. Cropping ears, slitting nostrils, heavy fines, and long prison terms in rodent-infested dungeons were also imposed, in accordance with the egregiousness of the offense. And, because Puritans and Protestant non-conformists were usually the most eloquent preachers, sermons were outlawed. Some innovative ministers tried to circumvent the prohibition against the sermon by substituting the "lecture," which became immensely popular. Soon the lecture, too, was forbidden.

In addition, Charles had married a Catholic, Henrietta Maria of France, and it was clear to serious Protestants that the Angilcan Church was looking more and more like the Roman Church with each passing day. On the horizon, the Puritans saw the possibihty of a return to the policies of Bloody Mary and a rekindling of the flames at Smithfield. The King's attitude toward the Puritan-dominated Parliament was growing increasingly hostile, as was their attitude toward him. Calling them a "nest of vipers," Charles dissolved Parliament in 1629 and put the opposition Puritan leaders in the Tower. Charles would not call another Parliament for 11 years, thus leaving the Puritans with no formal political channels to express their dissatisfaction with his regime. The Puritans had always sympathized with the cause of Separatists, such as the Pilgrims of Plymouth Rock. But most Puritans had thought, at least until now, that they could work within the system. They were, after all, a formidable political, intellectual, and economic power in England. But by 1630, it appeared to many that Charles had won, that he had effectively excluded them from the political process and that conditions within the English Church had become so debased that reform was hopeless. Prospects in England and on the continent for the survival of reformed Christianity appeared extremely bleak.

Meanwhile, John Winthrop was coming of age. He would become the central figure in the Great Puritan Migration to the New World. During his early years, however, young Winthrop was far more interested in women and in getting ahead in life than in the fate of his soul. He had been raised in a wealthy family on a large estate, and by age 16 had entered Trinity College at Cambridge. He was extremely intelligent and his career prospects seemed boundless. By age 18 he was a justice of the peace. Despite all this success, Winthrop was unhappy. He knew there was a void in his life, but it was a void he was unable at first to identify. While at Cambridge, he was struck by fever and thought he was going to die. He turned to God for help; but his spiritual growth ceased when his health improved. He began faithfully to attend church on Sundays, became well-read in theology and achieved a reputation as a devout man. But existence still seemed empty and he continued to be troubled: "I upheld the outward duties, but the power and the life of them was a manner gone," wrote Winthrop in his journal. "The more I prayed and meditated, the worse I grew - the more dull, unbelieving, vain in heart, etc. So I waxed exceedingly discontent and impatient, being sometimes ready to fret and storm against God, because I found not that blessing upon my prayers and other means that I did expect."

But then Winthrop began reading William Perkins, a Puritan writer, who pointed out that pagans, with their pious rituals, had done as much to deserve salvation as had people such as Winthrop, and that the average church-goer really had no reason to believe he was saved. We are not justified, said Perkins, in expecting any mercy from God. Perkins' writings seemed to speak directly to Winthrop, who, as he himself put it, had been a "hypocrite" in matters of faith. Winthrop came to the stark realization that what he really deserved was damnation. God's grace, as he described it, came like a steel razor from the blue, tore open his soul and revealed to him a floor crawling with vermin. Whatever good works, whatever religious duties he had diligently performed, paled in comparison to the evil that permeated his life and thoughts. He concluded that his reason for despair had nothing to do with humility, but with arrogance. He believed that as long as he went to church on Sundays and persevered against his weaknesses, he could overcome sin. But now he saw that he had no virtue by himself, and that, without God, he had no power to resist Satan. "The wages of sin is death," the Bible says (Romans 6:23), and Winthrop saw very clearly that his just destination was hell.

In the depth of Winthrop's despair, God suddenly seemed to reach down and grab the young attorney. It was as if in God's infinite mercy, He had said, "John, you live in Satan's world and alone you are doomed. Hold on to me and you will live. Please, John, lay hold to Christ's promise of salvation!" Winthrop stretched out his hand, and shouted, "O Lord, forgive me!" and went on to recall: "I acknowledged my unfaithfulness and pride of heart, and turned again to my God, and watching my heart and ways. O my God, forsake me not!" Tears welled up in Winthrop's eyes, as he realized that he had been saved. Winthrop decided that he would reject worldly ambition, for "I found that the world had stolen away my love for God." He would strike out on a path that was new, and devote every last breath in his life to God's glory. He had experienced what the Puritans meant by Christian conversion. It was not a merely intellectual understanding of the tenets of Christianity, but a spiritual rebirth. Jesus himself describes the phenomenon in the New Testament: "Truly, truly, I say to you, unless one is born again, he cannot see the kingdom of God. . . That which is born of flesh is flesh; and that which is born of the Spirit is spirit. Do not marvel that I said to you, 'You must be born again.' The wind blows where it wishes and you hear the sound of it, but do not know where it comes from and where it is going; so is everyone who is born of the Spirit" (John 3:3,6-8).

Winthrop could not understand Jesus' words before, but the wind of the Spirit had blown on his heart and he saw clearly now. He had had a personal encounter with God that radically changed his life, and which, in turn, empowered him to radically change the world: "Teach me O Lord," he cried, "to put my trust in Thee!"

In August 1629, an important conference took place at Cambridge University, the intellectual center for the Puritan movement in England. The meeting would have a profound impact on the future of America. The Puritans at Cambridge had talked often of settling in the New World, particularly since the Pilgrim Fathers had proven it could be done successfully. Their leader was 40-year-old John Winthrop. He and a number of Puritan businessmen decided at the conference to assume control of the Massachusetts Bay Company, which needed investors, provided the following conditions were met: Officers of the company would be selected solely from immigrants to New England; the stockholders would agree to sell all shares of stock to the settlers; and, most important, the colonists would take with them on the voyage the King's charter for the company:

> It is fully and faithfully agreed amongst us,... that ... we will be ready in our persons... to embark for the said plantation by the first of March ... to pass the seas (under God's protection) to inhabit and continue New England. Provided always, that before the last September next, the whole government together with the patent for the said plantation be first by an order of the court legally transferred ... [and will] remain with us... upon the said plantation.

This was the key provision in the compact, the writing of which came as naturally to the non-separahng Puritans as it had to the Mayflower Pilgrims. It would permit Massachusetts Bay to operate as an independent commonwealth. Winthrop was elected unanimously as governor, and the first ship, the *Arbella,* set sail in February 1630. By June, 14 ships were making the transatlantic journey. Historian Percival Newton, in his book *The Colonizing Activities of the English Puritans,* assessed the significance of the expedition: "The Massachusetts migration was an event entirely without precedent in the modern world; Virginia, Newfoundland, and Guiana had attracted merely adventurers and the needy." But these were people of substance, and Winthrop and his followers, as Newton put it, "guided as they felt by a Higher Power, were resolved upon a course that honey, they predicted, America would become a barren wilderness, merciless and brutal, unwilling to yield fruit to the sojourners, and would wreak havoc on the colony. As Winthrop told his passengers, "The Lord will surely break out in wrath against us, be revenged of such a perjured people and make us know the price of the breach of such a covenant." The weight of the world was on their shoulders. All civilized humanity was watching, most hoping they would fail. Should they embarrass God by their actions, "we shall open the mouths of enemies to speak evil of the word of God," said Winthrop; and then God would feel compelled to make an example of them, "a story and a by-word through the world." John Cotton echoed the warning, citing precedent from the Bible: "Do not degenerate as the Israelites did."

Both Winthrop and Cotton knew that God had given them a task that was not easy. Following the Lord's will was always difficult, as Adam and Eve found, as the Israelites and even Christ's own Apostles discovered. But, said Cotton, God keeps His commitments: "What He hath planted He will maintain." For to trust in God's promises was the essence of the covenantal relationship: "We are entered into a covenant with Him for His work," Winthrop told his people. And all who went agreed that God would, in turn, honor their commitment to His ways. They knew there would be hardships; but, as Cotton put it, the Lord "hath given us hearts to overlook them all, as if we were carried up on eagles' wings."

This was the first time a people, *en masse,* agreed to establish a society wholly on Christian principles. The spirit of those who went was expressed well in the opening lines of a poem, entitled "Upon the First Sight of New England," penned by an obscure Puritan settler:

> Hail holy Land wherein our holy Lord
> hath planted his most true and holy word; Hail
> happy people who have dispossessed
> yourselves of friends, and means, to find some
> rest for your poor wearied souls, oppressed of late
> for Jesus' sake, with envy, spite and hate...

For this would not be an empire such as Constantine's, where people were compelled to call themselves Christians. This would be an association of "saints," of people who had made a conscious decision to reject the ways of the world and devote their lives to the service of Christ. As Winthrop explained to his passengers: "It is by mutual consent through a specially overruling Providence, and a more than ordinary approbation of the churches of Christ to seek out a place of cohabitation and consortship under a due form of government, both civil and ecclesiastical." The people were committed to building a holy commonwealth, a voluntary assembly of Christian men and women, "knit together in this work as one man," to live under laws spelled out clearly in the Bible, and "to follow the counsel of Micah, to do justly, to love mercy, to walk humbly with God" (Micah 6:8).

In this light, we can see why the removal of the corporate charter from London to Boston was so critical. They did not want to form a corporation administered from England by a board of directors whose sole motive was profit. They sought to build a new society; one that would fulfill the promise of the Reformation, and enable an entire people to follow the example of Christ's

Apostles, of Francis of Assisi, of John Wycliffe, and of William Tyndale. Their aim was to create a society where such men would not be persecuted for their beliefs, but would rule instead. Had the charter remained in London, this project would have been doomed from the start.

Winthrop and his people landed safely, during strawberry season.[2] They prepared as best they could for the coming winter, and even got a crop planted. Indeed, they had brought with them 200 head of cattle. But still, the beginning was difficult. Lady Arbella, after whom the ship was named, died as the leaves were turning; her heartbroken husband, who had invested heavily in the expedition, soon followed her to the grave. Moreover, the dread symptoms of scurvy were rampant. Winthrop sent the supply ship *Lyon* back to Bristol with an urgent letter to his son John, still in England, saying that if provisions were not sent immediately, the colony would perish. The ship, loaded with grain, peas, barreled beef, and lemon juice to cure scurvy, reappeared in February, just in time to save the colony. Winthrop made the occasion a day of thanksgiving.

Two hundred of the 1,500 settlers died before the ground began to thaw. Nevertheless, distinguished graduates from Cambridge and Oxford, "silenced" by Laud, poured into the colony, and many brought whole congregations with them. The houses of worship they built were bleak. There was no organ music, no stained glass, and often no heating. The benches they sat on were hard. But nowhere in the world was the Gospel expounded more masterfully from the pulpit.

Because Massachusetts had in effect declared its independence from British rule by transferring the royal charter from London to Boston, it was crucial that they establish a government. Ordinances were framed by the General Court in March 1631. Fourteen years were needed for the colony to evolve from a trading company to a full-fledged commonwealth; but from the beginning, the Congregational principle of lay church rule planted the seeds of a democratic political system. By 1632, the governor,

2. John Cotton would not arrive until 1633.

his deputy, and his assistants were positions determined by general election, rather than appointments by the corporate board
of directors.

Some historians have disparaged the Massachusetts Bay
settlement for having restricted the vote to Christians. But this
stands to reason when one considers that the purpose of the
journey to New England was to establish "A Model of Christian
Charity." Given this goal, it would hardly make sense to permit
unbelievers to rule the colony. No doubt, a non-Christian would
have felt uncomfortable in Massachusetts Bay. But, then again,
no one was forced to live in Massachusetts Bay.

The Massachusetts Puritans were in fact the most advanced in their political thinking of any people of their period,
and they made essential contributions to the evolution of republican democracy. First, they abolished all hereditary privilege.
It made no difference whether a voter - or freeman, as he was
called then-was rich or poor, educated or uneducated. Social rank
was unimportant. The political franchise was narrow (by modern
American standards); voters had to be Christians, a certified
member of God's "elect." But, as Professor Ralph Barton Perry
points out in his landmark book, *Puritanism and Democracy,* the
electorate (that is, those who had final authority over the affairs
of the colony) cut vertically rather than horizontally through the
community. Thus the franchise could easily be expanded.
Moreover, the New England Puritans were less interested in
building a government on democratic than on biblical principles.
If wealth, social rank, and education were unimportant to Jesus
Christ, then they would also be unimportant in Massachusetts
Bay. If faith in Christ was critical for admission to the kingdom
of God, according to the Puritan logic, then it should be required
of voters.

The movement toward democracy in Massachusetts, in
other words, had nothing to do with following a liberal, or "Enlightenment," political philosophy. Rather, it was a natural by-
product of the Puritans making a conscious attempt to build a

commonwealth in accordance with God's precepts. Christian and democratic institutions are compatible, which is why the Whigs3 and the Puritans could so easily become allies against the Crown throughout the political struggles of the 17th and 18th centuries. Thus, we begin to see how American ways of government and American political thought can be traced directly to religious and political institutions in colonial New England. The movement toward political equality, meaning the "one-man, one-vote" principle, in New England stands in stark contrast to the aristocratic characteristics of New York, Maryland, the Carolinas, Georgia, and even Virginia, where feudal institutions were transplanted and remained, at least partially, until the American Revolution. It was in New England soil that the seeds of liberty were planted, took firm root, and eventually spread to other regions of the country.

Americans are fickle voters. A continuous source of amazement to non-democratic societies is how the United States can have so many changes in leadership and still maintain a viable government. A President who makes it through two terms is something of a rarity. The genius of the American system is that it has institutionalized revolution without bloodshed. The restless nature of the American electorate seems to have its origins in the politics of Massachusetts Bay. No voters demanded more exacting standards from their leaders than the Puritans. Winthrop, considered by many historians to be second in stature only to George Washington in the pantheon of American political leaders, was thrown out of office in 1634. Thomas Dudley defeated Winthrop for the governorship on the grounds that Winthrop had lent 28 pounds of gunpowder to Plymouth without a vote by the Court of Assistants. The campaign was a heated affair with charges and counter-charges. But in the end, the two leaders reconciled their differences. Winthrop held a banquet at his home in celebration of Dudley's victory, and wrote in his journal that Dudley was "a wise and just man." Winthrop would later regain his gov-

---

3. The Whigs emerged as a political force during the Puritan Revolution of the 1640s and the "Glorious Revolution" of 1688. They sided with Parliment against royal prerogative and allied themselves with the Puritans. They stood for protecting individual rights and religious toleration. Their champion was John Locke. Chapters 11 and 12 cover the origin of the Whigs in greater detail.

ernorship after a series of political gaffes by Dudley.

The General Court, which was made up of the "visible saints" (eligible voters) held annual elections for governor, deputy governor, and the governor's assistants. The General Court was the highest legislative authority, while the governor's assistants served as the Supreme Court. But a conflict arose between the Assistants and the General Court over a dispute about Goody Sherman's stray pig. As documented by Samuel Eliot Morison in his book, *Builders of the Bay Colony,* Robert Keayne, a rich merchant, confiscated the errant swine, which had trespassed on to his property. The Court of Assistants, composed mainly of wealthy merchants, ruled in favor of Keayne. But the less magisterial General Court claimed veto power, and overturned the ruling, something it had never tried in the past. This incident was America's first constitutional crisis, and all of Massachusetts was in an uproar. Winthrop argued for the veto as an additional check on the magistrates, thus making abuse of authority less likely. But if the Assistants were to give up their judicial supremacy, then the General Court would have to give them at least equal authority in legislative matters. Winthrop saw merit in this arrangement, and in a discourse on government, said he believed that "democracy is, amongst most civil nations, accounted the meanest and worst form of government." Some have cited this opinion to suggest that Winthrop was hostile to the vote, and favored aristocracy. Quite the contrary. Winthrop was a republican rather than a democrat, who believed there ought to be safeguards in the system preventing a tyranny of the majority. The law-making body was subsequently divided into the House of Assistants and the House of Deputies, and henceforth represented the first bicameral legislature in North America.

Thus, in the amusing squabble over the ownership of Mrs. Sherman's pig, we can see the origins of our Senate and House of Representatives, beginning a tradition of intense rivalry between the branches of government that continues to this day. But, as Winthrop recorded, the politicians of Massachusetts, though they badly wanted to have their way, still "feared God, and endeavored to walk by the rule of His word." They took seriously Jesus' warning to His disciples that "a house divided against itself shall not stand" (Matt. 12:25). Therefore, Winthrop noted, "In all differences and agitations they continued in brotherly love."

CHAPTER SEVEN

THOMAS HOOKER TRIES DEMOCRACY

Winthrop envisioned for his "City on a Hill" a tightly knit, unified community centered around Boston. But almost immediately upon arrival, the colonists began to disperse along the hills and rivers of New England. One of the most important migrations from the mother colony was led by the great Thomas Hooker to Hartford, Connecticut. Hooker was the most famous of all the English preachers to make the journey to New England. He was a learned scholar, widely published, and his preaching had electrified the English countryside, winning converts by the thousands. As Perry Miller recounts in his book, *Errand Into the Wilderness,* Samuel Collins, an agent of Archbishop Laud, warned in 1629 that Hooker had become too powerful, and threatened to undermine the established church: "I . . . have seen the people idolizing many new ministers and lecturers; but this man surpasses them all for learning. . . [and] gains more and far greater followers than all before him." Hooker was forced into exile. He traveled first to Holland and then, following the example of the Mayflower Pilgrims, made the holy pilgrimage to Massachusetts Bay. But even after his departure from England, Collins acknowledged that Hooker's "genius" still "haunts all the pulpits."

Hooker and Winthrop were good friends, which is why Winthrop was so bitterly disappointed when Hooker petitioned the General Court to allow his congregation to move to Connecticut. Winthrop argued that Hooker was breaking the covenant by leaving the colony. Moreover, said Winthrop, it was unwise for Christians to so divide themselves, leaving themselves open to attack from the Indians and perhaps even the British Navy: "The departure of Mr. Hooker would not only draw many from us, but also divert many friends who would come to us." But Winthrop apparently lost the argument, at least as far as Hooker's people were concerned. Whether Hooker got permission from the Massachusetts General Court to leave is not clear. In his May 1636 journal entry, Winthrop notes, without elaboration, that "Mr. Hooker, Pastor of the Church at Newtown, and most of his congregation, went to Connecticut."

As Perry Miller points out, Hooker was more radical in his Protestant beliefs than Winthrop. Though he was not himself an avowed Separatist, he had many Separatist followers. Hooker's views on the congregational polity were essentially democratic, and are explained in his great work, *A Survey of the Summe of Church Discipline.* We have only fragments of his *Survey,* as the bulk of the manuscript was lost in a trip across the Atlantic on the way to England for publication. It was intended as a manifesto, explaining Hooker's views on a congregational polity. His hope was to persuade the Church of England to organize itself along congregational instead of episcopal lines, and also to explain to English Church officials what he was doing in New England, which in essence was to demonstrate how he believed a truly Christian society ought to operate. The English Church, predictably, condemned as heretical Hooker's apologetics on behalf of "liberty of conscience.

Thomas Hooker is considered by many to have~played the role of John the Baptist for Thomas Jefferson in the sense that he laid the foundation for American republican democracy. Again, though, Hooker's primary concern was not politics, but the establishment of assemblies of worship resembling the churches found in the Book of Acts. Indeed, this was the consistent pattern behind the settlement of New England, with each colony attempting to create a more pristine Christian society, and each founder, usually a minister, trying to "out-Protestantize" everyone else. Hooker, for example, apparently felt that Winthrop's efforts in Massachusetts Bay had fallen short of the mark. According to Cotton Mather, "The very spirit of his [Hooker's] ministry lay in the points of the most practical religion, and the grand concern of a sinner's preparation for, and implantation in, and salvation by, the glorious Lord Jesus Christ."

By May 1637, the inhabitants of Connecticut were holding their own General Court. Hooker, unlike Bradford and Winthrop, did not keep a journal. So the facts of his Hartford ministry are fragmentary, derived from letters and notes taken by those who heard him. His most famous sermon, delivered before the Connecticut General Court on May 31, 1638, inspired the Fundamental Orders of Connecticut, which was the first written constitution in America, and very much resembles our own Federal Constitution. Direct quotes are impossible to reconstruct exactly, as they exist in a barely decipherable journal, written by 28-year-old Henry Wolcott. But the essence of Hooker's Election Day sermon was as follows:

> 1.The choice of public magistrates belongs unto the people by God's own allowance.
> 2.The election must be conducted by the people, but votes should not be cast "in accord with their humors, but according to the will and law of God."
> 3.Those who "have the power to appoint officers and magistrates also have the power to set bounds and limitations on their power" so that "the foundation of authority is laid in the free consent of the people," because "by a free choice the hearts of the people will be more inclined to the love of the persons chosen, and more ready to yield obedience."

On January 14, 1639, the Fundamental Orders of Connecticut were adopted. The deliberations of the assembly have perished, but, as Marion Starkey points out in her book, *The Congregational Way,* the principles are a mirror of the mind of Thomas Hooker. The Fundamental Orders included many provisions essential to free and open government. Each town was to have proportional representation, and each was to send its elected representatives to the government in Hartford. In the event that the governor failed to call a meeting of the General Court, or attempted to govern contrary to established laws, the freemen were entitled to "meet together and choose to themselves a moderator," after which they "may proceed to do any act of power which any other general court may do." This was an important affirmation that the power of government resided with the people, not the magistrates. Always stressed was the voluntary nature of the covenant the people were entering into, that the purpose of government was to serve, not rule, the people, and that to do this the administration of government must be regular and orderly, not arbitrary: "The Word of God requires that to maintain the peace and union of such people there should be an orderly and decent government established according to God, in order to dispose of the affairs of the people."

The Fundamental Orders of Connecticut was the most advanced government charter the world had ever seen in terms of guaranteeing individual rights. But while certainly the effect of the charter was to ensure the establishment of free and democratic government, its primary purpose in the minds of the people of Connecticut was to establish a commonwealth according to God's laws and to create an environment conducive to spreading the Gospel: We "therefore associate and conjoin ourselves to be as one public state or commonwealth; and to do for ourselves and our successors and such as shall be adjoined to us at any time hereafter, enter into a combination and confederation together, to maintain and preserve the liberty and purity of the Gospel of our Lord Jesus which we now profess, as also the discipline of the churches, which according to the truth of the said Gospel is now practiced amongst us; as also in our civil aifairs to be guided and governed according to such laws..."

The Fundamental Orders of Connecticut represented the first known time when a working government was framed com pletely independently, without a charter or some other concession from a previously existing regime, but by the people themselves. It provided for regular elections, while setting strict limits on the power of those elected. In Massachusetts, the franchise was limited to proven church members, "visible saints." In Connecticut, however, voters merely had to be inhabitants of "honest conversation," according to Perry Miller, though they could not be Quakers, Jews, or Atheists. Elected officials had to be property owners, believers in the Trinity, and of good behavior. And the governor had to be a member in good standing of an approved congregation. Today, these requirements would seem severe, but in the 17th century such an easygoing regime was unprecedented.

Hooker criticized other New England congregations for being too quick to censure and excommunicate. His impulse was always to lower standards for church membership, believing it was far better to let in a few "hypocrites" than mistakenly to exclude true Christians. "He that will estrange his affection, because of the difference of apprehension in things difficult, he must be a stranger to himself one time or other," wrote Hooker in the preface to his *Survey.* "If men would be tender and careful to keep off offensive expressions, they might keep some distance in opinion in some things without hazard to truth or love." Hooker thought church discipline should be as uncoercive as possible. During his entire ministry only one person was excommunicated.

All this, however, does not mean that Hooker was a theological liberal; far from it. Hooker believed with Paul the Apostle that Scripture was absolutely inerrant - "All Scripture is inspired by God . . . "(2 Tim. 3:16)-and that for every act of church government a specific chapter and verse must be cited. No church officer was to act according to his own discretion, but had to point to a biblical mandate. This approach lent itself to the creation of constitutional government. For God is not a capricious ruler, but spells out in clear terms the laws His people are to follow and the conditions for eternal life. By reading the Bible, one can know exactly where one stands with regard to salvation, or damnation.

Though Hooker was a democrat who believed fervently in protecting the people's right to be wrong, he was not anything approaching a moral relativist. Not only did he believe there was a definite right and wrong, he also believed there was one, and only one, way to Heaven. In a long sermon on the prodigal son, Hooker described man without Christ as damned and undeserving of mercy. "If the Lord may damn him, He may, and if He will save him, He may." Moreover, good works could not save man from his fiery fate, because every good work would be canceled out by a hundred sins: "You cleave to these poor beggarly duties and (alas) you will perish for hunger." "The Devil slides into the heart unexpected and unseen because he comes under a color of duties exactly performed . . . Salvation comes from faith in Christ, or as John 14:6 says: "Jesus said to him, 'I am the way, and the truth, and the life; no one comes to the Father, but through Me.'" But, as Hooker put it, Christ came "not to call the righteous, that is men who look loftily in regard to what they do Christ came to call and save the poor broken-hearted sinners."

Hooker was convinced, however, that more sinners would be saved in a forgiving society than under the more regimented Massachusetts Bay, and certainly more than in England under the watchful eye of Archbishop Laud, where outward appearance (rather than genuine conversion) determined whether one was an Anglican in good standing.

Though God Himself is infinitely humane, as illustrated in the Gospel when Jesus forgives Mary Magdalene and heals the sick, Hooker warned that "mercy will never save you unless it rules you too." This idea became the underlying principle of Connecticut's government. It also established a tradition of American generosity and mercy unparalleled in history. German soldiers at the end of World War II, for example, threw their rifles down and eagerly surrendered to the American side rather than risk capture by the Russians. And after defeating them in war, America rebuilt Japan and West Germany's industrial base at enormous expense. No other people have been as magnanimous toward its enemies as has the American people, though we have often paid dearly for what most of the world would consider hopeless naivete. Mercy, forgiveness, and almost limitless charity are distinctly American characteristics that can be traced to the heart of Puritan society in 17th-century New England.

The Puritan respect for the importance of the individual soul - which included the non-Christian soul - was essential for the development of American constitutional democracy. Jesus taught that with God not one sparrow is forgotten, which is a major difference between Christianity and the pantheistic religions of the East, such as Hinduism, in which nature is god. In pantheistic religions, all of nature is part of one unified living organism, in contrast to the Christian view in which every individual is sacred and distinct, and is, therefore, to be treated with utmost reverence. This was especially true of Puritanism, the focus of which was the conversion experience, and the personal relationship to Christ. For the Puritan, the soul was the stage on which the spiritual drama occurred, and where, in the end, he was saved or damned depending on the decision he made to accept or reject Christ's offer of salvation. The decision for Christ marked a crucial turning point, and was the beginning of a transformation of the individual. Some, indeed Christ Himself, called this transforming experience being "born again." It was the first step on a radically new journey. Thus, we can see why Thomas Hooker thought "liberty of conscience" so critical to the biblical commonwealth. Salvation was a matter between the individual and God, not the individual and the state. One did not move one inch closer to Heaven when forced to pray.

The role of the state, in Hooker's mind, was to permit God's grace to easily penetrate the individual heart, to create social conditions in which all Christians could be priests; and this brings up another point of vital importance. These Protestants did not want to eliminate the priesthood, as is commonly suggested; they wanted to expand the franchise to include all believers. The Protestant believes he has direct access to God through Scripture and prayer, and that the Holy Spirit will steer him clear from serious error. As John's Gospel states: "When He, the Spirit of truth, comes, He will guide you into all the truth" (John 16:13). It is everyone's duty, thought Hooker, to preach and baptize. Moreover, if all believers could be priests, then all people could also be rulers. If the spiritual franchise could be expanded, then so could the political franchise.

The existence of Hooker's colony, its ability to attract settlers, and its constitutional protection of individual liberties put pressure on Massachusetts Bay to adopt a more formal constitution of its own. Winthrop, of course, wanted regular elections. But once elected, he thought it was up to the magistrates to make decisions according to their own interpretation of the Bible. Hooker, however, took issue with Winthrop, thinking it gave the Bay government too much discretion. Hooker recognized that many civil matters were not explicitly covered in Scripture, which meant that laws had to be carefully crafted after much deliberation and by following Scriptural principles: "That in the matter which is referred to the judge, the sentence should lie in his breast, or be left to his discretion, according to which he should go, I am afraid it is a course which wants for both safety and warrant," said Hooker. "I must confess, I look at it as a way which leads directly to tyranny, and so to confusion, and must plainly profess, it was my liberty, I should choose neither to live nor leave my posterity under such a government."

The voters of Massachusetts agreed with Hooker, that the colony needed to codify a formal body of law, provide for due process, and delineate specific penalties for particular offenses. As John Cotton put it, "If you tether a beast at night, he knows the length of the tether by morning." At first Winthrop resisted the movement to further restrict the government on the grounds that magistrates ought to have flexibility to deal with situations as they came up. But in the end he gave in, acknowledging in a journal entry in 1639 that "the people . .. desired a body of laws, and thought their condition very unsafe while so much power rested in the discretion of magistrates."

The Massachusetts "Body of Liberties," drawn up by Nathaniel Ward of Ipswich, was passed in 1641. It included 98 specific propositions, the purpose of which were to protect what they considered to be the sanctity of life, liberty, property, and reputation - foreshadowing the Bill of Rights. This historic charter declared it a violation of common law to impose taxation without representation; said that no one shall be deprived of life, liberty, or property without due process of law; and guaranteed the right of the accused to be tried by a jury of one's peers. The "Body of Liberties" also forbade cruel and unusual punish-ment, the mis-treatment of animals, and the beating of one's wife, "unless it be in his own defense upon her assault"! In 1644, the Bay adopted the secret ballot, with Indian corn representing *aye* votes and beans signifying the *nayes*.

The immense contribution the Puritans of New England made to the world's understanding of how to write a constitution cannot be overstated. When one studies the precise nature of the laws crafted by these early assemblies, and considers the sophis-ticated level of political discourse, one cringes in shame to wit-ness the sheer ignorance displayed in congressional debates today. We hear many references to lofty phrases like "inalienable rights" and "general welfare" by our demagogic politicians who have little demonstrated understanding of what these terms mean.

The Puritans of colonial America had an understanding of freedom that was far in advance of our own. They saw, for ex-ample, that the spirit of freedom and the spirit of Christianity reinforced each other. But they also understood that religious and civil authority operated in separate spheres. They had started to recognize, before any other nation, that the Holy Spirit did not need His power enhanced by government officials; that to have the government engaged in the regulation of matters religious was more often than not to put hypocrites in charge of the moral health of the people, and thus actually undermined the cause of Christianity. Winthrop and Hooker consistently pointed out that Jesus is perfectly content with the power He already wields. He did not ride into Jerusalem with an army, He came on a donkey. His authority rests in His Spirit convicting men's hearts, not in His wish to see people burned at the stake for disputing an ecclesiastical pronouncement. Though it is true that much New England law came directly from the Old and New Testaments,[1] the tendency of the Puritans was to erect a wall of separation between the responsibilities of church and state, to paraphrase Jefferson. They saw the roles of magistrates and clergy as distinct, which is why ministers in Puritan New England were prohibited from holding a civil office.

But the Puritans also believed that liberty would not survive unless it was firmly grounded in a healthy fear of God and a spirit of Christian charity. For if a man is not restrained by fear for his soul, what is to prevent him from pursuing his own interests at the expense of everyone else? A large chasm exists between what is lawful and what is ethical. And while the policeman and the courts can punish people for committing egregious offenses against society, only religion can regulate the more subtle area of morals. Government's highest responsibility is to safeguard liberty, while salvation is the supreme aim of the individual. Moreover, for a people to remain free, they must vigilantly attend to matters concerning their character and souls. The citizen must pursue with diligence not just his own interests, but the interests of his neighbor.

John Winthrop, as much as any, embodied this ideal. He was charitable beyond reasonable expectation, and frequently sacrificed his own welfare for the good of the community. When the Massachusetts treasury was out of funds, he donated the proceeds from the sale of his Groton Manor to pay public expenses. When he saw others in need, he gave them money, food, and

---

1. Indeed, we would expect this, given that the settlers of New England were Bible-believing Christians.

shelter from his own resources. His generosity toward others was unsurpassed, yet he was so frugal and austere concerning his own comforts that his friends often called his attention to Paul's admonition to Timothy, who apparently had a similar disposition: "No longer drink water," says Paul, "but use a little wine for the sake of your stomach . . . " (1 Tim. 5:23). John Winthrop was a superior man of impeccable character. William Hubbard, an early historian of Massachusetts Bay, provided us an appropriate summary of Winthrop's life: He "had done good in Israel, having spent not only his whole estate. . . but his bodily strength and life in the service of the country." Winthrop saw clearly that as self-sacrifice was an essential Christian trait, so self-sacrifice was also vital to the preservation of liberty and independence.

What we see emerging in early New England, almost unnoticed, was an utterly new political culture. Alexis de Tocqueville saw this clearly, and compares the conditions of Europe with those of New England in 1650: "Everywhere on the Continent at the beginning of the 17th century absolute monarchies stood triumphantly on the ruins of the feudal or oligarchic freedom of the Middle Ages. Amid the brilliance of the literary achievements of Europe, then, the conception of rights was perhaps never more completely misunderstood at any other time; liberty had never been less in men's minds. And just at that time these very principles, unknown to or scorned by the nations of Europe, were proclaimed in the wilderness of the New World, where they were to become the watchwords of a great people."

* * *

The Puritans knew that conditions of political and economic well-being depended on an educated population. The American belief that every citizen must have a certain amount of education, and a certain degree of literacy and mathematical competency, is a Puritan legacy. In Europe, education, especially advanced education, was limited to the extreme upper crust of society. The lower classes, it was thought, were unfit to be put through schools. Education in Europe was to be reserved for the ruling class. Oxford and Cambridge were England's only two universities.

In the Puritan mind literacy was important not only to ensure a reasonably informed electorate, essential for the survival of democratic government; but it also played an important role in the individual's walk with the Lord. The Puritans stressed the individuals personal relationship with Jesus. To read the Bible or follow the logic of a sermon requires a certain familiarity with basic concepts. That a religious movement, which shunned philosophy, was strictly fundamentalist, and believed completely in the inerrancy of Scripture, produced the most educated nation of people the world had ever seen is one of the remarkable paradoxes, and lessons, of history.

The building of schools was one of the first orders of business when Winthrop and his followers arrived in Massachusetts. Puritan dissidents from Cambridge and Oxford provided excellent teachers. By 1640, there were 113 men with university educations living in New England, and 71 in Massachusetts. This was a much larger concentration of educated men than could be found in England, or anywhere else. The Puritans thought it vitally important that every congregation have a learned pastor who could inspire, point out doctrinal errors, and defeat the forces of darkness. The Massachusetts School Act of 1647 stated: "It being the chief project of that old deluder Satan to keep men from knowledge of the Scriptures, as in former times keeping them in an unknown tongue, so that in these latter times, by persuading them from the use of tongues, so that at least, the true sense and meaning of the original might be clouded with false glosses of saint seeming deceivers; and that learning may not be buried in the grave of our forefathers, in church and commonwealth, the Lord assisting our endeavors."

Harvard was founded in 1636, after newly arrived John Harvard donated 777 pounds and a library of 400 volumes for the purpose of training Puritan ministers. King Charles had effectively purged the Puritans from the English universities. Hence the need to establish a second Cambridge. "The main end of the scholar's life and studies," said the Harvard Rules and Precepts, "is to know God and Jesus Christ which is eternal life. Therefore, to lay Christ in the bottom is the only foundation of all sound knowledge and harmony." In addition to reading the Scriptures, history, literature, and theology, Harvard students were expected to achieve proficiency in mathematics and the sciences: calculus, geometry, astronomy. Knowledge in every area, for the Puritan, far from undermining his religious faith, served to magnify God's glory and always shed new light on the maguificence of His creation. Scholarship and scientific inquiry aided the Harvard student in searching out the Holy Spirit.

The founding of Harvard was yet another Puritan challenge to royal authority. In England, the king had monopolistic power over the granting of degrees, as Oxford and Cambridge were arms of the government and private alternatives were illegal. Harvard had no royal charter, and hence no authority in King Charles' mind to award college diplomas. But the Puritans in the Bay did not recognize the King's education monopoly, and Harvard granted its first degree in 1642. The fact that Harvard continued to award college diplomas despite official protests from England was, in effect, an affirmation of New England's independence from Crown rule. Harvard's existence was a perpetual source of irritation to royal authorities, particularly since more than half of its graduates during the 17th century became ministers of a dissident faith.

The construction of a printing press in 1639 in Harvard Yard allowed the proliferation of publications, mostly sermons, Psalm books, and almanacs. This material was viewed as subversive by officials in England, as it clearly did not conform to the *Book of Common Prayer*. Obvious from the start was the Puritan penchant for rebellion against British rule, and particularly against impositions from the English Church. But King Charles could do little about transgressions in New England, as he had his hands more than occupied with the increasingly powerful Puritan movement at home. As a result, New England operated for the most part as an independent nation, and continued to evolve into a new and distinctive society, consciously and defiantly creating itself.

New England's reputation as a center of American learning is a legacy of the Puritan stress on diffusing knowledge as broadly as possible. Yale was established in 1701, also for the purpose of training Congregational clergy, in response to the emergence at Harvard[2] of what some thought to be erroneous Arminian theology (that opposed strict Calvinist predestination, but favored election and salvation by grace).[3] The two universities found themselves in competition with each other for students and introduced for the first time market forces to higher learning. The effect was to encourage very low tuition. It is more profitable for an institution to educate many at less cost per student than to admit only the few who could afford an expensive education. Hence, college tuition in the colonies was about one-tenth what it cost to educate someone at Oxford or Cambridge. At Dartmouth, established by another Congregational minister to bring the Gospel to the Indians, it was common for students to work their way through college. The result of this uniquely American approach to education was to spread, rather than deepen, knowledge. And while the quality of education was less than what, say, an earl or duke might receive from Oxford, it brought the possibility of higher education to the general population-in contrast to England and the Old World, where the opportunity for schooling of even the most elementary soft was non-existent for the great majority of people.

In the Puritan view, the purpose of education was not to groom the children of a ruling aristocracy in order to set them

---

2. William and Mary was founded in 1693, but did not operate successfully until the middle of the 18th century.
3. Strict Calvinists feared that Arminian theology left too much room for the human will, thus implicitly diminishing God's omnipotent power. In addition, Arminianism, by suggesting that people chose their own fates, either by accepting or rejecting Christ (instead of being predestined for damnation or glory), tended to lead to a theology of salvation by works rather than faith. Arminian thought influenced John and Charles Wesley, the founders of Methodism, and in fact would hardly be considered liberal theology by the standards of today.

apart from the general population, but to supply the communities with knowledgeable ministers, doctors, teachers, lawyers, businessmen, and civic leaders. Education in New England was not to be a special privilege limited to a few, but a vehicle to elevate everyone in the community. The proliferation of schools and the availability of instruction made it impossible for a powerful aristocracy to establish itself in New England. It should be obvious why this development, Puritan in origin, was so essential to the emergence of democracy in America. As Tocqueville observed, "In America it is religion which leads to enlightenment and the observance of divine laws which leads men to liberty." Government by the people requires an educated people, which helps explain why democratic experiments in the Third World in recent years have mostly failed.

CHAPTER EIGHT

TROUBLE IN NEW JERUSALEM

Progress toward a free and open society in America is typically presented in modern history texts as coinciding with the failure of the so-called "Puritan oligarchs" to keep a grip on their people. Freedom, we are told, is purely the product of Enlightenment thought and the valiant efforts of a few noble people who battled the Puritan ruling establishment for "liberty of con science." This view of New England history is clearly false, but the figures most often cited in this context are Roger Williams and Anne Hutchinson, two religious dissidents who were expelled from Massachusetts Bay for persisting in preaching a theology that the General Court thought erroneous. Usually Williams and Hutchinson are portrayed as doctrinal liberals. This presentation of American history is consistent with the view that man was liberated when he freed himself from the chains of "religious superstition." The problem with this history is that it is unhistorical.

To begin with, neither Roger Williams nor Anne Hutchinson objected to Massachusetts being a strict Bible commonwealth. Their complaint was that Massachusetts, too, had fallen short of the church model provided in the Book of Acts. Both thought that Massachusetts was not Christian enough, that it had failed in its mission to establish a "City on a Hill," a beacon for all the world to follow. Neither was a proponent of humanist thought in Christianity, and neither was motivated by a concern for lack of freedom of religion. Quite the contrary; their invective was directed against what they perceived to be corruption and impurity within the polity of Massachusetts Bay. They thought the people and their leaders too worldly, too ready to compromise on doctrine in order to build church membership, and too inclined to ignore or dilute the difficult passages in the Bible.

Roger Williams, who arrived in 1631, attacked the churches of Massachusetts for failing to sever completely their ties with the Church of England, which he saw as beyond repair because of its commitment to be all-inclusive and permit the unregenerate to worship alongside the saved. Williams' position was that the Massachusetts Bay church had been too lax in admitting "non-elect" people, mixing "herds of the world" with the "flock of Christ." He went so far as to denounce the residence oath on the grounds that "a magistrate ought not to tender an oath to an unregenerate man." Williams was also more hard line than the mainstream New Englander on such aspects of Calvinist theology as predestination and irresistible grace. He believed that church and state should be utterly separate, not because of a desire for religious liberty, but because he believed the state poisons Christianity, and that Jesus, not some cabal of government officials, selects His people. Williams was what was known as an Anabaptist; that is, he was a radical Separatist. He represented an extreme end of the Protestant spectrum, indeed too extreme for the General Court of Massachusetts Bay.

Williams was actually very popular, even among the leaders of the colony. He was a friend of John Winthrop and Thomas Hooker and was perhaps closest to William Bradford. They knew genius when they saw it, and no doubt thought he was making some valid points. Williams probably would not have been expelled had the Bay not received news that King Charles was planning to send the Royal Navy, seize the company charter, and take over the government. The presence of a virulent Separatist, such as Williams, continuously ranting against the English Church would confirm the King's bias against the practices of this maverick colony. The Bay did not comprehend the dimensions of Charles' political problems with the Puritans in England and, therefore, could not have anticipated that Charles would never get around to dealing with the Bay. At the time, however, it appeared to the leaders of Massachusetts that the survival of the colony was at stake, and the last thing they wanted was an articulate and flamboyant dissident in their midst.

The General Court argued with Williams at length, and even brought in Thomas Hooker to reason with him. They gave Williams ample time to change his views, or at least agree to temper his most extreme rhetoric; but as the process continued, his stance grew even more intractable. He denounced as "hypocrites" several respected leaders. The General Court, feeling there was little choice, ordered him expelled. Williams was given six weeks to leave, much to the sadness of William Bradford, with whom he would correspond for the rest of his life. Williams wound up staying much longer than six weeks, but was finally told that if he did not depart soon he would be shipped off to England. In January 1636, he and five of his followers bought from the Indians a plot of land at Narragansett Bay and founded "Providence."

As it turned out, Rhode Island did become a haven for various dissident Christian denominations, in part because Williams was not at all interested in building a political community. By then, he had come to the conclusion that all human institutions were evil and ought to be avoided. "Oh remember whither your principles and conscience must in time and opportunity force you!" said Williams. "'Tis but worldly policy and compliance with men and times (God's mercy overruling)" which leads men to "the murdering of thousands and tens of thousands were your power and command as great as once the bloody Roman emperor was."

This sentiment remains strong in certain Christian denominations in America, who believe politics and government to be so corrupt and ungodly that Christians are advised not to participate. But this position is counterproductive. While certainly all human institutions are fallen, how much more corrupt will government be if left to non-Christians? If Lenin, Hitler, and Mao had been Christians, the world would be a far better place - far more hospitable to the spread of Christianity. If Christians refuse to involve themselves in the affairs of state, the totalitarians and authoritarian despots will gladly step in. Wililams' error was to permit the perfect to be the enemy of the good, for human institutions always will be flawed. To forsake society and community altogether, as Williams did, is detrimental not only to freedom's prospects, but also to Christianity. Christ, after all, waited until the Roman Empire was at its pinnacle to make His entrance into the world, no doubt seeing the spread of civilization, however imperfect, as the best vehicle to also spread the good news of eternal life.

Ultimately, Williams rejected the label Anabaptist for himself, thinking it too sectarian and institutional sounding, preferring instead to be called merely a "seeker." Williams is often called a pioneer of "religious liberty." But one should not equate liberty with the rejection of civilization. The credit for beginning the evolution toward republican constitutional democracy in America, leading ultimately to separation of church and state, goes to Winthrop and Hooker, who progressively broadened the political franchise and loosened standards for church membership as time passed, and as it became apparent that by doing so the commonwealth would not degenerate into anarchy. Williams may have inadvertently contributed to this process; but one can hardly give him credit for promoting civil liberties of any kind, given that he was uninterested in civil affairs and shunned society altogether. Moreover, Williams would be shocked if he knew that his legacy would be routinely cited by revisionist historians as a victory for the cause of liberal humanism in religion. His sin, in the minds of the magistrates of the Bay, was not that he was a humanist or some sort of theological liberal, but that his religious enthusiasm was too extreme.

The same can be said of Anne Hutchinson. The various twists and turns within Puritan theology seem alien to the 20th-century mind, which is one reason we have not delved deeply into theological distinctions in these pages. But to ignore completely the doctrinal issues is also a mistake, because they are critical to understanding the mind of the 17th-century Puritan and the sub-stance from which a distinctly American character and stream of political thought was forged.

Anne Hutchinson got herself into difficulty when she launched a campaign against the minister of the Boston Church, John Wilson, whom she despised because she thought his preaching was not at all compelling. This was a serious misjudg-ment, because Wilson was both influential and popular, though Hutchinson was right about his preaching, which was lackiuster and difficult to hear (he had a tendency to mumble his words). Her dispute with Wilson might have been ignored if she had not gone on to make pronouncements on the qualifications of mini-sters throughout the colony. According to her count, there were only two truly Christian - "sealed" - preachers in all of Mas-sachusetts. They were John Cotton, whom she called "the voice of the beloved," and her brother-in-law John Wheelright. The rest were hypocrites, liars, and on their way to perdition. But she singled out Wilson (no one knows exactly why) as especially pernicious. One day she caused a scene by abruptly leaving a Boston meeting after it turned out that John Wilson was preach-ing when she expected it to be John Cotton.

For a woman in the 17th century to be launching such in-vective against a prominent member of the community was un-heard of. John Winthrop tried to defend her behavior on the grounds that women must be given more latitude because of their weaker intellects. But even though the Bay leadership was inclined to make allowances for "female troubles," it was thought that Hutchinson had gone beyond the pale. She seemed to be passing judgment on others, which the Bible says is the sole pre-rogative of the Lord. The General Court convened to investigate her behavior, and to ask who she thought had given her the authority to decide whether John Wilson, or anyone else, was "sealed" or not? Anne answered that she had been given "an immediate revelation" from God, and that "the voice of His own Spirit" had spoken to her soul.

This answer sealed her fate in the minds of the General Court. For not only was she treading very close to something like the "inner light" followed by the Quakers, but apparently she had elevated herself to the status of prophet, by claiming she could receive divine revelations not available to everyone else who read Scripture. The Bible, in the Book of Revelation, addresses a warning to "everyone who hears the words of the prophecy of this book," saying: "If anyone adds to them, God shall add to him the plagues which are written in this book; and if anyone takes away from the words of the book of this prophecy, God shall take away his part from the tree of life and from the holy city, which are written in this book" (Rev. 22:18-19).

The Puritans believed these words ought to be applied to the Bible in its entirety; that God's revelations were inscribed in the Scriptures, were accessible to everyone, and were not exclusive to any particular individual. The General Court ruled that Anne Hutchinson was a heretic, and a dangerous one at that. She was banished from the colony as a "woman not fit for society." She traveled first to Roger Williams' settlement in 1638, but found Rhode Island as unsuitable for her version of Christianity as Massachusetts. She then set off for Long Island where she was killed by Indians.

Hutchinson, like Williams, in many history texts is included in the pantheon of forerunning secularists crusading for religious freedom and hounded out of the Massachusetts theocracy by intolerant oligarchs. Hutchinson was many things, and dead wrong on a number of counts. But one thing she wasn't was a secularist. Nor was she the least bit concerned about expanding either church membership or the political franchise. She was the opposite of a civil libertarian. According to her count, there were only two ministers in Massachusetts who would be forgiven for their sins and given eternal life with God. She was expelled because she was a religious fanatic who spent much of her time slandering the reputations of good and honorable men. She had violated both the laws of the Bible and of acceptable conduct needed to hold society together. To characterize this episode as "The Persecution of Anne Hutchinson," and to present her as a lone heroine battling for liberty of conscience, or as some sort of early feminist up against the "Old Boys Network," as is commonly done, is an abomination of the truth.

The expansion of New England was accomplished almost entirely under the auspices of migrating congregations. There were, of course, the highly publicized dissidents who left the Bay under unfavorable circumstances, such as Williams and Hutchinson. But most, like Thomas Hooker, adhered fairly closely to the Christian practices of the mother colony. Some settlements were less theocratic, while others, like the religious settlement in New Haven, established by John Davenport and Theophilus Eaton, were more strict and less lenient with deviants. By 1640, English Puritan settlements dotted the Atlantic coast from New Netherland to Maine.

John Winthrop was the architect of the New England Confederation. Formed in 1643, its purpose was to settle trade and boundary disputes that might develop among the various Puritan settlements, and to provide a mutual defense against possible aggression on the part of the Spanish, French, or Dutch colonies. After the first meeting at Boston, Hooker wrote to his "Honored Friend John Winthrop Esquire, Governor of the Plantations on Massachusetts Bay." Hooker praised Winthrop for his "candid and cordial carriage in a matter of so great consequence" and his "special prudence to settle a foundation of safety and prosperity in succeeding ages." The New England Confederation would play a major role in King Philip's War of 1675-76, thwarting the Spanish monarch's colonizing ambitions in North America. It also introduced the federalist principle, which would become another cornerstone of American constitutional democracy, making it different from all other forms of government.

Surprisingly, the most serious threat to the independence of early New England came not from King Charles, but from the English Puritans during the ascendancy of their leader Oliver Cromwell during the 1640s and 50s. Charles was beheaded in 1649, and Cromwell assumed his role as Lord Protector of the empire. One would think that New Englanders would have considered this a great victory for the cause of Reformed Christianity. But Puritans who prevailed in England under Cromwell's leadership were largely Presbyterian, while those who settled New England were predominantly Congregationalist. Presbyterians and Congregationalists considered themselves allies on most theological matters - broadly speaking they were Calvinist. But they had different conceptions of church government. Presbyterianism was really Low Church Anglicanism, which means, in essence, that most Presbyterians of that day believed firmly in a national church, but one that was more stark in appearance, more Protestant, and administered by presbyters rather than bishops. Congregationalists adhered strictly to the principle of the autonomous local church. This difference between Presbyterians and Congregationalists helps explain why Puritans in America succeeded in building a free society, whereas Puritan rule in England failed.

In this light, John Winthrop's insistence on maintaining neutrality for Massachusetts during the civil war in England between the Puritans and the Crown is significant. Winthrop went so far as to punish a privateer for firing upon a royalist ship in Boston Harbor. And when some Puritans in Parliament offered Massachusetts special favors for supporting their cause against Charles, Winthrop convinced the General Court to decline on the grounds that it would be hazardous to the independence of the Bay to suggest that Parliament had any jurisdiction over the colony. In Winthrop's mind, Parliament had no authority to grant favors to Massachusetts, because it was a self-governing commonwealth. To Cromwell and most of his largely Presbyterian followers, Congregationalism seemed too loose a way to conduct church affairs, which they thought needed tighter controls so as to prevent both political and doctrinal chaos.

Thus, when Dr. Robert Child, a Presbyterian, arrived in Massachusetts, he was welcomed as a Protestant reformer, and friend of the Winthrop family. But bad feelings rapidly arose when he discovered that as a Presbyterian he could not be a church member, and therefore could not even vote. This festered into a serious problem for Massachusetts because Dr. Child was an intellectual of towering stature, even by New England standards. He had a master's degree from Cambridge, an M.D. from the University of Padua, and had completed further graduate work in Holland. Moreover, the younger John Winthrop had persuaded Dr. Child to invest and settle in New England. So one can imagine Child's chagrin when upon arrival in 1645 he discovered he was excluded from the political affairs of the colony. He could have moved to Hooker's settlement and voted, but he chose to stay in Massachusetts Bay and fight. He quickiy gained a following of people who were in a similar situation.

Child challenged the Bay's independence from Parliament, and argued that "civil liberty and freedom be given to all." Child demanded that all members of the Church of England (who, being largely followers of Cromwell, were now mostly Presbyterian) be admitted to the Massachusetts congregations, and then announced that if this were not done he would appeal directly to "the honorable house of Parliament.', In one respect Child's grievance was legitimate. One could sympathize with his desire to vote, and it would have been wise for Massachusetts Bay to let him do so. Indeed, if he had confined his complaint to that issue, in time he probably would not only have been given church membership with all its advantages, but might have been elected governor. His mistake was to overreact to what was really nothing more than a glitch in the system, and to challenge New England's independence from the British government. The General Court reacted angrily to Child's threat of appeal to the British authorities and fined him 50 pounds. It also issued the following statement, which no doubt would have startled English officials had it reached their eyes: "Our allegiance binds us not to the laws of England any longer than while we live in England, for the laws of the Parliament of England reach no further, nor do the King's writs under the great seal."

Child decided to leave the colony for the home country. Still, Winthrop saw that it was crucial to institute safeguards against central administrative control, such as could be imposed by a Presbyterian-dominated British government.

In 1648, ministers from the Bay, Plymouth, and Connecticut called a "synod" (a term that was later changed to "an association of ministers" to avoid Presbyterian implications). The result was the Cambridge Platform, an historic charter codifying the Congregational Way as the accepted form of church organization. It defined Christ's church as the body of believers, and specified that no visible church larger than the individual congregation would be recognized; that the selection of officers was the sole prerogative of the congregation; and that church discipline, such as excommunication, was strictly up to the particular church and was not a civil matter. John Cotton expressed well the spirit of congregationalism when he said in one sermon that "no particular church standeth in subjection to another" and that "all the churches enjoy mutual orderly communion amongst themselves." Under the congregational system, a synod carried with it no official authority, was strictly advisory and the individual congregations were free to accept or reject its recommendations. If, however, a particular church trespassed beyond standards agreed to at the synod, the other churches might decide to withdraw their fellowship. The Cambridge Platform further italicized the federalist concept as a central feature of American civilization. It was both an improvement on and an affirmation of the New England Confederation conceived by John Winthrop.

The tendency of Protestant theology was always toward smaller and smaller religious establishments. Roger Williams and Anne Hutchinson took this tendency to an extreme by rejecting the fellowship of practically every Christian, and ultimately society.

John Clark's story is somewhat different. He was another Anabaptist disrupter, friendly with both Williams and Hutchinson. He followed Williams to Rhode Island, but decided to return to Boston in 1651 to propagate his Baptist beliefs. He and some of his followers were fined, probably less for their views than for the fact they were making public nuisances of themselves. Clark subsequently published a small tract titled *Ill News from New England,* in which he outhlined abuses of civil liberties taking place in the Bay and argued that Christ gave no man the authority to compel the consciences of others. Clark's arguments convinced enough New Englanders of the merits of his case, and soon other Baptists were also preaching, for the most part unmolested. By 1686, most Puritans had decided that Baptists were indeed brothers in Christ and permitted them to establish meeting houses. By 1700, there were ten Baptist churches operating successfully in Boston, Plymouth, and Rhode Island.

The Baptist view was about as far as reformed Protestant Christianity was willing to go in terms of separatism. The Quakers were the most radical, relying less on the Bible than on what they called their "inner light." This approach violated the central Puritan tenet, of which there could be no compromise, which is reliance on the written word of God as the sole standard by which the conduct of human affairs should be judged. There is no more precedent in Scripture for the Quaker "inner light" than for Anne Hutchinson's "immediate revelations." Both could lead to dangerous religious enthusiasms, and, more alarming, elevated the opinion of the individual above the Bible. What common denominator is there, what moral absolutes can one appeal to, what standard of right and wrong can we refer to if everyone is guided by their "inner light"? The Quaker approach seemed a prescription for both moral and social anarchy. In the Puritan view, the Baptists, though not held together very tightly through an institution, were connected to the body of believers through Scripture.

Agreement about the supremacy of the Bible over all human pronouncements and all man-made traditions was the thread that held Protestants from all denominations together. New Englanders came to believe that there was room for argument about church structure; but to dispute the ultimate supremacy of God's written word, to make Him secondary to the "inner light," was outside the realm of discussion. As the American Revolution approached, Puritanism in America found itself tending more and more toward the more virulent Baptist Separatism, a position that seemed more and more correct with every encroachment by the Anglican Church on American religious practices.

An important difference between the New England settlers and the Spanish, French, and Dutch colonists, was that the English considered the New World to be home. The other Europeans saw their stay in America as temporary, and eagerly waited for the day when they could return to their motherland. The English Puritans planted roots in American soil and their number increased steadily throughout the 17th and 18th centuries. Though unanticipated, this turned out to be a tremendous boon to the British colonizing enterprise, as English-speaking people increased their advantage in terms of sheer manpower over the competing European powers. London had little difficulty in routing the Dutch in New York and winning the French and Indian War because of the indigenous population of dissenting Protestant Englishmen who fought willingly on the side of England in order to preserve their way of life.

Cotton Mather in 1684 was the first European on record to use the term "American" to describe his nationality. He was proud to wear the label. But he also considered himself an Englishman, as did the other New England Puritans, and this worked to the tremendous benefit of the British government. How foolish the British were to treat the colonists in America as second-class citizens, as competitors rather than allies. If England had permitted its American colonies to trade freely and to worship as they saw fit, unmolested by burdensome taxes, nosy regulators, and Anglican clergy, London would have had no better friend in the world.

Modern historians, in painstaking fashion, have combed through the history of the New England Puritans and picked out their faults. Certainly the Puritans had shortcomings. They were, after all, human. We can find instances of intolerance in their heritage. Indeed their daily lives were very strict by the standards of cosmopolitan America. But by 17th-century standards, even 17th-century English standards, there were no more forgiving people anywhere. Archbishop Laud sent thousands to rot away in King Charles' dungeons for failing to adhere strictly to every item in the *Book of Common Prayer.* Seventeenth-century Spain and France was no barrel of laughs, and life grew progressively grim as one traveled east into the heart of Islam and the Orient. Only with extreme reluctance was anyone ever expelled from Massachusetts Bay. It is pure myth that the Puritans prohibited alcoholic drinks. A Harvard student could be fined five shillings for drunkenness, unless it was "a very aggravated drunkenness," in which case a student might be expelled. But the Puritans enjoyed liquor, consumed in moderation, and derived much of their income from the sale of rum. Nor were the Puritans preoccupied with hellfire and damnation, but actually tended to be very cheerful about life and spoke often ofthe "tidings of great joy" given them by their faith in Jesus. And when they wore drab clothing, it was more often because they lacked money and lived in the wilderness than because of religious conviction. When they could afford brightly colored clothes, they generally bought them and wore them cheerfully to look their best—in order to attract the opposite sex.

The Puritans would be the first to admit that their people often strayed from the spirit of Christ, that perversions and corruptions often crept into their communities, that some of their ministers and government officials became more enamored with personal power than with following the path of righteousness.

But these were exceptions. What Puritanism stood for over the course of 200 years was personal integrity, sincerity of purpose, living in accordance with the Gospel, and always seeking God's will. The Puritan was far quicker to judge his own behavior than to judge the actions of others. His intellectual strength came from his mastery of the Bible. His moral power came from living the Bible. Perhaps this has something to do with why the Puritan heritage has been so thoroughly denigrated in modern times.

CHAPTER NINE

THE PROTESTANT SPIRIT OF CAPITALISM

We have discussed at some length the Puritan contribution to America's political institutions: written constitutions, separation of powers, regular elections, the secret ballot, the federalist principle, religious toleration and separation of church and state. But there is also a strong connection between the rise of Puritanism and the emergence of capitalism. To fully appreciate this fact, it is worth reflecting briefly on conditions in Europe prior to the economic revolution, which began to take place following the Protestant Reformation. Living standards for most people in medieval Europe were poor. About 90 percent of the people spent their waking hours working in agriculture, trying to acquire food. Whether or not one could eat on a particular day was a major source of insecurity. Poor weather often meant starvation.

The abject poverty of the average medieval sert, though, had nothing to do with lack of native intelligence or ability, but with the social and economic system with which he had to contend. The medieval ethos was decidedly hostile to commercial activity. The merchant was seen as a scurrilous character in feudal Europe. To most, he seemed to provide nothing of obvious value, serving as middleman who skimmed his profit off the labor of others, buying cheaply and selling to someone else for more than it was worth. His contracts were not enforced in the medieval court system. In an effort to protect the unsuspecting peasant from being scalped by shady middlemen, charging interest on money was prohibited by the Catholic Church, as was the selling of insurance. But such laws made it very difficult for a merchant to hedge his bets against possible future calamity.

In addition, there were rigid economic controls imposed on the population. Among the most pernicious regulations involved the "just wage" and "just price" theories, promulgated mainly through the Roman Church. It seemed, on the surface, a sensible doctrine given the impoverished and desperate condition of the vast majority of the people. Hence, except for a small minority, "just wage" and "just price" regulations were uniformly accepted and enforced. The idea that a price could be settled through negotiation between buyer and seller was an alien notion in medieval society. Wages and prices were set by custom. Every service and every product had a fixed price, even if external circumstances made the prices unworkable. A drought, for example, might make it necessary for the farmer to raise his crop prices in order to turn a profit. But this notion was completely antithetical to the medieval understanding of a just social order. The result was economic havoc, food shortages, and regular famines.

In addition, anyone engaged in trade was required to belong to a guild, which was similar in some respects to a modern trade union - except that gaining access to a guild was all but impossible. One acquired his position in this structure through inheritance. The vast majority of people in the Middle Ages were barred by law from entering into markets, as the force of heredity perpetuated all authority and privileged position. The guild enforced all regulations of the trade - prices, wages, rules for workmanship - and administered punishments to transgressors. Those engaged in trade at all were lucky and few, the entire point of the guild being to protect the few market jobs that existed. The great majority of people were marooned on a manorial plantation in indentured servitude, under the authority of a lord or baron.

What we now call feudal Europe evolved naturally from

the break-up of the Roman Empire. As law and order from the sixth through the ninth centuries disintegrated, the crying social need was for safety, which only the powerful landowners could provide. The small and isolated individual was forced by circumstances to exchange his freedom, as well as the freedom of all his descendants, to a particular lord, who, in turn, would provide protection and social identity. The tenant agreed to become the lord's hereditary serf. The giving away of the freedom of all the serf's descendants was an essential part of the bargain, because it was the lord's guarantee of continued agricultural service.

Sometimes these landowners were church authorities, sometimes friends or relatives of a king or prince. Usually land was accumulated in the form of grants from a king to a lord or monastery in return for their loyalty. The armed castle or manor was the focus of medieval life. The Southern plantation in the American colonies was a descendant of this system, antiquated and outmoded by the time of the American Revolution.

Typically, a serf and his family would be given a tract of land to cultivate, from which they would be permitted to keep a small percentage of what was produced, usually subsistence level, sometimes less. The amount taken by the lord in duties, taxes, and actual goods varied from manor to manor. It was understood by all, however, that everyone worked for the benefit of the lord-not themselves, and certainly not for profit.

The Catholic Church is often blamed for the quality of life of the average serf, as it was the dominant force of the age. The official Church, to be sure, did Christianity no service by embroiling itself in power politics, by selling indulgences, by using what amounted to slave labor to build its magnificent cathedrals. But as corrupt as it sometimes was, the Catholic Church was the one unifying social and religious force without which the individual became isolated, defenseless, and spiritually adrift. The Church was not merely one aspect of civilization. It was civilization. The Church was the only systematic machine spreading literacy and advancing learning. It was a source of comfort and enlightenment for the vast majority of people. Indeed, there were many brave missionaries in the Church, selflessly spreading the Gospel among barbaric tribes throughout Europe. Without the likes of Dante and Thomas Aquinas, two titanic intellectual powers, our understanding of spiritual truths would not be as rich. Without living examples such as Francis of Assisi and John of the Cross, the hope of actually living a life worthy of the men of New Testament fame would seem a distant dream.

Because civilization had been in decline for so long, one of the Church's main missions was to rediscover its classical heritage and copy it down. During the early Middle Ages, all intellectual efforts went toward relearning old concepts. With good reason, this project placed strong emphasis on order, custom and continuity. Intellectual and material progress cannot be made-indeed the Gospel cannot easily be spread - if the foundation of society is ignorance and chaos, as was the case from about the 6th to 11th centuries. Monks, who were the most learned class of people during this period, labored in the monasteries to meticulously preserve Scripture and reconstruct texts from vanquished Greek and Roman culture.

Since the Church's main preoccupation was the rebuilding of classical civilization on a Christian foundation, rituals, serving as a memory mechanism to preserve tradition, became very important and grew increasingly elaborate. Over the centuries, legal and social relations also became bewilderingly complex, and had little to do with economic considerations.

The idea that new products could be developed, larger markets found, or that a service could be delivered more efficiently, cheaply, and with higher quality if competition were permitted and agreements enforced was not part of the medieval experience, or its understanding of a just social order. The prejudice the businessman endured in English society - one day to be a great trading culture-was apparent in Shakespeare's *Merchant of Venice,* in which Shylock, "the Jew," tricks Antonio into accepting unreasonable and deadly terms on the delivery of a cargo. Naturally, justice prevails in the play and the merchant of Venice is comically disgraced.

This anti-market culture made the amassing of wealth through a combination of skill, luck, and sure calculation all but impossible. Ever since Adam Smith published *The Wealth of Nations* in 1776, in which he set forth an economic model based on his observation of human behavior, we have referred to the inexorable laws of economics. But medieval society had no understanding of how wealth could be created, or of the forces that drive men to strive to make better lives for themselves. A good example of this was the response of feudal policy makers to the first of the major plague epidemics, which eventually wiped out about one third of Europe. Instead of permitting wages to rise with the accompanying labor shortage, the English Parliament enacted the Statute of Laborers in 1350, requiring a cut in what workers were to be paid. Thus, the living standards of the general population was worse off than it needed to be, as people were prevented from earning what the market would have permitted.

The Roman Church was not alone in failing to recognize the benefits of allowing economic freedom. The nominally Protestant government of Henry VIII was at least as suspicious of trade as was Rome. The English aristocracy wanted taxes, customs, and a military. But it did not want fluid class mobility or a destabilization of the existing social structure. Not until after 1688 could the protection of private property for the lower classes be defended as a right in England's courts. Though the royal court permitted trade in luxury items such as silk, glass, spices, and tobacco, the production of essentials, such as food, lumber, and coal were actually discouraged by a proclamation of 1585 forbidding the breaking of fresh ground. The Statute of Artificers, passed in 1563, excluded from industry all those who had not undergone seven years of apprenticeship, thus nationalizing the guild system. A statute of 1533 limited the number of sheep one could own, and there were numerous restrictions on the transport of food from the farms into London. In this light, it is not surprising that the prospect of famine was a continuous worry for the average citizen. Many of these economic regulations were actively promoted by the Anglican clergy, who said they were looking after the interests of the little man who was in danger of being taken advantage of by the crafty merchant. The church-state establishment, whether it happened to be Roman Catholic or Episcopal Protestant, had a decided bias against the trader, in part because government and church officials were not dependent on commerce for their positions in society, and because trade inevitably creates an independent class of people, less beholden to the paternalistic state for their livelihoods. Trade threatens governments because money equals power for the individual; and trade threatens privilege because money also equals status.

One of the most important developments of the 16th and 17th centuries was the emergence of a new class of traveling peddlers, often operating outside city limits; middlemen who supplied clothing, food, and other goods to the towns. They were often harassed by officials and even tougher laws were passed against their trading in established industries. But they flourished anyway. Some were Jewish, and made their way in the underground economy because they were ostracized from the mainstream culture. But the great majority were dissenting Protestants. There is a strong connection between the independent wayfaring merchants and the independent Protestants who rebelled against the English Church. The Stuart kings spent much of their energy denouncing the activities of these middlemen, and attempted to legislate out of existence not only their churches, but their professions as well.

Many of them stayed in England, and eventually waged war and won against the Crown in the Puritan Revolution of the 1640s, after which attempts to regulate commerce broke down and the spirit of capitalism began to permeate all areas of English life. As we shall see later, the destruction of the royal and ecclesiastical bureaucracy by Oliver Cromwell during the 1640s was one of the decisive events in the history of progress towards a free society. But many non-conforming Protestants left England for America, where they proceeded to build from scratch the greatest commercial empire the world has ever seen.

At first glance it would appear that the Puritans were good businessmen because they were largely excluded from positions of political influence, that commerce was, therefore, their only vehicle to social advancement. No doubt, their circumstances as religious dissidents in England encouraged them to choose business over pursuing positions in the king's court. But there is more to the Protestant proclivity toward commerce than their situation as outcasts. Catholics in Europe were never good merchants even when they were out of power. There is no evidence in England that Catholics felt especially inclined toward business, and they were far more hated than Puritans in English society. English Catholics remained poor, while English Puritans prospered. Moreover, the Puritans (as opposed to the Separatists) were not in continuous disfavor. The Puritans dominated the House of Commons during the reign of the Stuart kings. In fact, the Stuarts were generally disliked more than the Puritans. Oliver Cromwell was popular for most of his 12-year reign. The evidence suggests that the Puritans were exceptionally good capitalists regardless of whether they were in or out of fashion in English society. Max Weber, in his classic study, *The Protestant Ethic and the Spirit of Capitalism,* makes the case that the central force driving the Puritan to be industrious was theology.

The rejection of privilege, hereditary or otherwise, is essential to both the Protestant and the capitalist spirit. The bishop was as anathema to the Puritan as the courtier seeking royal favor was to the free marketeer. Indeed, the Puritans combined hostility to the clergy with a rejection of aristocracy. John Calvin put the same value on a worker as on a minister, and taught that all honest callings are sanctified by God and should be pursued with equal diligence. Calvin himself was a socialist. But his work ethic was modified by the New England Protestants to say that if work is good, then wealth is a just reward. Moreover, it was soon discovered by the settlers of Massachusetts Bay that wealth was good not only for the individual, but for the entire community, so long as it was pursued in a lawful, honest, and Christian spirit. For reward encourages work, and work is a holy endeavor.

It might seem, at first, that the capitalist ethic and the Christian ethic are contradictory. As the Apostle Paul says, "The love of money is a root of all sorts of evil" (1 Tim. 6:10). Indeed, luxury and avarice were continuous targets of attack by Puritan preachers. Isn't capitalism about greed and the acquisition of luxuries? The answer is a most emphatic *no.* The great industrialists and traders of American history have not lived in luxury. Quite the contrary: a good capitalist makes sacrifices, forgoes immediate consumption, and invests his time, effort, and resources in an enterprise that might or might not work. At heart, he is an ascetic. A spendthrift is not a good businessman. Capitalism is really about discipline and restraint, which is one reason we look at a nation's savings rate to determine the health of an economy. The following paragraphs were written by a prominent American colonist, and they shed light on what Max Weber meant by the Protestant Work Ethic:

"Remember this saying," wrote the colonist: "The good paymaster is lord of another man's purse. He that is known to pay punctually, as exactly to the time he promises, may at any time, and on any occasion, raise all the money his friends can spare. This is sometimes of great use. After industry and frugality, nothing contributes more to the raising of a young man in the world than punctuality and justice in all his dealings; therefore, never keep borrowed money an hour beyond the time you promised, lest a disappointment shut up your friend's purse forever.

"The most trifling actions that affect a man's credit are to be regarded. The sound of your hammer at five in the morning, or eight at night, heard by a creditor, makes him easy six months longer; but if he sees you at a billiard table, or hears your voice at a tavern, when you should be at work, he sends for his money the next day."

This advice was offered by Benjamin Franklin. Franklin was no Puritan. Far from it. Indeed, his advice to the young tradesman was utilitarian, not spiritual. But the Puritan would not have been troubled at all by the practical nature of Franklin's advice. For the Puritans, the Bible was not only a road map to salvation, it was also a blueprint for living. In the Book of Proverbs, for example, we find equally practical advice: "Do you see a man skilled in his work? He will stand before kings" (v.22:29). Virtue not only helps us win eternal rewards, it also improves our prospects here on earth. Paul was very careful to say that it is the "love of money" that is a root of evil, not the money itself. In fact, Paul was strident in warning that "if anyone does not provide for his . . . household, he . . is worse than an unbeliever . . . " (1 Tim. 5:8). A successful enterprise, in the Puritan mind, reflected good character. Duty, honor, discipline, integrity, and restraint were essential capitalist, as well as Puritan, virtues.

The Protestant Work Ethic created reliable patterns of behavior, important for the development of a market system. An alarm clock appeared in a poem of 1654, indicating a new importance placed on regularity. It was certain that a good Protestant would carry out the terms of an agreement with diligence, care, and honesty, thus following Calvin's views on how one is to conduct his daily affairs: "We shall not rush forward to seize in wealth or honors by unlawful actions, by deceitful and criminal arts, by rapacity and injury to our neighbors; but shall confine ourselves to the pursuit of those interests, which shall not seduce us from the path of innocence." This attitude dominated the lives of the early settlers of New England. Whereas the Catholic Church (and the Anglican Church)-essentially medieval institutions - regarded the merchant, until relatively recently, with intense suspicion, the Puritans lifted social stigma from the trader. It was all right to charge interest on money and still be a Christian. A minister had no greater claim on salvation than a banker. While the Catholic tendency was always to acquiesce to tradition and to clerical superiors, the 17th-century Puritan and the entrepreneur responded to a personal calling. The Puritan was single-minded; he forged ahead regardless of conventional opinion; his spirit, often ferocious, was not dissipated by failure. These qualities also enhanced greatly the prospects of his business ventures.

Capitalism and Puritanism fed off each other. Both developments placed responsibility on individual initiative; and both involved clean breaks from the paternalistic and static feudal order. Both were highly destructive of hierarchy and empowered the individual to determine his own fate. Was it the Reformation that created the cracks in the medieval hierarchical system that permitted the rise of the merchants; or was it capitalism that broke up the old arrangements, making possible the Protestant rebellion against the medieval Church? My reading of history is that freedom - whether economic or religious -is always threatening to those in positions of power, and that freedoms tend to rise and fall together. How can we have freedom of conscience if the state can confiscate our property? We can't. The rise of Protestantism and the rise of capitalism were part of the same movement. One could not have survived without the other.

As soon as the Puritans arrived in Massachusetts, they began building fisheries in Marblehead. They quickly discovered a market for dried codfish that became so important an industry that someone carved a statue of a codfish, placed it in a "meeting house," and dubbed it "The Sacred Cod," demonstrating a sense of humor even about Christianity (which forbids idol worship). Massachusetts Bay also prospered in the raising of cattle, poultry, horses, pork, corn, and other vegetables. Lumber became an important industry, as did ship building. Soon, New England's vessels could traverse the Atlantic more rapidly than the British Merchant Marine. There was no one in the world who could compete with unfettered Puritan merchants, a fact that can be documented by New England's astounding growth. New England's population in 1630 numbered about 1,500 settlers; by 1680, this number had increased to 68,000; and by 1710, approximately 115,000 industrious people lived in New England, which, with Boston as its trade center, had become a significant economic power. So successful were the New England industries that the British government felt forced to place draconian trade restrictions on the colonists in the form of the notorious Navigation Acts. In contrast to the asceticism of the medieval monk who retreated to the monastery for prayer and contemplation, the New Englander believed his business, his craft, and the support of his family to be an entirely Christian enterprise.

The capitalist spirit alone was inadequate for ensuring the triumph of the market over a world of hostile forces, and more than the profit motive was needed to tame the American wilderness. The Puritans believed it had to be a holy endeavor. They were not interested in placing a few isolated trading posts on the edge of a wild continent; they wanted to build a model society, one founded on the precepts of God. For they understood very clearly the close connection between civilization, the Christian faith, and private property. The ownership of property teaches man responsibility, reinforces in his mind the importance of law, raises man above brutish existence, enables him to pass a better life on to his children, and affords him the leisure to meditate on matters concerning the soul. Perhaps better than any other people, the Puritans of New England understood that piety, liberty, and commerce were three essential pillars of a lasting and flourishing culture; knock one down, and civilization falls.

CHAPTER TEN

GOD AND THE TOBACCO SOCIETY

Virginia was the other major early British attempt to colonize North America. The expedition was generally promoted as an opportunity to share in the work of God. There was a widespread worry in English ruling circles that the natives in the New World risked conversion to the Catholic Church by the Spanish and the French. Thus, a founding principle of the colony was stated in the company charter, which was the ". . . propagating of the Christian religion to such a people as yet live in darkness and miserable ignorance of the true knowledge and worship of God, and may in time bring the infidels and savages living in these parts to human civility and to a settled and quiet government." And, according to an official statement published by the Virginia Company, entitled *A True and Sincere Declaration,* the "principal and main ends," of the settlers, " . . . were first to preach and baptize into the Christian religion, and by propagation of the Gospel, to recover out of the arms of the Devil, a number of poor and miserable souls, wrapt up unto death in almost invincible ignorance; to endeavor the fulfilling an accomplishment of the number of the elect which shall be gathered from all corners of the earth; and to add our mite to the treasury of Heaven." Keep in mind that Virginia was among the most religiously lax of the English colonies in North America. Such statements of purpose were taken for granted, and caused no division in 17th-century Anglo-American culture.

Though the spreading of the Gospel was one reason the English government granted a charter to the Virginia Company in May 1607, there were also other goals: 1) to get the poor of England off the streets; 2) to create new markets for British wool products; 3) to obtain raw materials such as gold and lumber inexpensively; and 4) to find a shortcut to the Indies and thereby cut costs on Oriental spices, herbs, and oils.

The New Englanders had one overarching reason for coming to the New World, the establishment of a pure Christian community; everything was subordinate to that one goal. The Christian mission for the Virginians, however, was but one aim among others, an important one being to turn a profit for themselves and the stockholders of the corporation. Thus, the community of early Virginia would not be homogenous, or "knit together as one body," as John Winthrop put it. The expedition attracted a wide range of personalities, from diverse back-grounds with different motives. There was no sense of the covenantal community as there was in New England. Some were English gentlemen, while others were artisans, debtors, adventurers, mercenaries, and even criminals. Hence, we see division and quarreling among the sojourners almost from the start, and few wanted to work. The New England sense of Christian love and holy endeavor was noticeably absent in early Jamestown, which is why it was not as resilent as the New England communities during times of hardship.

The initial Jamestown colony, established in 1607, was a disaster, decimated during its first six months by disease, starvation, desertion, and internal strife. The governing council could not get along with each other or the settlers. Many suspected that council President Edward Maria Wingileld was a secret papist or an atheist since he carried no Bible and prohibited preaching. So difficult were conditions that it wasn't long before all the council members had fled back to England - at which point Captain John Smith proclaimed himself President of Virginia. Smith had actually arrived in Virginia as a prisoner, under arrest for suspicion of hatching a plot to usurp control of the colony. He was almost hanged *en route* by his rivals, who had constructed gallows for him during their stop at Nevis Island.

Captain Smith is one of the most colorful characters in American history. He had fought against the fearsome Turks on the eastern frontier of Europe. After one especially bloody conflict, he was discovered by pillagers half-dead among the corpses. He was then sold into slavery to the Crimean Tartars. He escaped by beating his master to death with a club, and then traveled back across Europe, through Spain to North America, where he joined a band of pirates under the command of a Frenchman. But Smith was actually less interested in plunder than in knight-errantry, quests for glory, and encounters with enchanting brown-skinned women.

Smith got along very well with the Indians and would exchange food for assorted trinkets. These red men were a fearsome sight. The right sides of their heads were shaved (with shells), while the hair on their left sides grew long. What clothing they had was made from skins and leaves. Both men and women, according to Smith's account, had "three great holes" in each ear, in which some warriors inserted live snakes or dead animals. A bird's feather, or the dried hand of an enemy, might provide the head-dress. They took scalps, and malefactors were sometimes boiled to death. An enemy would be quartered, flayed live, and then burnt. These Indians had a remarkable leader named Powhattan, who had built for himself an empire of some 9,000 people. It is thought that Powhattan was responsible for the eradication of several Spanish expeditions, and perhaps of Sir Walter Raleigh's "lost colony."

Smith was captured on one of his solo expeditions into the forest, surrounded by some 200 "grim" warriors, and taken to see Powhattan. The chief seemed to admire the fearlessness of the bearded white man, and gave him an Indian-style banquet. Following the meal, however, two boulders were rolled out. Smith's head was seized and placed on the rocks; he was certain he was about to be executed in some horrible fashion. But, according to Smith, the beautiful *"Pocahontas,* the King's dearest daughter, when no entreaty would prevail, got his head in her arms and laid her own upon his to save him from death: whereat the emperor was contented he should live." Smith described Pocahontas as "next under God . . . the instrument to preserve this colony from death, famine and utter confusion."

Another instrumental figure in the early settlement of Virginia was the Reverend Robert Hunt. The corporate planners had wanted the famous chaplain Richard Hakluyt to "watch and perform the ministry and preaching of God's word in those parts." But Hakluyt could not be persuaded; so the assignment fell to Hunt, who proved himself to be a major unifying agent in the initial settlement. Hunt was a powerful preacher and often called the idle settlers to repent: "We are all laborers in a common vineyard..." He even put Captain Smith to work at building a house of worship. As Smith himself wrote: "When I first went to Virginia, I well remember we did hang an awning (which is an old sail) to three or four trees to shadow us from the sun. Our walls were rails of wood, our seats unhewn trees till we cut planks, our pulpit a bar of wood nailed to two neighboring trees. In foul weather, we shifted into an old rotten tent, for we had few better. . . This was our church, till we built a homely thing like a barn." This was hardly Westminster Abbey, and is evidence of how America's wilderness conditions had a purifying effect on Virginia's Anglican Church, weeding out the ecclesiastical extravagances to which the Puritans objected. William Bradford and John Winthrop would not have felt terribly out of place in the church of the Reverend Hunt. For, as another settler noted, "One cannot observe strictly all the usual formalities in making a beginning under such circumstances."

Hunt's church services were mandatory. He took care of the sick, and took to heart Christ's invocation: "To the extent that you did it to one of these brothers of Mine, even the least of them, you did it to Me" (Matt. 25:40). He spent much of his time hearing confessions and administering the last rites over typhoid and malaria victims. Even the swashbuckling Smith marveled at the way Hunt conducted himself, "that honest, religious, courageous divine," who during the course of the journey and living in the forest, lost "all but the clothes on his back, [but] none did ever hear him repine his loss." Hunt also tried to set a good example for others by taking on difficult physical tasks. He built Virginia's first grist mill for grinding corn. He knew that the colony's prospects for survival depended on the settlers ability to sustain themselves.

But Hunt's example was to little avail. Most of the settlers were content to pan for gold in the hopes of getting rich quick, and relied on the generosity of the Indians for sustenance. That the natives bothered was puzzling, since they were often treated poorly by the settlers. It would be 20 years before Virginia would plant a crop capable of feeding its inhabitants. At one point, the settlers had accumulated enough yellow ore to fill a ship, only to discover later that it was pyrite, "fools gold." The effort had been a waste and had distracted them from planting a crop, vital to their survival. These men did not have the Puritan virtues of thrift and industry - demonstrating that these virtues are not just godly, they're immensely practical. What a contrast in character between the settlers of Virginia and the settlers of Massachusetts. Meanwhile, death in the colony was so frequent that burials were done secretly and with no ceremony. By the fall of 1607, only 30 settlers remained of the initial 104 who had arrived only six months before. By any objective measure, the colony had been a disaster.

In 1609, the Virginia company was reorganized, with the prominent British merchant Thomas Smythe as treasurer and Lord De La Warr (Delaware) appointed governor. Smythe, a brilliant businessman, launched a massive advertising campaign for "subscriptions" to the colony. He saw that the quest for profits alone could not sustain the enterprise, and so began to rely more on religious rather than strictly commercial appeals. He saw that faith, patriotism, and commercial success were all intertwined and vital factors in Virginia's prospects for survival. "The eyes of all Europe are looking upon our endeavors to spread the Gospel among the heathen people of Virginia, to plant an English nation there, and to settle a trade in those parts, which may be peculiar to our nation, to the end we may thereby be secured from being eaten out of all profits of trade by our more industrious neighbors [the Dutch]," said one circular letter. The craze for Virginia began.

So successful was Smythe's promotional scheme that an alarmed Spanish ambassador wrote to Philip III that "there is no poor little man nor woman who is not willing to subscribe something for this enterprise." Fifty-six companies and more than 650 individuals invested in the colony. Hundreds of people, including women, children, clergymen, craftsmen, soldiers, and prisoners volunteered for the voyage for various reasons, ranging from religion and patriotism to adventure and economic opportunity. A fleet of nine ships set sail in June 1609 with 800 passengers. The expedition's leaders were on the *Sea Adventure,* which a storm separated from the other ships and carried to Bermuda Island, marooning them for 10 months. The episode inspired Shakespeare to write *The Tempest.*

Meanwhile, the rest of the fleet had arrived in the summer of 1609, and the colony faced its first constitutional crisis. Captain Smith refused to relinquish his presidency, pointing out that the appointed governor had been lost at sea. Chaos resumed. The new settlers refused to acknowledge Smith, and Smith's followers refused to submit to the new settlers. But it wasn't long before a disgusted Smith, having suffered a gunpowder wound to his leg that needed attention badly, and seeing his inevitable deposal, decided he had seen enough of Virginia and sailed home.

The death rate continued to increase. For every 10 new settlers who arrived, nine died, including the Reverend Robert Hunt who was their main source of spiritual and moral inspiration. On his memorial was written: "He preferred the service of

God to every thought of ease at home. He endured every privation, yet none ever heard him repine . . . He planted the first Protestant church in America, and laid down his life in the foun dation of Virginia."

Without the elevating sermons of Hunt, conditions in Jamestown grew even more desperate and, as the winter of 1609 approached, more bodies turned up frozen to death in their beds. The specter of starvation pervaded the colony. According to one account, corpses were dug from their graves and eaten: "And amongst the rest, this most lamentable, that one of our colony murdered his wife, ripped the child out of the womb and threw it into the river, and after chopped the mother into pieces and salted her for food." Governor De La Warr eventually arrived; he concluded that a better sense of community was needed, and stricter discipline. As one company official observed, the settlement was "full of mutiny and treasonable inhabitants." But De La Warr, too, was soon stricken with fever; he sailed back to England after only a 10-month stay, during which disease and starvation killed 150 more colonists.

De La Warr's successor was Sir Thomas Dale, a tough veteran of the Netherlands War. He promised to bring order and discipline to Jamestown with "Lawes Divine, Morall and Martiall." Dale, no doubt, went beyond the pale in policing the religious lives of the people, who were required to worship twice on Sunday under military escort and fill their days with prayer. Anyone who took the Lord's name in vain could expect a bodkin to be thrust through his tongue. A third blasphemous remark earned the death penalty. To demonstrate his seriousness, Dale executed eight offenders. He also employed the settlers in a strict work regime, under military escort. These were extreme measures, but then again the situation in Jamestown was desperate and the settlers had proven they were incapable of policing themselves. The price for liberty is responsibility; the colonists, by not planting crops when they should have, had abdicated their responsibilities, and as a result also lost their liber ties. Dale's regime was severe, but he was alarmed at the disastrous condition of the colony and sought to bring some order to the chaos. He wanted Virginia to survive.

But Dale did not rely solely on the stick to encourage thrift and industry among the colonists; he also employed the carrot. He abolished the original system of indentured servitude, under which settlers would be expected to work for seven years, receiving only the bare necessities of life for their labor, in exchange for being included on the expedition. At the end of seven years of hard labor, one might receive a small plot of land, if anything at all. So there was no incentive to produce. Instead of working for the benefit of the company, many workers shirked their responsibilities and spent their time panning for gold and cheating the Indians. Jamestown was a great example of how socialism undermines the moral fiber of a community. Virginia, under Dale, restored the right to private property, and awarded those who finished out their seven-year contracts with 50 acres of land. By 1617, after six years of Dale's reign, Virginia numbered about 1,000 European settlers eagerly building homes and new lives for themselves.

In the meantime, Dale had become enamored with the Indian princess Pocahontas. He had devoted much effort trying to persuade her to convert to Christianity. Dale wanted to marry her. He was then informed by newcomer John Rolfe that he, too, was hopelessly in love with the beautiful 18-year-old. Rolfe was nervous about how the stern Thomas Dale might react to the news that he had competition for the hand of the brown-skinned lady. So Rolfe approached the situation delicately. He sat down and carefully crafted a letter to Dale asking for permission to wed Pocahontas. Rolfe assured Dale that his affection for her "was in no way led" by "the unbridled desire of carnal affection," but by "striving for the good of this plantation, for the honor of our country, for the glory of God and Jesus Christ, of an unbelieving creature, namely Pocahontas, to whom my hearty and best thoughts are, and have for a long time been so entangled and enthralled in so delicate a labyrinth..."

It was a testimony to the selflessness of Dale's character that he acquiesced to Rolfe's plea. In a ceremony presided over by the Reverend Richard Buck, Rolfe married her, renamed her Rebecca, and had her baptized into the Christian faith amid much fanfare and feasting between the Indians and the white men. This relationship turned out to be a significant landmark in the history of Virginia, for it was Pocahontas who introduced Rolfe to tobacco. She showed him the pipe, the cigar, and the cigarette. Tobacco swept Europe by storm, and was even hailed as a cure for all kinds of ailments. As early as 1618, Virginia exported 50,000 pounds (weight) of tobacco to England. Dale eased the martial law restrictions, and gradually Virginia changed from a trading post run along military lines to a culture that began to resemble the more familiar plantation aristocracy.

Sir Edwin Sandys, a feisty visionary, was made treasurer of the Virginia Company in 1619. Sandys was a vocal Puritan leader in the House of Commons. He advocated abolishing the single corporate colony in favor of a settlement by individuals and easy acquisition of land. In addition, he helped bring greater religious tolerance to America. Being a Puritan himself, he understood what it was like to be part of a persecuted religious sect. The year before Sandys became treasurer, Sir George Yeardley had taken over the governorship of Virginia and promptly awarded 50 acres of land to each settler. The company, under the influence of Sandys and Yeardley, also abolished Dale's martial law style of rule, and created a General Assembly and a House of Burgess, which was elected by all the "free men" (male inhabitants) and had the power to pass local laws. This assembly met in a church, and its laws could be vetoed only by the company's directors in London. In 1619, 90 women arrived, giving the men of Virginia the opportunity of starting families and ensuring the future of the colony. By 1621, Virginia's population had reached 4,000.

But then catastrophe struck. Three thousand Virginian settlers suddenly disappeared, according to the records of the colony. Because the local government had neglected the defense of the community, the settlement was massacred in a series of bloody Indian attacks beginning in 1622. Jamestown was virtually wiped out, and John Rolfe was among the dead. The colonists had relied too heavily on the good relations they had established with Powhattan and on the marriage between Rolfe and Pocahontas to keep the peace. They did not know that Powhattan's successor, Opechancanough, resented British encroachment on his cornfields. On Good Friday, the Indians arrived as usual to trade furs and meat with the settlers. Suddenly, they turned on the colonists, killing them in their fields and homes, beginning a long history of perpetual war between the red and white men.

The disaster caused the company to come under political attack in England. It was thought that both the board of directors and the local colonial assembly had ignored its most basic responsibility: the protection of its citizenry against potential aggressors. The corporate charter was revoked, and the colony fell under the Crown's direct control. This did not affect political conditions much, as the Crown maintained its elective assembly. But it took many years for Virginia to rebuild.

Virginia has sometimes been called the Anglican colony - also the Crown colony. The image passed down to us regarding colonial Virginia is one of wealthy High Church gentlemen managing their estates-of England transplanted. It is true that Virginia was not born out of dissent, as was Massachusetts. Virginia was seen by many as something of a patriotic endeavor, and most Virginians were openly hostile to the new "Christian Zion" being built in Massachusetts Bay. It is also true that the Anglican Church was the official church of the land, established by law in 1624 and supported by tax revenue.

But on closer examination, we see that the religious tradition that grew up in Virginia during the course of the next century and a half did not much resemble the High Church

Anglicanism of the home country, and actually looked far more like the Puritanism of the Northeast than these early Virginians would have liked to admit. This is important because it helps explain why many of America's most illustrious revolutionary leaders were Virginians: George Washington, James Madison, James Monroe, George Mason, and Thomas Jefferson, to name a few. It also helps explain why these men were not more hesitant in throwing off the shell of Anglican orthodoxy. Over time, Virginians, though many were Anglican in name, had developed an uncomfortable relationship with the home church and had adopted many Puritan habits and modes of thought. Though the Anglican Church in Virginia was not founded as a pilgrimage of dissent, it took on distinctly American Protestant characteristics over time and eventually became non-conformist in substance-even while it retained the Anglican label.

The Anglican Church in England was very definitely episcopal in structure - hierarchical and lavish. Not so in Virginia, which did not even have a bishop until 1783, after the American War of Independence. Church authority in colonial Virginia was diffused through the local church vestries, which in essence were boards of elders governing the affairs of the local parish. Theoretically, each member of the clergy was supposed to travel to England to be ordained. But the expense and distance made this procedure impractical, and so ministers were simply appointed by the vestry. By law, positions in the local vestry were elected by the laity. Generally a minister held a one-year contract, which was renewed by the vestry if he proved satisfactory. Thus, the Anglican Church in Virginia was very nearly congregational in structure, federal rather than monarchical. The parishes were also independent from each other, mainly because the vast distances between churches in Virginia made Catholic-style organization unworkable.

The Anglican Church in England was remote from the common man, and the English clergy was prone to absenteeism, dereliction of duty, and some were notoriously corrupt. This was not true of the Anglican Church in Virginia, where the local parish was central to community life. Virginians guarded their local churches jealously, kept a tight reign on their ministers through the vestries, and demanded preachers whose sermons could inspire and elevate the spiritual lives of the people. This system, according to American historian Daniel Boorstin, produced ministers "decidedly superior to their English contemporaries." As in New England, Virginians learned politics in their churches (Episcopal in name only), which were laboratories in representative democracy. All but three of the more than 100 delegates to the Virginia constitutional convention in 1776 were vestrymen in their local church. For Virginians, self-government in religious matters was just as important as self-government in political affairs.

To ascribe Virginia's decentralized church structure solely to the pressures of the geography, however, would be a mistake. On close examination we find that exactly the same class of people settled Virginia as settled New England. This has been pointed out in Thomas C. Hall's book *The Religious Background of American Culture,* in which he says "'Cavalier Virginia' is a myth." Virginia was not settled predominantly by English gentlemen, as we have so often heard, but by tradesmen, artisans, and farmers. The Virginia aristocracy that developed was almost completely self-made, and was a natural product of the rural plantation economy. The great majority of the people were lower class in origin, and came from precisely the segment of the English population that was overwhelmingly Puritan in their religious views.

Puritan notions flourished in Virginia's sermons, and Alexander Whitaker's *Good News from Virginia* (1613) is indistinguishable in its tone and thesis from the diaries of William Bradford and John Winthrop. That Virginia survived those terrible early years, wrote Whitaker, proved "that the finger of God hath been the only true worker here; that God first showed us the place, God called us hither, and here God by His special Providence hath maintained us." Such a tract would have been an embarrassment to English High Churchmen, but not Anglicans in America.

The church buildings in colonial Virginia were every bit as austere as the churches of New England; the traditional Anglo-Catholic symbols were wholly absent; many congregations would sit while singing but stand when praying; and instead of kneeling, Virginians grew accustomed to taking communion in their seats - all characteristics of Puritanism and anathema to the Church of England. As in Massachusetts, there were laws in Virginia against Sabbath-breaking, missing church services, fornication, adultery, blasphemy, profanity, and drunkenness. There was even a law stating that "no man shall disparage a minister whereby the minds of his parishioners may be alienated from him and his ministry prove less effectual, upon pain of severe censure of the governor and council"-thus further italicizing the spirit of New England pervading Virginia life. It should be noted that these laws were not imposed on the people of Virginia by the government in London, but were enacted by Virginia's elected representative assemblies. Such laws were not in any way considered oppressive by the general population. Most Virginians were not only eager to submit to such religious strictures, but would have considered their absence evidence of alarming moral decay. Virginians, in other words, took their Christianity seriously.

Moreover, the Puritan strain in Virginian Christianity, apparent from the beginning, grew more pronounced as time passed. The Scotch-Irish, persecuted in their native land by both the Anglican and Catholic Churches *for* their strict Calvinist beliefs, found a home in Virginia. Then came the Baptists, with their Separatist creed, and the "New Light" preachers who lambasted the Anglican establishment for complacency and spiritual laxity. Thomas Jefferson reported in his *Autobiography* that by the time of the American Revolution three quarters of Virginia's population was dissenting Protestant. At least half of the members of the official Anglican Church were sympathetic to Puritan beliefs. For evidence of this, we need only recall Patrick Henry's celebrated attacks against Virginia's Anglican establishment and the taxes that supported it. Moreover, his assault on the "spiritual tyranny" made him one of the most popular politicians in Virginia, so rampant was the hostility toward the "Romish" church - especially when word came that London was planning to send a "dreaded bishop." For by the time of the American Revolution, the established English Church with all its pomp had become an exotic anachronism in American life, as the culture of dissent had cut across all denominational boundaries. Though no one, to my knowledge, said them, these words would have been an appropriate American refrain: "We are all Puritan-Separatists now!"

There were, however, some significant differences between New England and Virginia. Virginia's major industries, tobacco, indigo, rice, and later cotton, did not compete with British manufacturers; in fact, they enhanced British commerce by providing raw materials at rock bottom prices. Thus, London always looked upon Virginia favorably - in contrast with New England, where the colonists deliberately thwarted the protectionist Navigation Acts and undercut British manufacturers by building better ships at far less cost.

In religion, Virginians stressed tradition more than dogma. Sentiment moved them more than precise intellectual distinctions; habit more than philosophy. Virginians did not begin as self-consciously hostile to the Anglican Church. Virginians were perfectly content to call themselves Anglicans if it made London happy - and so long as the English episcopacy did not intrude excessively into Virginia's religious practices. Virginia's eventual rebellion against the Anglican establishment was spurred less by theological differences than by the Crown's attempt to use the church to consolidate its grip over the colony and uproot habits and customs long established. There was no intellectual equivalent of Thomas Hooker or Cotton Mather in early Virginia. Whereas New England was passionate and urgent in its Christian mission, Virginia was content to be steadfast.

The lazy character of Virginia's Christianity was further enhanced by the plantation culture. Communities in New England were tightly-knit homogenous units; but in Virginia they were spread out. Twenty miles often separated churches. Whereas government in New England revolved around the town meeting, in Virginia we see the development of county government, which required a more extensive administrative apparatus and tended to place political authority in the hands of the large planter families, sometimes called the "Tobacco Aristocracy." As a result, Virginia tended to cultivate an upper class of skilled leaders; while New England, with its direct participatory democracy, reared a population more generally educated in political alfairs. This helps explain why the rank and file of New England would be far more active than the rank and file of Virginia in the War for Independence. New Englanders, as a group, had a better and more precise understanding of the issues involved in the collision with Britain; while Virginia contributed more serene and circumspect statesmen, the archetype of which was George Washington.

Without the almost relentless Puritan mind of New England, always dividing the world into good and evil, there probably could have been no American Revolution. But without Virginia's virtues of loyalty, sobriety, and its general bias in favor of traditionalism acting as a brake on New England's ideological purity, the American Revolution might have gone too far. While Boston was yelling "Charge!" Virginia was counseling caution. The two tendencies balanced each other very well; thus the colonies were able to avoid the sometimes excessive Puritan zealotry that drove Cromwell's revolution in England, while at the same time steering clear of the excessive docility that characterized so much of America's South.

It was the lack of ideological (and theological) rigor in Virginia, however, that permitted the perpetuation of the abominable institution of slavery. The "Tobacco Aristocracy" was more attached to their habits and the expediencies of plantation farming than the letter of Scripture. It is ironic, in a way, that Virginia was saved by the very weed that would later seduce them away from the "golden rule" of their religious creed and the principles of liberty for which they would later fight. They were able to tolerate slavery because Virginians, unlike New Englanders, generally avoided thinking things through to their logical conclusion. Thus, George Washington owned slaves until it was pointed out to him that this was a contradiction of all he and America stood for and had them freed. Virginians tended to accept life as it was rather than remake it into something it should be. This was Virginia's weakness as well as its strength.

CHAPTER ELEVEN

BRAVE OLIVER'S "CRUEL NECESSITY"

Most histories of American political development focus on the American Revolution in isolation. But the American Revolution succeeded in large part by building on the legacy of Oliver Cromwell's Puritan Revolution of the 1640s, the first war waged on behalf of representative government. Cromwell, by defeating the armies of King Charles I, shattered forever the medieval doctrine of the "divine right of kings," a doctrine that was inherently opposed to republican democracy. One cannot overstate the magnitude of this achievement. In stead of the sovereignty of the king, who received specially dispensed divine authority at birth, the English Puritans advanced a new doctrine, the "sovereignty of the people subject to God." The Puritan creed denied privilege. Whether rich or poor, powerful or weak, we are all priests and kings with equal authority from God. The Puritans cited often Peter's proclamation to fellow believers: "You are a chosen race, a royal priesthood, a holy nation, a people for God's own possession. . . "(1 Peter 2:9).

Cromwell stood in opposition to the extravagant excesses of the Renaissance, and led an anti-humanist movement against man's impulse to deify himself. For him, the law derived from Heaven reigned supreme, even over kings. Says Psalms: "Now, therefore, O kings, show discernment; take warning, O judges of the earth. Worship the Lord with reverence, and rejoice with trembling. Do homage to the Son, lest He become angry, and you perish in the way, for His wrath may soon be kindled" (Psalm 2:10-12). "The Lord is our judge, the Lord is our lawgiver, the Lord is our King," says the Prophet Isaiah (v.33:22). This was the cornerstone of the Puritan world-view, and its logic drove them to put to death a priest-king in 1649. When the execu-tioner's axe crashed down on King Charles' neck, the organic unity of the Middle Ages - in which church, state, ruler, and pastor were all combined into one mystical, seamless garment - split apart and could never again be repaired. An age came to an end and a new era was born.

In putting together the pieces, the Puritans began a move-ment in England to strictly define (if not yet completely separate) the functions of church and state in order to free the individual soul to make its peace with God unencumbered, as the Apostle Paul wrote, by "philosophy and empty deception, according to the tradition of men, according to the elementary principles of the world, rather than according to Christ" (Col. 2:8). Liberty was an important political aim of the Puritan Revolution in England, but it was not the final goal. The attainment of liberty for the indi-vidual was a means to the ultimate Puritan aim of achieving the fullest expression of divine truth. The Puritans were discovering the principle - so basic to American thinking and enshrined in our First Amendment - that variety of expression in religious faith strengthens the spiritual life of a nation; and that the gov-ernment, far from aiding worship, actually impedes one's access to God even if the state is ostensibly Christian. The eyes of Puritans were glued on the next world, but once liberty of con-science for them took on a theological dimension, there was no question that the Puritans would defend this right to the death - a lesson King Charles I failed to grasp until for him it was too late.

Perhaps more than any war in Western history, the Puritan Revolution in England was fought over abstract ideas, which is why Cromwell's achievement looms so important in shaping our own understanding of what constitutes good government. We see

in the Puritan spirit the seeds of the American passion for republican constitutional democracy, which drives us with an almost
messianic zeal to try and export its principles to other nations
deprived of its blessings. As was proven by the fact that 200,000
Americans died in World War II and another 50,000 lost their
lives fighting for the freedom of others in the rice paddies of
Southeast Asia, Americans historically have believed liberty to
be more precious than life itself. This phenomenon can be
explained only by attaching religious significance to the inalienable rights of men. This attitude of mind, indeed the entire
American political order, owes much to Cromwell's Puritan
Revolution in England.

Cromwell's victory over the King's armies provided the
colonists with the intellectual and moral justification for defending
their republican institutions against the designs of grasping
Anglican bishops and a conniving monarch. More importantly,
Puritan ascendancy in England provided the theological frame-
work as well as the necessary precedent for America's rebellion
in 1776 against King George III, whose actions were not protected
by divine sanction. Cromwell's revolution fell short of its stated
aim, which was the creation of a Bible-based commonwealth undefiled by human additions. But his destruction of the royal bureaucracy, and the mystique that surrounded the king's office, changed
the mind of the world, paved the way for the emergence of Whig
political ideas, and laid the foundation for a distinctly American
political creed. It is important, therefore, to look briefly at events
in 17th-century England in order to understand why the American
political and social order developed the way it did.

Oliver Cromwell was born at Huntington in eastern
England on April 25, 1599. His father, Robert, was a landlord, a
justice of the peace, and a member of Parliament during the reign
of Queen Elizabeth. He died when Oliver was 18. But Oliver's

mother, Elizabeth Steward, lived until she was 89, long enough to witness the greatness of her son.

Oliver had dark, brooding eyes, a ruddy complexion, and auburn hair. He had short legs, but a massive trunk and shoulders. Country living had made him an expert horseback rider and hunter. His temperament was moody, subject to bouts of wild merriment and sudden descents into silent despair. His favorite reading was the Bible. Even as a young man, he filled his correspondence with Scriptural citations, not feeling the need to quote full verses since Scripture was the language of the day. He attended Cambridge University for one year until his father died, when he returned home to take care of his mother and family. He also studied law for a time at Lincoln's Inn in London. In 1620, he married Elizabeth Bourchier, the daughter of a London merchant, and his love for her burned strongly throughout his life. "Thou art dearer to me than any creature," he wrote in a letter. She never concerned herself with her husband's politics or religious life, but was a devoted wife and mother.

Cromwell did not experience genuine Christian conversion until he was 30. Sir Philip Warwick, a friend of the Cromwells, observed that "the first years of his manhood were spent in a dissolute course of life, in good fellowship and gaming, which afterwards he seemed very sensible and sorrowful for, and as if it had been a good spirit that had guided him therein. . . he declared that he was ready to make restitution unto any man who would accuse him or whom he could accuse himself to have wronged." Eight years later Cromwell wrote to his cousin of his new birth: "You know what my manner of life hath been. Oh, I lived in and loved darkness, and hated the light; I was a chief, the chief of sinners. This is true: I hated the godliness, yet God had mercy on me."

We do not have any record of his spiritual struggle, but can conclude from the quality of the man that emerged that the experience must have been intense. It appears that his grim confrontation with his soul made him seriously ill, to such an extent that it took him a number of years to fully recover his health. He became driven by a passion for righteousness; but he also had an instinct for mercy and kindness. He might lash out suddenly in anger, but would be quick to repent and admit his fault. One can catch a glimpse of Cromwell's character in a letter he wrote to a friend consoling him on the death of a son: "There is your precious child full of glory, to know sin nor sorrow any more. He was a gallant young man... God give you His comfort."

Cromwell was elected to the Puritan-dominated House of Commons in 1628 for the Huntington borough. He had already achieved a reputation for his fiery attacks on Charles I's bishops. He showed open hostility toward his local bishop at Ely and donated large sums of his own money to "lecturers" and itinerant Protestant preachers. Cromwell believed the pompous pageantry of the Anglican clergy blasphemed God's name by trying to steal His glory.

Meanwhile, the outrageous behavior of King Charles contributed to the opinion of the Puritans, including Cromwell, that the wings of the monarchy needed to be clipped. Charles had started circumventing the independent "common law" courts in favor of the infamous Crown-controlled court of the "Star Chamber," which under Charles became a symbol of arbitrary justice and ecclesiastical arrogance. The Star Chamber court was established by the Crown ostensibly to administer justice more swiftly. Instead, it became an instrument of tyranny, not bound by standard procedures for protecting the rights of the accused. Under the Stuart monarchy, the Star Chamber became the main vehicle for the centralization of royal power and the punishing of political dissidents. Archbishop Laud, especially, used the Star Chamber ruthlessly to enforce adherence to the rituals of the Anglican *Book of Common Prayer*.

Contributing to the unpopularity of Charles' regime was his incompetence in foreign policy. After a disastrous naval conflict with Spain he bungled into a war with France, which he also lost. Said one member of the House of Commons: "Our honor is ruined, our ships are sunk, our men perished, not by the enemy, not by chance, but by those we trust." Thus, by the time Cromwell began his political career, Charles' government, in the Puritan view, was thoroughly discredited. Moreover, Parliament had opposed both military campaigns and had denied the King funds to carry them out. Charles, however, by-passed Parliament by imposing forced-loans, which were declared illegal by the judiciary, thus creating a constitutional crisis over who had the final authority in matters of foreign policy - the Crown or Parliament. Charles then compounded the crisis by arresting 70 knights and gentlemen who refused to contribute to his war efforts. In 1628, the House of Commons passed the famous Petition of Right, which declared henceforth that there shall be no taxes without the consent of Parliament; no imprisonment without cause; no martial law in peacetime; and no quartering of subjects in the homes of citizens. Charles signed the document, but then put the opposition Puritan leaders in prison and dissolved Parliament on March 2, 1629. He would not call another for 11 years.

Political conditions in England went from bad to worse. The vast majority of Englishmen, many of whom considered themselves staunch Anglicans, suddenly found themselves labeled Puritans for opposing the increasing rigidity and hierarchical structure of the English Church. Archbishop Laud reviewed all printed material on religious matters. In 1637, he obtained a Star Chamber decree forbidding the printing of any book without his approval. Unauthorized printers were imprisoned, pilloried, or whipped. Extemporaneous preaching and praying were outlawed. William Prynne, a leading Protestant dissenter, was tortured and mutilated. Worst of all, from a Protestant perspective, Laud made it clear he wanted closer links with Rome, and Mass began to be said openly in London.

There is evidence that Cromwell seriously considered following John Winthrop, Thomas Hooker, and thousands of other Puritans in their massive migration to the New World. But he loved England too much, and so elected to stay and try to rescue his homeland from its apparent drift toward monarchical absolutism and "popery." He was bred for resistance, not retreat. Moreover, exciting news was coming from Scotland. In 1637, Charles commissioned Archbishop Laud to dictate to the Scots that they cease their itinerant religious practices and conform to Anglican ways. But Scotland said "No." In fact, the entire nation formally covenanted to have nothing to do with any "Romish" innovations. Charles decided to invade, but he was out-maneuvered and beaten by a well-disciplined and fierce Scottish covenanting army. Charles was then forced to promise the Scotsfree assemblies, free parliaments, and freedom of religion.

Archbishop Laud, however, persuaded Charles to break the agreement and call what became known as the "Short Parliament" in order to raise money for another campaign against Scotland. Parliament refused and instead presented him with more grievances. Charles dissolved Parliament again, and raised revenue by unilaterally increasing customs duties, known as ship money, which caused much unhappiness and resistance among merchants. As Charles prepared his invasion, however, the Scottish army launched a preemptive strike, crossing England's border. The King's army panicked at the sight of the disciplined Presbyterian ranks and Charles suffered another humiliating defeat.

The King was again out of funds and forced to call another Parliament, which became known as the "Long Parliament" because it sat until 1653. Cromwell was elected to represent the borough of Cambridge. This Parliament made the "Short Parliament" appear friendly by comparison. In fact, one of the King's favorite ministers, the Earl of Strafford, was tried for treason, found guilty, and beheaded. The King, now expressing an understandably more conciliatory attitude, agreed to sign the Triennial Act guaranteeing regular meetings of Parliament and promising that Parliament would not be dissolved without its own consent. He also accepted bills declaring ship money and other arbitrary taxes illegal, and was very contrite regarding other grievances condemning almost every aspect of his ad-ministration.

Rebellion broke out in Ireland in October 1641, which may have been the final incident that turned England against Charles. The Irish Catholic army was brutally butchering English Protestant women and children. News of the numbers came into London: 50,000-100,000-150,000 English people slaughtered. These rumors were exaggerations, but the flow of English blood was substantial. Charles failed to address the Irish Catholic revolt, and reports came in that the Irish army would soon be in London. Thousands of municipal officials and gentry marched on London with petitions and hysterical demands that the King do something to halt the Irish invasion. Many Puritans believed the Catholic uprising in Ireland was part of a conspiracy on the King's part to install an absolutist Catholic monarchy in the pattern of Spain or France.[1] This, too, was an exaggeration, but one which many believed.

A month after the start of the Irish revolt, Parliament assembled again in London on November 22, 1641, and presented Charles with the "Grand Remonstrance," which consisted of more than 200 clauses. Cromwell was most pleased with the provision censuring the bishops "and the corrupt part of the clergy, who cherish formality and superstition." Charles rejected the remonstrance, and brought impeachment proceedings in the House of Lords against the principal authors of the Grand Remonstrance in the House of Commons (Pym, Strode, Holles, Hampden, and Hazerig). The House of Lords told Charles he had no legai precedent to remove these men from office because they had done nothing wrong. Charles then moved in with an armed guard to arrest the Puritan leaders on the floor of the House and try them for treason. Forewarned, Pym and his fellow Parliamentarians escaped and took refuge in friendly Puritan households in London. Charles arrived with his soldiers, swords drawn, saw the empty seats, and merely noted "the birds are flown." A week later the King left London to raise an army. He intended to close down

---

1. This bloody rebellion bred a disdain for the Irish in Cromwell that was out of character for him in all other respects. With the slaughter wrought by the Irish uprising of 1641 forever impressed on his mind, he would later in life crush another Irish rebellion in brutal fashion. This event brought out the dark side in this revolutionary leader and would forever taint his otherwise enormous contributions to representative government, rule of law, and religious toleration.

Parliament with armed force and, thus, remove the major obstacle to centralizing royal power. England was on the brink of civil war.

Puritan leaders in Parliament concluded that they had no choice but to raise an army as well. They prepared to defend themselves not only from Charles, but also from the threat of an invading Irish Catholic horde with whom he was suspected of forming an alliance for the purpose of imposing a political and "papist" tyranny. Cromwell was not yet prominent enough to be noticed by Charles, but he had begun to distinguish himself in the eyes of his Parliamentary colleagues as a gifted political organizer. In July 1642, he was commissioned to go home to his constituency in Cambridge to recruit soldiers. At age 43, Cromwell had found his calling and a whirlwind of immeasurable velocity was unleashed upon the world.

There were grey streaks in his hair, lines on his brow:"Look at those strange, deep, troubled eyes of his, with their wild, murky sorrow and depth - on the whole wild face of him; a kind of murky chaos; almost a fright to weak nerves," wrote Thomas Carlyle in his *Historical Sketches*. His clothes were plain, almost slovenly. But John Hampden, a member of Parliament, predicted of Cromwell, even before he took to the battlefield: "That sloven whom you see before you, hath no ornament of speech; that sloven, I say, if we should ever come to a breach with the King (which God forbid), in such a case, I say, that sloven will be the greatest man in England."

What to many must have seemed like the end of the world, a nation at war with its king, the Puritans saw as a glorious opportunity to rid England of its impurities and fulfill the aspirations of the Protestant Reformation. No one expressed Puritan dreams better than John Milton, Cromwell's friend and future secretary. "God," he wrote, "is manifestly come down among us to do some remarkable good to our church and state." It would be up to the Puritans to show the world a Christian commonwealth, Milton thought: "Let not England forget her precedence of teaching the nations how to live," a commission no one saw more clearly than

Cromwell. In July 1642, Cromwell contributed 100 pounds of his own money for arms and obtained a vote in Cambridgeshire allowing the town of Cambridge to raise two companies of volunteer militia.

On October 23, Cromwell made his first military appearance at the Battle of Edgehill under the command of the third Earl of Essex Robert Devereux. The Parliamentarians fought the Royalists to a standoff in a gruesome and bloody affair. We have few details about Cromwell's role, but he did learn that the Parliamentarians could not win without better generalship; that heavy armor was of little use; that the greatest weapon was not the sword or musket but the horse; and that relentless attack was the best defense. Most important, Cromwell observed, the cause of Parliament was doomed if its ranks did not show more discipline.

In 1643, he was given the rank of colonel and rapidly gained a reputation as a military organizer. He recruited his fighting men mainly from dissenting churches: Independents, Separatists, Baptists, Antinomians. Cromwell did not himself join any sect after severing his ties with the Anglican Church, but felt a natural kinship for those who steadfastly refused to permit anyone-bishop, priest, or layman-to come between them and the Lord Jesus Christ. He believed Paul, who told Timothy, "There is one God, and *one mediator* also between God and men, the man Christ Jesus" (1 Tim. 2:5, italics mine). Cromwell wanted his recruits to possess the same furious zeal that he had "for liberty of the Gospel and the laws of the land."

Cromwell always treated his regiments fairly and paid them on time. He also exercised strict discipline. If they swore they were fined; if drunk, placed in stocks; deserters were whipped. Any offense against a civilian or property was sternly punished; for this, he said, was not a war against Englishmen. He subjected his men to rigorous and continuous drills and exercises, and they became the best trained regiment in England. He also made an important military innovation. Cromwell learned to retreat, reform his men in the midst of battle, and launch second and third charges, thus keeping continuous pressure on his opponents. Previously, it was thought that the chaos of battle made such precise maneuvering impossible. Cromwell's army baffled plodding Royalist forces with its speed and flexibility. Here was a new kind of man in England, totally without fear, and one utterly certain of the righteousness and providential nature of his cause. He prevailed at the Battle of Gainsborough over a previously unbeaten Royalist foe by reforming his lines in a moment of crisis and surprising his fatigued opponents with a subsequent charge more ferocious than the first.

Cromwell proved himself a revolutionary genius on the order of Lenin. But instead of communist cells, he recruited from the small independent churches consisting mostly of tradesmen, farmers and small landowners. He felt at ease with the Puritan common-folk, called "Roundheads" by their aristocratic detractors. "My troops increase," he wrote happily. "I have a lovely company," full of "honest, sober Christians." He created a new theory of revolution that would be passed on to Samuel Adams and the American Sons of Liberty in the next century. During his entire military career Cromwell would never lose a battle, though often far out-numbered.

In 1644, Cromwell was given the rank of Lieutenant General and made a member of the war cabinet, called the Committee of Both Kingdoms. Cromwell served under the Earl of Manchester, who was Commander in Chief. "Brave Oliver," as he came to be called, distinguished himself again at the Battle of Marston Moor, where the New Model Army defeated decisively the King's Commander in Chief Prince Rupert. In a letter to his brother-in-law, Cromwell concluded of the victory: "Truly England and the church of God hath had great favor from the Lord in his great victory given unto us. . . . It has all the evidences of an absolute victory obtained by the Lord's blessing."

But Cromwell criticized his commander, Manchester, for his lethargy and for failing to take full advantage of the disarray in

Royalist ranks. Victory, Cromwell believed, should have been more resounding. Cromwell, who had begun to achieve legendary status, proposed that no member of Parliament - such as Manchester - be permitted to hold both civilian and military posts simultaneously. His proposal was accepted, and the New Model Army was reconstituted under the leadership of Sir Thomas Fairfax, with Cromwell as second in command. The stormy-eyed Puritan went on to destroy Charles' two remaining armies at the battles of Naseby and Langport. Charles then fled to Oxford, which was soon surrounded by the forces of Cromwell and Fairfax. Charles managed to escape, leaving the city in disguise. But he was captured by Scottish covenanters and turned over to Parliamentary authorities in January 1647.

Cromwell thought a *modus vivendi*[2] might be worked out between Parliament and Charles. After the enemy had fallen, he knew it was his Christian obligation to sheathe the sword and extend a hand of reconciliation. He wanted, however, a promise from Charles that no longer would England's religion be dictated by grasping priests and hypocritical bishops; nor would Charles subject his countrymen to arbitrary royal or Star Chamber decrees. John Milton, the revolution's most famous theorist, expressed Puritan objectives when he said: "Our liberty is not Caesar's. It is a blessing we have received from God Himself," in a passage that gave rise to our phrase, the "blessings of liberty." Being "peculiarly God's own," said Milton, "that is truly free, we are consequently to be subjected to Him alone, and cannot, without the greatest sacrilege imaginable, be reduced to a condition of slavery to any man." Milton concluded, therefore, that "absolute Lordship and Christianity are inconsistent."

Cromwell and his son-in-law Henry Ireton visited Charles twice. Cromwell assured the King that he was not committed to any particular form of government, only, as Ireton put it, to "the defense of our own and the people's just rights and liberties" as "called forth and conjured by several Declarations of Parliament." Indeed, Oliver found that he rather liked the King and was deeply

---

2. A manner of living.

moved by Charles' concern for his family. After their discussions, in which Charles seemed amenable to Puritan demands, Cromwell assured the King that both the monarchy and the House of Lords would remain as constituted, and insisted only that he submit to laws duly enacted by Parliament. Most importantly, he would have to promise never again to employ the coercive powers of the Episcopal Church. Religious toleration, added Ireton, would have to be universal, even for papists. Charles committed to nothing, but suggested he was flexible. Charles went on to ruin the cordial atmosphere, however, by escaping from his comfortable quarters in Hampton Court Palace and fleeing to the Isle of Wight, where he took up residence at Carisbrooke Castle. A rift then developed between Parliament, which was predominantly Presbyterian, and Cromwell's Roundhead army, consisting mainly of Independents. Charles seized on this opportunity and, from his Carisbrooke Castle headquarters, began complicated negotiations between Parliament, the leaders of the New Model Army, and the Scots. He was not above promising one thing to one group and the opposite to another, which served his objective of intensifying discord within Puritan ranks. Charles concluded an agreement with the Scots, who promised to restore him to power in return for the establishment of their Presbyterian religion. This news alarmed Independents in the New Model Army, who wanted neither an Anglican nor a Presbyterian national church. An enraged Cromwell, reflecting the sentiment of his troops, stood on the floor of the House of Commons and called the King "an obstinate man, whose heart God had hardened." The King's supporters, encouraged by the Scottish agreement, raised another army and commenced the Second Civil War.

On April 29, 1648, Oliver Cromwell called a prayer meeting at Army Headquarters in Windsor. After a reading from Proverbs, the soldiers concluded that they had relied too heavily on human wisdom in their dealings with the King and had ignored the providence of God. "We were led," according to the journal of one in attendance, "to a clear agreement among ourselves, not any dissenting, that . . . if ever the Lord brought us back again in peace, to call Charles Stuart, that man of blood, to an account for that blood he had shed and mischief he had done to the utmost, against the Lord's cause and the people in these poor nations."

While Cromwell was in the field, the Independents and small Protestant sects expelled from Parliament the Presbyterians and anyone who advocated further negotiations with Charles. The so-called "Rump" Parliament was then formed, consisting of only one-eighth of its former membership. Cromwell was alarmed by the high-handed actions of his followers, but was persuaded that in time of civil war unity of purpose took precedence over established procedure. The Royalist forces were stronger than expected, outnumbering the Roundheads. But Cromwell, with fighting men of superior quality, crushed a Royalist uprising in Wales, defeated an invading Scottish army, and then moved into Scotland and restored order. The last of the King's supporters were defeated at the Battle of Preston in August 1648. Charles was promptly arrested.

Incredibly, Cromwell gave Charles yet another chance to save himself. Cromwell took to heart Jesus' admonition to forgive one's enemies and to show mercy. He had little interest in becoming an oiigarch. His main concern was for the safety of the realm and for creating political conditions that would permit Christian people to preach the Gospel freely. On Christmas Day 1648, Cromwell sent an envoy named Basil Denbigh to ask Charles to agree to give up the royal veto and abolish the episcopacy. Cromwell promised to spare the King's life if the concessions were accepted. Charles refused, still believing he was the divinely ordained head of both church and state and, therefore, beyond human reproach. Had he agreed to the restrictions on his power, Cromwell probably would have given back his throne. What more could a chief of state ask after losing two civil wars, both of which Charles had started? Cromwell originally had no desire for vengeance against his defeated opponent. But Charles was recalcitrant and unwilling to negotiate; he had also proven himself a frequent liar, a double-crosser, and extraordinarily arrogant. Hesitant until the last moment, Cromwell in the end gave in to the arguments of his son-in-law Ireton: there was no choice but to try Charles for high treason. After all, if Charles had won, there is no doubt Cromwell, Ireton, and many others would have been in exactly the same position, facing the executioner's axe.

Charles Stuart was found guilty as a tyrant, murderer, traitor, and public enemy of the Commonwealth of England. When Charles refused to plead, Cromwell (along with 134 others) signed the death warrant. The sentence was carried out on the morning of Tuesday, January 30, 1649, on a scaffold outside Whitehall. With the assistance of his executioners, Charles put his hair inside a white satin cap. He then removed his cloak, placed his head on the block and prayed devoutly. He stretched out his hands, and the axe blade fell swiftly on the back of his neck, severing his head from his shoulders. Thus ended Charles Stuart's life at the age of 48. The assembled crowd groaned in horror; it was a "cruel necessity," Cromwell lamented.

The impossible seemed to have occurred: God's vicar on earth had been put to death by his own subjects. Cries of anguish went out from ruling circles and pulpits throughout continental Europe. But Cromwell believed that Charles had abdicated his duty to serve and protect God's children. He had committed murder, started two civil wars, and drenched poor England in a torrent of blood. He had routinely plundered the people's liberties, and had brought ruin and misery to his countrymen for his own vanity and exaltation. As Paul says in his letter to the Christians in Rome, "there is no authority except from God, and those which exist are established by God" (Romans 13:1). It was clear to Oliver that God had not ordained Charles' reign, as was obvious from the way he ruled. Just as the Lord in the Old Testament commanded the future king of Israel, Jehu, to "destroy" the tyrannical house of Ahab (2 Kings 9-10), so Cromwell believed the Lord had raised him up to remove permanently a tyrannical Charles Stuart from his throne. Moreover, Cromwell's right to do so had been codified in a court of law and executed. In 1776, Thomas Jefferson would claim this same right to rebel in the Declaration of Independence. Cromwell soon discovered, however, how difficult it was to construct a new political order on the ruins of the old.

One of the most intellectually powerful movements during the Cromwellian era was an Independent Puritan sect called the "Levellers," who wanted complete religious freedom, annual Parliaments, broader suffrage, and fewer taxes. They were very similar to Wycliffe's pre-Reformation Lollards. The Levellers had a small socialist wing, called "Diggers" or "True Levellers." But the great bulk of Levellers believed strongly in property rights and favored only the political levelling of privileged position, the elimination of titles of nobility, and the expansion of democratic ideas and constitutional protections. Their spokesman was John Lilburne and their logic was compelling; Cromwell, who liked Lilburne, was receptive to their arguments.

This movement was important because a faction of Levellers and Independents in the House of Commons initiated a new constitution caHed an "Agreement of the People," which proposed that the present "Rump" Parliament dissolve itself, that a new Parliament be elected every two years, and that a one-man, one-vote system be instituted, excluding only paupers and obvious social misfits. There would also be complete freedom of conscience and equal protection under the laws. This "Agreement of the People" was a forerunner of the United States Constitution. But England was not ready for the Leveller democratic program; and while Cromwell sympathized with men such as Lilburne, he ultimately accepted the more moderate position offered by the majority in Parliament: England would abolish the aristocratic monarchy and the House of Lords in favor of a 40-member council, and establish a "Commonwealth and Free State." In addition, the English Church would become Presbyterian rather than Episcopal.

This settlement greatly disappointed the Levellers, who felt abandoned by their leader. To them, the establishment of Presbyterianism was no victory; it was little more than a re-affirmation of Laud's government-run church, albeit a more austere version. "We fought two civil wars to achieve this!" was the Leveller cry. Cromwell put down an attempted mutiny by executing three Levellers in his army. Rarely have military insurrections been defeated with so little bloodshed. The episode saddened him greatly, though, because he was inclined to agree with the general thrust of their complaints, which in essence was that the Puritan Revolution had fallen well short of its stated aim of stripping the state's authority to tyrannize consciences.

But as chairman of the first Council of State, Cromwell felt his first duty was to keep the peace. In order to do so, he had to balance interests and continuously search for middle ground. To govern, he had to remain within the English consensus. The majority in England thought that completely eliminating the state church was utopian, anarchistic, and would probably lead to another civil war. As it was, Cromwell had to contend with Royalist uprisings in Ireland and Scotland. In addition, Charles' son and heir to the throne, Charles II, raised a formidable army of his own and invaded England in an effort to reclaim the Crown for the House of Stuart. Cromwell defeated young Charles' forces at the battle of Worcester in 1651; but he was learning that the creation of a free republic involved more than beheading a king. Theologically, Cromwell was a radical reformer, but operationally he was conservative. He wanted to move England toward Leveller ideals, but had the sense to do so cautiously.

Not until 1653 did Cromwell have the luxury to ponder the science and practice of governing. By this time, Presbyterians and Independents in the House of Commons had grown increasingly quarrelsome. Seeing a widening ideological chasm between the two Protestant camps, and wishing to avoid more social strife, Cromwell dissolved the Rump in 1653, calling it a conclave of "corrupt and unjust men . . . scandalous to the profession of the

Gospel." He then assembled a so-called Assembly of Saints, which he hoped would rule "in fear of God." This body consisted of a few religious "fanatics"; but, contrary to the conventional portrait, the members of the Assembly were mostly sober-minded, moderate men. Cromwell admonished them to "be pitiful. . . and tender towards all though of different judgments . . . Love all, tender all, cherish and countenance all, in all things that are good . . . And if the poorest Christian, the most mistaken Christian, shall desire to live peaceably and quietly under you - I say, if any shall desire but to lead a life of godliness and honesty, let him be protected." John Locke could not have articulated any more plainly the principle of religious toleration. The Assembly of Saints then proceeded to abolish church patronage and mandatory tithes.

But political unrest was becoming rampant throughout the land. Dispossessed Royalists and Anglican clergy were very unhappy with the state of affairs for obvious reasons. Presbyterians, who still believed in the idea of a state church, were alarmed at the apparent trend toward the total disestablishment of religion. Meanwhile, on the extremist wing of the Puritan side, a group known as the Fifth Monarchy, which was rapidly gaining followers, wanted to abolish the common law of England altogether and substitute the unadorned laws of Moses. Having no notion of how to deal with the nation's problems - and its increasingly polarized politics - the Assembly of Saints abdicated their governing responsibilities and turned all authority over to Cromwell. Many moderate Puritans wanted to crown him king, a prospect that displeased Cromwell enormously. Hadn't they just fought two civil wars and beheaded a king in large part to abolish monarchy and privilege? "My own power," he lamented, "was again by this resignation as boundless and as unlimited as before; all things being subjected to arbitrariness, and myself the only constituted authority that was left, a person having power over three nations without bound or limit set." Cromwell worried that much of England had set him up as a false god. He had a Puritan understanding of the frailty of man and knew how dangerous it was to place unlimited political power in the hands of any one individual. The Assembly of Saints was a noble experiment in government. The problem was that they were unwilling to govern.

With extreme reluctance Cromwell accepted on his shoulders the awesome responsibility of bringing England into the modern age. "It matters not who is our Commander in Chief if God be so," Cromwell remarked, with a tone of resignation. If he had wanted, he could have set himself up as a dictator with absolute power. But Cromwell, because of conviction and character, did not choose that course. He was determined, instead, to bring order out of the chaos and place England under the rule of law. With the help of the Army, most notably Lieutenant General John Lambert, he established the "Instrument of Government," which was a modified version of the earlier rejected "Agreement of the People." "For the people I desire their liberty and freedom as much as anybody whomsoever," said Cromwell. "This liberty and freedom consists in having government, those laws by which their lives and goods may be most their own."

The Instrument of Government is rarely discussed in histories of America's political system, but it had an important influence on the thinking of the authors of the U.S. Constitution. Perhaps one reason it is almost never mentioned is that it illustrates so conclusively that the origin of limited government emerged directly out of Protestantism. Under the Instrument of Government, the executive power remained with Cromwell, the Lord Protector and Council Chairman. But he had no right to veto Parliament's bills, a power he voluntarily relinquished. There are precious few examples in history of men willingly giving up power. Moreover, the Protector served at the pleasure of the Council. This was hardly broad-based democracy in the modern American sense, but it was a gigantic step in that direction and was a far more representative method of selecting the executive than the previous system of inheritance.

While Presbyterianism was England's official creed under the Protectorate, congregations selected their own ministers and toleration became the law of the land. Anglicans, for example, were permitted to practice the rituals in the *Book of Common Prayer,* just as Congregationalists, Baptists, Independents, Levellers, Diggers, and other Protestant sects were permitted freedom of worship in their own homes so long as they did not disrupt the peace. English Catholics and Quakers were not legally protected, but in practice they too were permitted to worship so long as they did not promote social discord. Cromwell once remarked: "I have plucked many [Catholic priests] out of the fire, the raging fire of persecution, which did tyrannize over their consciences, and encroach by arbitrariness of power over their estates." Cromwell also became good friends with George Fox, founder of the detested Quaker sect. Jews were readmitted to England. Thus, even though Cromwell saw his political mission inextricably tied to his faith, he did not see this at all incompatible with liberty. His policy toward the faith of others, including those with whom he disagreed vehemently, was the most tolerant England had ever seen. It was a tolerance that sprung to a great degree from his own Christian beliefs.

As important, from America's perspective, were Cromwell's tremendous achievements in foreign policy. He had a fatherly affection for Puritan New England. Even though New England often shunned his offers of assistance, he still provided his American brothers both military and economic protections from the aggressive colonial policies of France and Spain. During a two-year period, 1649-51, Cromwell built 40 warships, making England a formidable naval power, and he dramaticaliy ex panded British commercial activity. Under Cromwell, the English began beating the Netherlands in trade and reduced Portugal and Brazil to political insignificance. France was seriously battered and Cromwellian forces seized Jamaica from Spain. He did not want the world to fall to the Catholics, whom he saw as not only heretical but totalitarian. To him, British colonization was an

essential evangelical mission. His victories he saw as divine providence, declaring in 1654: "As all the nations on this matter, and
they will testify, and indeed the dispensations of the Lord have
been as if He had said, England, thou art my first born."

In August of 1658, Cromwell fell deathly ill with bron-
chitis. Much of England was on its knees praying for the fallen
leader. He asked his doctors not to look so melancholy. "I am
safe," he said. "I am the poorest wretch that lives, but I love God,
or rather am beloved of God," and added: "The Lord has filled me
with as much assurance of His pardon and His love as my soul
can hold." Tottering on the brink of eternity, one of Cromwell's
last prayers was not for himself, but for his country.

"Lord," he said, "though I am a miserable and wretched
creature, I am in covenant with Thee through grace and, if I may,
I will come to Thee for Thy people. Thou hast made me, though
very unworthy, a mean instrument to do them some good and
Thee service; and many of them have set too high a value upon me,
though others wish and would be glad for my death. Lord, however Thou dispose of me, continue and go on to do good for them.
Give them consistency and judgment, one heart, and mutual love,
and go on to deliver them, and with the work of reformation, and
make the name of Christ glorious in the world. Teach those who
look too much on Thy instruments to depend more upon Thyself.
Pardon such as desire to trample upon the dust of a poor worm,
for they are Thy people, too. And pardon the folly of this short
prayer, even for Jesus Christ's sake, and give me a good night if
it be Thy pleasure." On September 3, Oliver Cromwell fell into a
coma and never again awakened.

CHAPTER TWELVE

THE BLOODLESS REVOLUTION

Cromwell's reign created the seeds of a modern nation. But he was unable to resolve the relationship between the executive and Parliament. He believed that the liberties of the people could better be protected by a government of many than a government of one; and therefore, Parliament ought to supersede the executive in authority. But Parliament during his reign never wanted the responsibility of governing. They trusted Cromwell more than they trusted themselves to manage the affairs of state. Even over his objections, Parliament always abdicated its own duly constituted authority. Moreover, the British were still monarchists, not republicans, at heart, and 12 years of Puritan rule was not sufficient by itself to change centuries of English thought and custom. Charles I could be dismissed as an anomaly, and not representing an inherent flaw in the principle of Crown supremacy. After all, one could point to the many good kings and queens in England's past.

After Cromwell's death, his son Richard was given the office of Lord Protector, which, like his father, he did not want. The Puritans were never comfortable in power because to rule was in fundamental conflict with their basic creed, which was to level human authority. A man without the force of personality or the desire to govern, Richard Cromwell resigned after only a few months in office. The Puritan movement had no leader to replace Cromwell and had not satisfactorily answered the constitutional problems created by overthrowing the King. Unable to organize, the Puritans gave up power to a determined General Monek, who had assembled a formidable army and occupied London. Charles II promised to abide by the concessions his father had made, and a reconstituted pro-Royalist "Free" Parliament restored the Stuart monarchy. On May 25, 1660, 13 years after the beheading of his father, Charles II returned from exile and landed on Dover Beach. Exhausted by years of political and social turmoil, the English people willingly accepted a return to old ways.

King Charles II, with his now overwhelmingly Loyalist and Anglican House of Commons, moved quickly to restore the bishops to their old positions and take revenge on the Puritans. Puritan ministers were immediately ejected from the English Church, and in 1661 the Corporation Act was passed barring non-members of the English Church from holding public office -an effort to ensure a pro-monarchy and pro-episcopal Parliament. In 1662, the Act of Uniformity was passed, demanding "unfeigned assent and consent" to all tenets of the official Anglican *Book of Common Prayer*. This excluded many Puritans who disagreed with some practices of the English Church, but were willing to call themselves Anglicans. Those who did not conform to official church rites were expelled. If the Anglican Loyalists had learned one lesson from the Cromwellian period, it was that the English Church needed to be more rigid in its theology, form of worship, and administrative apparatus.

Added was the Conventicle Act of 1664 forbidding clergy who were excommunicated by the Act of Uniformity from preaching to gatherings of more than five people. The Five Mile Act, passed the following year, prohibited these expelled clergy from traveling within five miles of any location where they had at one time held worship services. This package of laws made up what came to be called the Clarendon Code, named after Charles' Chancellor - who paradoxically counseled against the most severe aspects of the legislation because he feared another Puritan back-lash. Taking Clarendon's advice, Charles-who was far more politically astute than his father - issued in 1672 a Declaration of Indulgence that permitted non-conformists to worship with the appropriate license. But his Anglican-dominated Parliament, declaring that the King did not have the authority to unilaterally repeal Parliament's statutes, countered by passing the Test Act, which Charles agreed to sign. The Test Act strengthened the Corporation Act, declaring that the Anglican Church's religious rites would be used as a political litmus test to exclude non-conformists from public office.

Against this background, John Locke's friendship with Anthony Ashley Cooper, the first Earl of Shaftesbury, takes on importance. It was Shaftesbury who drew Locke's attention to the political arena. Shaftesbury was the man of action, while Locke was a man of ideas. The combined efforts of these two individuals helped establish a whig (republican) political tradition in England that would find an especially favorable reception in the American colonies and provide a philosophical and moral justification for America's decision to break with England.

John Locke was raised in a Puritan home. His father had fought on Cromwell's side during the Puritan Revolution. Locke studied at Oxford during the reign of Oliver Cromwell, and his ideas on politics were certainly influenced during this period. But Locke's main interest as a young man was science, not politics. He worked closely with one of the founders of modern chemistry, Robert Boyle, and became a physician. It was as a medical doctor that Locke first came to the attention of the statesman Lord Ashley (later the Earl of Shaftesbury), who hired Locke to tutor his son and serve as the family physician. Locke rapidly gained Ashley's confidence and began advising him on political affairs.

Though the facts of Ashley's early political life are sketchy, it seems he was involved in establishing the "Little Parliament" in 1653, and then in December of that year persuaded Parliament to turn its powers over to Cromwell. Ashley was then appointed to Cromwell's Council of State, established by the Instrument of Government; he was also elected to serve in the "Assembly of

Saints." He was not, though, a zealous Puritan, but rather a Puritan-leaning Anglican. Though he had supported Cromwell, he decided ultimately that the Protectorate was not right for England. Some middle ground, he thought, was preferable, and so he stood for constitutional monarchy, the Protestant succession, religious toleration, civil liberty, and the supremacy of Parliament. He was also a politician of consummate skill-though often reckless and Machiavellian in his tactics.

Shaftesbury grew alarmed at Charles II's government on two counts. First, Charles, following his father's practices, had formed a close friendship with the French monarch Louis XIV. In fact, Louis was subsidizing Charles, thus freeing the English Crown from dependence on Parliament for revenue. Second, Charles was suspected of having secretly converted to the Catholic Church during his exile in France, a view that seemed to be confirmed by the fact that French Catholic money was steadily flowing into Charles' treasury. The great fear-among both Episcopal Anglicans and Puritans - was that Charles was conspiring with Louis to bring the English Church back into communion with Rome. Moreover, Charles was suspected of having gained an appreciation of the French monarchial dictatorship while in exile there. John Locke, meanwhile, assisted Shaftesbury in writing treatises designed to excite the English people to oppose Charles' attempts to circumvent Parliament and subvert England's Protestant religion.

Titus Oates's "exposure" of the so-called "Popish Plot" threw fuel on the fire of English paranoia about the Catholic threat. Oates charged that he had evidence of Charles' secret plan to move England back into the Roman fold. His charges were unfounded, but Shaftesbury capitalized on them brilliantly and his followers - who formed the nucleus of an emerging Whig or "country" political party- swept three successive parliamentary elections. Charles was suddenly in serious political difficulty, as he had only about 30 supporters in the entire House of Commons (despite all the anti-Puritan legislation designed to ensure a

Royalist Parliament). To make matters worse for Charles, Shaftesbury then initiated a series of bills to ease restrictions on dissenting Protestant groups.

The issue that brought the conflict between Charles and Shaftesbury to a head was the matter of who would inherit the throne. Charles had no legitimate heir; so his brother James II, the Duke of York, held the greatest claim. But James II had converted to the Roman Catholic Church, and thus appeared totally unacceptable from both an Anglican and Puritan per spective. Shaftesbury's candidate for king was Charles' illegitimate son, the Duke of Monmouth. Monmouth became the darling of the Whig cause for two reasons: he was a Protestant, and his bastard birth undermined the principle of hereditary succession. The Puritans were skeptical, however, because of the immorality it implied. Though they had nothing personally against Monmouth, it seemed inappropriate to reward the fruit of promiscuity with the Crown. Even the Anglican Church was squeamish about this stain on Monmouth's character. In Shaftesbury's view, though, Monmouth's illegitimate birth was an asset because it would make the executive an essentially elective rather than a hereditary office.

But Charles II was a good politician. He saw Shaftesbury's attempt to exclude James from succession as the perfect opportunity to eliminate Shaftesbury permanently from the political arena. When Shaftesbury confronted the King on the floor of the House of Lords, an episode chronicled by Stuart Prall in his excellent book, *The Bloodless Revolution,* Charles seized the moment and fought back. With all his ministers present and the full dignity of the office behind him, the King stared at Shaftesbury. "Let there be no disillusion," he said. "I will not yield, nor will I be bullied. Men usually become more timid as they grow older. It is the opposite with me, and for what may remain of my life I am determined that nothing will tarnish my reputation. I have law and reason and all right thinking on my side." And then, pointing at an assembly of bishops, he concluded: Most importantly, "I have the Church, and nothing will ever separate us."

Shaftesbury had miscalculated, thinking the King would back down. He would not. Charles sensed that England would not support Shaftesbury to the point of setting off another civil war. The legacy of the Puritan Revolution was double-edged: Cromwell had established that a nation could eliminate its king; but only at a heavy price. The Church, the gentry, the aristocracy, and the merchant class all stood to lose from war. Exclusion of James II from the throne was not worth the cost. Moreover, King Louis of France would likely have come to the assistance of the embattled English monarch with arms and men. Shaftesbury had gambled and lost. On July 2, 1681, Shaftesbury was arrested, denied common law Habeas Corpus protections of due process, convicted in the King's court of treason, peijury, and seditious libel, and sent to the Tower. Prior to Shaftesbury's trial, John Dryden published his famous satirical attack on Shaftesbury, entitled *Absalom and Achitophel,* a work that is largely responsible for the unfavorable and unjust image of Shaftesbury in history. After a year in prison Shaftesbury was released in poor health and died in Holland in January 1683.

A politically rehabilitated King Charles II began a program of restructuring the boroughs to guarantee the election of a Loyalist (later called Tory) Parliament. Through a series of what were essentially executive orders, Charles revoked corporate and borough charters from his political enemies and awarded them to his Tory supporters. Charles and the Loyalists then proceeded to exercise their restored power without restraint. The Puritans and non-conformist Protestants absorbed the full brunt of the King's wrath. It was the old story, so reminiscent ofpast Stuart behavior. Dissenting Protestants could be brought up on charges and fined or sent to prison. Property and business assets of the accused were frequently seized to pay fines. The prisons were overcrowded, disease-ridden, cold, and filthy beyond human tolerance. Charles seemed to have repealed Cromwell's legacy, and appeared to be pulling England's political system back into the

Middle Ages.

Times of persecution and social upheaval often produce great literature, and the period of the Stuart Restoration was no exception. Reflecting on the fading Puritan dream in England, an aging John Milton wrote his great allegorical poem *Paradise Lost*. He seemed to have concluded that God was unhappy with the way in which the Puritans had mishandled themselves in government. Perhaps they had reveled too much in their victory over the King; and instead of establishing a Christian commonwealth that guaranteed the civil liberties of all Englishmen, their failures resulted in a Stuart despotism more tyrannical than ever. Milton illustrated the point in a famous passage in which Eve is unable to resist the flattery of the serpent and eats the apple, arguing that she no longer needs God to govern her life:

> But of this Tree we may not taste nor touch;
> God so commanded, and left that Command
> Sole Daughter of his Voice; the rest, we live
> Law to our selves, our Reason is our Law.

As God punished Adam and Eve for deliberately breaking His command, Milton thought, so He must also be punishing England and the Puritans for their transgressions by giving Satan free reign of the countryside through the instrument of Charles II. It was a punishment the Puritans deserved, thought Milton, as the title of his poem *Pairadise Lost,* and not *"Paradise Stolen,"* suggests.

The most moving work of Puritan literature, written during the Restoration period, was John Bunyan's *Pilgrim's Progress,* published in 1678. Samuel Coleridge called it the best evangelical Christian work "ever produced by a writer not miraculously inspired." Bunyan, a Separatist Protestant, wrote the book while serving time in one of Charles' dungeons. It constitutes the first English novel, and is the story of a troubled soul's painful search for salvation. In the end, and after many trials, the searching sinner of Bunyan's tale is mercifully spared by God's providence. Other than the Bible, *Pilgrim's Progress* was the most widely read book in the colonies. Indeed, the wrath the Puritans endured under Charles II seemed to serve a definite purpose, rekindling the pure and humble Christian spirit that they may have lost while in control of the government. Power tends to breed arrogance. No longer in a position of political authority, the Puritans had no choice but to return to the itinerant religious practices of preaching and persuasion that had made them such a dominant intellectual and moral force in English culture. To men such as Milton and Bunyan, God's ways were not pointless or arbitrary: He was humbling His children for a reason, for some great future purpose.

But the writer most responsible for developing a distinctly Whig political philosophy was John Locke, also of Puritan stock. He applied Protestant theology and principles to the ordering of government. Since Shaftesbury's friends were all in grave danger in England so long as the Stuarts remained in power, Locke followed his patron to Holland. In 1684, Locke's name appeared on a list of 84 traitors sent by the English government to the Hague. To avoid arrest, he went into hiding where he continued scribbling down his thoughts on a variety of subjects, from religion to politics.

Locke was a pious man, who venerated the Scriptures. He authored paraphrases of Paul's epistles to the Romans, Galatians, Ephesians, and Paul's two letters to the Corinthians. He also wrote a book entitled *The Reasonableness of Christianity,* in which he ventured to prove that the Christianity of Scripture, free from corrupt human mixtures, makes sense. Locke's Christian convictions are also apparent in his two *Treatises of Civil Government,* which contain 102 biblical citations to add weight to his case. *Civil Government,* which he began writing in 1682 (though it was not published until 1690), is Locke's most important work in terms of the development of American constitutional theory.

Locke strongly favored the separation of the executive, legislative, and judicial functions of government as a way to avoid the concentration of power and make less likely the rise of a tyrant. Locke wrote his book with the Stuart monarchy in mind. *Civil Government* was a devastating refutation of the divine right of kings, for which he substituted the "social contract" as an alternative. He based the idea on "that Paction which God made with Noah after the Deluge." He was also well aware of the church covenants of Congregational and other independent Protestants as well as the Mayflower Compact signed 60 years earlier by the Pilgrim settlers of Plymouth, Massachusetts. The social compact, according to Locke, involves a group of people voluntarily joining together into a community for their own protection and to pursue common aims. The "consent of the people," thought Locke, is the only legitimate basis for just government.

Locke began his argument with the proposition that God intended man to own private property, and referred the reader to Genesis: "God gave the world to Adam and his posterity in common," said Locke. He then went on to cite Paul's first letter to Timothy: "God . . richly supplies us with all things(1 Tim. 6:17). But, Locke added hastily, this is by no means a prescription for socialism, as man also possesses property in the form of his own exertions. Thus any individual who takes what God has provided equally to all and tailors it to his own purposes becomes the sole owner of that property. A farmer, for example, who builds a fence and cultivates the land for the production of food becomes the legitimate owner of the land. According to Locke's view: "God, when He gave the World in common to all mankind, commanded man also to labor . . . God in His reason commanded him to subdue the Earth, subdue it for the benefit of life, and therein lay out something upon it that was his own, his labor. He that in obedience to this command of God subdued, tilled and sowed any part of it, thereby annexed to it something that was his property, which another had no title to, and could not without injury take it from him." Moreover, "thou shalt not steal" and "thou shalt not covet" are commandments of God designed to protect private property.

From his reading of Genesis, Locke noted that man at one time existed outside the bounds of civil government, was in a "state of nature" and completely free. But once sin entered into the world through Adam's indiscretion, the safety of men and their property became tenuous. Man's fallen state required that he give up some of his freedom and prudently subject himself to civil government, without which his ability to enjoy the fruits of his labor and defend his rights "is very uncertain and constantly exposed to the invasion of others." Locke added: "For all men being kings such as he, every man his equal and the greater part no strict observers of equity and justice, the enjoyment of the property he has in this state [of nature] is very unsafe, very insecure. This makes him willing to quit this condition, which however free, is full of fears and continual dangers."

Frail and defenseless individuals, in Locke's view, were forced by the brutish circumstances of existence to band together for their own mutual protection to form civil societies, entrusting to some sovereign agent the power to wield the sword against bandits and foreign invaders. But Locke, wanting to confine the duties of government to a narrow compass, was quick to add that the power of government is by no means absolute; the people had entered into a mutual and binding trust with each other and had established a regime with precisely defined obligations. If this trust or "compact" is at any time broken, the people have the right to withdraw their allegiance - even to rebel and depose their ruler - an astonishing notion to those who believed the monarch's authority flowed from divine right.

To the question: Who shall judge the king? Locke replied, "The people shall be the judge," though in the end, said Locke, "God in Heaven is Judge. He alone, 'tis true, is Judge of the right. But every man is judge for himself. . . whether he should appeal to the Supreme Judge, as Jephthah did" and wage war against an oppressor (Judges 11:27-33). "I will not dispute now whether princes are exempt from the laws of their country," wrote Locke, "but this I am sure, they owe subjection to the laws of God," and added: "No body, no power, can exempt them from the obligations of that Eternal Law. . . Whatever some flatterers say to princes of the world, who all together, with all their people joined to them, are, in comparison to the Great God, but a drop of a bucket, or a dust on the balance, inconsiderable, nothing" (Isaiah 40:15). Rebellion, for Locke, was a measure of last resort, to be exercised only when all other means of redress had been exhausted. But, in his view, to appeal to the ultimate Judge, the Maker of Heaven and earth, was a legitimate option.

Locke's argument for disobeying a king was actually a conservative one. While Royalists believed rejection of the monarch's authority was the same as disobeying God, Locke thought little harm would come from acknowledging the people's prerogative to exercise their ultimate right to reject the civil authority, because "people are not so easily got out of old forms as some are apt to suggest." "Great mistakes," said Locke, "will be born by the people without mutiny or murmur." Only "a long train of abuses, prevarications and artifices, all tending the same way," that is towards subverting the people's God-given liberties, could make the people "rouse themselves." Indeed, thought Locke, that's the way it should be.

Locke was merely applying Protestant religious principles to the world of politics. If the individual has the authority to interpret Scripture for himself, without a human agent acting as intermediary, isn't it also up to the individual to determine his own relationship to the government and indeed to the rest of society? Under extreme circumstances, thought Locke, the conscience of the individual, informed by Scripture and right reason, can supersede the government and even the collective judgment of the group because society is a voluntary union, from which anyone can exit if he so chooses. Locke was making here the modern distinction between the state and the collection of individuals that form society, a distinction the medieval world did not make.

Locke's treatise was aimed specifically at undermining political support for the regime of Charles II. But the American colonists applied these same Lockean principles to great effect when making their case for severing their relationship to the British government and establishing a new political order, one better designed to defend the people's rights to "life, liberty and property," Locke's words which appear in the Fifth and Fourteenth Amendments of the U.S. Constitution. No political philosopher has been more widely quoted in American political discourse than John Locke, which is why it is important for Americans to have at least a bare understanding of events in England during this period. For it was events, which he witnessed and took part in, that were decisive in shaping his political views.

In this sense, Locke was more a social scientist than an abstract political philosopher. He sought first to observe events, and then develop a theory to explain them. The radical ideologue, by contrast, adheres to a theory regardless of the facts, and then tries to make events conform to his theory. Locke was no radical. He was a conservative, and often criticized radicals who labor to destroy without proposing a viable alternative. "A building," he said, "diseases them. They find great fault in it, and welcome, if they will, but endeavor to raise another in its place."

Locke was not doctrinaire politically, but adjusted his views continuously in light of the facts. Indeed, he initially supported the restoration of the Stuart monarchy, believing that Cromwell's Protectorate was too radical a change in England's body politic. Locke was a pure scientist, who transferred the skills he learned as a chemist and physician to the world of politics. He observed that the medieval order had broken down, had become dysfunctional, and that the vast majority of people were becoming increasingly dissatisfied with the despotic nature of the Stuart monarchy. The divine-right doctrine was clearly dead, both morally and politically. Locke saw his task as: a) providing moral and philosophical justification for those who already opposed the monarchy;

and b) providing a sensible alternative, the "social compact," meaning the consent of the people, which seemed to have the sanction of common sense, historical precedent, and Holy Writ. Locke merely codified and popularized a political doctrine that events had started to bring into being.

The relationship between the men of action and the men of ideas is critical in judging the prospects of a revolution succeeding in replacing the old regime with an improved regime. If action precedes the theory, then the revolution stands a chance of success. On the other hand, if theory or ideology precedes events, particularly if the ideologues are militantly wedded to their theories, then there is virtually no chance that the new regime will be freer and more tolerant than the old. Communist revolutions, for example, attempt to impose a preconceived Marxist ideology on reality and explain every event through the lens of communist dialectical materialism. The result has been tyranny and mass murder because the communist's sense of the truth is never altered by the facts. Locke, though, had no wish to inflict an abstract ideology upon the world, but instead formed his views largely in response to actual political developments emerging from Shaftesbury's conflict with Charles II. Republican ideas of government never could have taken root in Anglo-American life had they not flowed naturally from the course of events and already existing patterns of thought.

Although the King defeated Shaftesbury, he did so narrowly, and the existence of the Whigs as a formidable political party was clear. After Shaftesbury's confrontation with King Charles II, as Stuart Prall points out in his book, there began to develop an understanding in English politics that four complementary and interacting elements are necessary to modern functioning constitutional government. First, there must be general elections at regular intervals. Second, there must exist at least two strong political parties attempting to advance specific programs for government. Third, there must be enough common ground between the parties to ensure that the winners do not seek to eliminate the losers, nor would the losers feel compelled to take up arms against the winners. Fourth, office-seekers must feel free to campaign against the party in power.

Shaftesbury, in a sense, was the first realistic alternative to a sitting monarch, and had a party of followers who became known as Whigs. Locke, working closely with Shaftesbury, provided the philosophical program. Supporters of the King and national church (Tories) were then forced to respond with programs of their own to counter Whig initiatives. What was still lacking, however, was the spirit of cohesion and compromise, whereby whichever side won, it would not attempt to eliminate the other; and the losers would peacefully accept defeat in the hope that they might achieve victory in some future election. The fact that the losers did not take up arms in this case was not because of a new conciliatory spirit, but because Shaftesbury's followers knew there was no hope of defeating the King militarily. Moreover, Charles had no interest in establishing a constitu tional government. He liked the old way, where officeholders owed their positions to him and not some opposition party. His wish was for centrally-administered government; he had no patience for the political give-and-take of coalition building and persuasion so integral to democracy.

The attempt to exclude James II from the throne had paved the way for the emergence of Sir Edward Seymour as leader of the Tory party. The Tory interest distinguished itself from the royal interest in that it saw its mission as preserving the Anglican Church from creeping Catholicism. Seymour also believed that a nation ought to be governed by accountable politicians and not remote royal administrators. Thus Shaftesbury's defeat was not in vain. The "exclusion issue" had planted the seeds of the two-party political system. When Charles II died in 1685 and the Duke of York, James II, succeeded him, the new King had working against him a consolidated Whig/Puritan opposition and the embryo of a Tory/Anglican party which, though friendly to old ways, had its own constituents and political agenda distinct from the Crown's.

Immediately after his succession, James began attending Mass ostentatiously, making it a state occasion. He also demanded that his ministers accompany him. Some did, others refused. The Earl of Rochester, a Tory leader, spent his Sundays in the country so he would not have to attend. The Earl of Ormonde, another Tory, waited for the King outside the chapel. Even more alarming, from a Protestant (Anglican or Puritan) perspective, was that James would openly seek the advice of French Jesuits and entertain them at Court. The Jesuits were seen as a highly effective subversive force whose main mission was to advance both papal and French interests in Protestant countries. They were, from the Protestant perspective, the Catholic equivalent of the K.G.B., created to undermine the achievements of the Reformation. The Jesuits, at one point, had hatched a plot to overthrow Queen Elizabeth, an incident that had not escaped the memories of the English people.

In addition, James, like Charles, received large subsidies from the French treasury, making it appear as though he was a pawn of both Rome and Versailles. The steady supply of French revenue enabled James to dissolve Parliament on July 2, 1687. He then began removing Protestants and placing Catholics into key positions in the military and the Anglican Church. The culmination of James' policy to advance the Catholic interest in England was the issuing of a Declaration of Indulgence on April 4, 1687, which repealed by decree the odious Test Act (which required all holders of public office to conform to all Anglican Church rites). At first glance, this would seem a great boon for the cause of religious toleration - which is exactly the motive James claimed for himself. But very few believed religious toleration was his true aim - a view that seemed confirmed by recent events. James, it appeared, wanted to clear the way for moving Catholics (who in the 17th century did not believe in religious toleration) into all areas of government. Many saw the Declaration of Indulgence as the logical first step toward his eventual goal of re-establishing

Roman Catholicism as the official religion of the English state.

That same year, James launched a radical program to alter the religious composition of the universities. He ordered the board of directors of Oxford's Magdalen College to appoint Anthony Farmer, a Catholic sympathizer, to the presidency. The board refused, and instead appointed their own Protestant nominee, administering the traditional oaths in violation of the Declaration of Indulgence. William Penn, the Quaker founder of Pennsylvania and a true friend of religious toleration, attempted to mediate the dispute. Naive about the King's real aims, Penn hoped James and the college could arrive at a compromise. Penn's efforts failed, and James placed Magdalen College under Cathohc administration.

Questions raised by the Magdalen College episode and the Declaration of Indulgence were similar to those leading to Cromwell's revolt and later the American War of Independence. William Penn saw religious toleration as an inalienable right, granted by the Lord Himself, and the Declaration of Indulgence as therefore desirable, no matter what the King's true intentions. Penn, a member of the much-persecuted Quaker sect, believed it necessary to go to virtually any length to arrive at religious toleration, even if this meant breaking duly established English law, precedent, and custom. Tories, who wanted an established Protestant church, disagreed with Penn. But most Whigs, advocates of religious toleration, differed with Penn as well: what good is toleration if the price is the subversion of law and the consolidation of royal power for future acts of despotism?

The Catholicization of Magdalen College mobilized against James not only Whigs and Puritans, who were a perpetual thorn in the side of royal prerogative, but also many Tories who began to panic over the seemingly inevitable dissolution of the Anglican Church. A number of Tories began corresponding with William of Orange in Holland, seeking his assistance in a *coup d'etat*. William's right to the English throne rested with his wife, Mary, eldest daughter of James. William of Orange was England's hope for a bloodless revolution. The unexpected news in November 1687 that James' Queen was pregnant established the prospect of Roman Catholic succession and made the overthrow of James all the more urgent in the minds ofEnglish Protestants. The incident that sparked the English Revolution of 1688 was the reissuing of the Declaration of Indulgence by James on May 7, 1688, and his subsequent order that it be read from every church pulpit. Thus, James was ordering the Anglican clergy not only to condone previously outlawed Catholic practices, but to assist him in bringing the Anglican Church back under papal jurisdiction.

A central Anglican and Tory assumption had been that the Crown and the Church combined to form the same reality, which was the English nation. But, as Dr. Prall demonstrates in his study of the period, James had created a situation in which the Crown could not be defended without opposing the Church, and *vice versa*. If the clergy had chosen loyalty to the King, it would also have been choosing the elimination of the Anglican Church. The clergy chose self-preservation, and the established Church allied itself with the Puritan non-conformists. It was rapidly becoming apparent that Protestantism in England could not be guaranteed without the deposition of James II and without religious toleration, at least among Protestants. An Anglican Tory named Sir John Reresby went so far as to concede in May 1688 that "most men were now convinced that liberty of conscience was a thing of advantage to the nation." For an Anglican Tory, this was a revolutionary idea and in opposition to the entire concept of a unified church and state which he had fought to defend in the past. Virtually all of England, it seemed, had adopted Whiggery in its essentials, if not all its particulars.

The Archbishop of Canterbury and six of his bishops petitioned the King to withdraw the order to read his Declaration from the pulpit. James prosecuted the bishops for seditious libel. But on July 10, they were acquitted in a humiliating defeat for the Crown. That same day, some of England's highest ranking Tory leaders sent an invitation to Prince William to rescue England from its tyrannical king. The case made to William was that it was not the people who were rebelling against the Crown, but the Crown which had declared war against the people, subverting their constitution and destroying their church. Indeed, this was precisely the thesis of John Locke's *Civil Government.* The vast majority of Englishmen were inclined to agree with Locke that King James II had broken the "social compact." Prince William calculated that the time was ripe to invade.

Before he arrived with his Dutch fleet, William sent ships ahead with copies of a declaration to be distributed among the English people so that they would not panic. This was a revolutionary document, after which America's Declaration of Independence would be patterned; essentially, it was a catalogue of abuses by the King and his "evil advisers." Most important, however, from the standpoint of marking an advance in political theory, it made the Lockean distinction that the nation, rather than the king, ought to be the object of the people's loyalty.

James turned virtually everyone in England against him when he attempted to rally the Irish Catholic army to defend his interests against his political opponents and the Dutch invasion. To the average Englishman, the Irish were sub-human savages who, as Macaulay put it, "did not belong to our branch of the human family." When Prince William landed, James saw he stood no chance and tried to flee for France, which turned out to be a series of comic mishaps. He was captured by fishermen who were patrolling for Catholic priests and returned to London, much to William's irritation. Twelve days later, William allowed James to sail into exile.

The kingdom was without a king. The major worry was the possible degeneration of society into anarchy. A Parliamentary convention assembled on January 22, 1689, and stood at the crossroads of history. What proceeded was the most momentous debate about the nature of constitutional government in the history of England. The substance of Locke's *Civil Government* was debated item by item and put to the vote. The central issue was the nature of the monarchy. Did this institution exist by divine right, or by "original contract" between the people and the king? "Original contract" won in both the House of Commons and the House of Lords.

A related issue was the nature of the throne's *vacancy*. The Whigs wanted it declared that James had *abdicated* rule and that a new leader needed to be *elected*. The Tories, however, saw the word *abdicated* as lethal to the principle of hereditary succession and therefore deadly to the doctrine of rule by divinely dispensed privilege. The Tories wanted James declared legally dead, which would mean that Mary was already queen and that the throne was not really *vacant* at all. Such a discussion sounds arcane to modern ears, but it was by no means frivolous to the 17th-century Englishman. The nature of the throne's vacancy cut right to the heart of the relationship between government and society.

The Whigs won the day merely by pointing out that the King was not dead, but had deserted his post, a view that was not only correct ideologically but squared with the facts. The Tories in the House of Lords, in a final effort to rescue the hereditary principle, asked the House of Commons to adopt the following amendment: James II had deserted his administration, but this did not change the fact that he was still king. One Whig pointed out that if this were true, the present Parliament was an illegal assembly since it had not been convened by the King himself. If James' authority was still acknowledged as legitimate, England was in a *de facto* state of civil war. This was an intolerable idea to both Whigs and Tories. Even the most hard line Tory never wished to see James on English soil again. Both law and practicality dictated that the throne was vacant and that someone other than James had to be given the Crown.

Mary made it clear that she would not accept the throne if it meant excluding her husband, William. With the mobs gathering in the streets, and fearing civil war, the Tories conceded that under dire circumstances Parliament could alter the line of succession and *elect* a king. But the Tories did not suffer a total defeat. Just as Mary would not exclude William, so William would not exclude Mary. Moreover, William had no interest in surrendering royal prerogative to Parliament. He had a vested interest in reasserting, as far as possible, the doctrine of divine right. Even the most doctrinaire Whigs saw that they could not "elect" William unless they also honored Mary's hereditary right to be queen. To do one to the exclusion of the other would create a volatile situation, possibly plunge the kingdom into anarchy, and pave the way for the emergence of a military dictatorship, as is likely to be the case when both law and custom are uprooted. It was resolved that both William and Mary should sit on the throne, one by Parliamentary election and the other by divine right. This compromise passed both houses swiftly and was made law on February 7, 1689.

While the Tories in the House of Lords were busy arguing about what legal precedent permitted such a settlement, the Whigs in the House of Commons established a committee headed by Sir John Sommers, a Whig, to draw up an oath to be taken by the new King and Queen and to draft a Declaration of Rights. Following in the tradition of its predecessors, the document catalogued 28 grievances against James II and listed 22 specific legislative measures for their redress.

The importance of the Revolution of 1688 - called the "Glorious Revolution" by its supporters-was not the expansion of the list of officially recognized rights. This was merely the logical extension of a centuries-old tradition beginning with *Magna Carta* and extended by the Petition of Right and other such documents. Both John Locke and the most staunch Tory, after all, agreed that people had rights. The argument was over how these rights were to be best protected. The question under discussion was the nature of the social contract between the ruler and the people. In the minds of the Tories, the king was God's provision for man's protection, was responsible for defending the rights and interests of his subjects and realm. But for writers such as Locke, the king was not a party to any contract, but a civil servant set up under it, serving at the whim of the people.

The events of the Glorious Revolution established the overthrow of a king as legitimate (at least under extreme circumstances). Moreover, these events proved that he could be deposed without going to war. A bloodless revolution, in other words, was possible-which ultimately leads us to the next step, which is a constitutional democracy. Democracy is nothing more than a series of legal revolutions where the people can, at regular intervals, opt to overthrow their governors. There are no guillotines and no reigns of terror in democratic revolutions, which take place under controlled legal procedures. The social stability rests in the very facts that the jobs of officeholders are unstable and fluid, but that they can lose their jobs without losing their heads.

Though important progress had been made, England was by no means yet a republican democracy. The idea that political sovereignty should rest with the people still would have struck most members of the British ruling class as ludicrous. That most risky of all experiments in political science would have to wait another century until the Philadelphia Convention of 1787.

CHAPTER THIRTEEN

A HOLY EXPERIMENT IN LAISSEZ-FAIRE

William Penn's dream was to build a Quaker "City of Brotherly Love." King Charles II owed Penn's father, Admiral William, who was not a Quaker, 16,000 pounds in loans and back salary. Finding it an easy way to get out from under his debt, Charles, in 1681, gladly granted William Penn the younger-who had inherited a small fortune from his father-proprietary ownership of the land west of the Delaware River and north of Maryland. This would be the site of the Quakers' "Holy Experiment" in government.

The Quakers were an extreme Puritan sect founded in 1650 by George Fox, so extreme, in fact, that they almost ceased to be related to other Protestants. They rejected priests, rituals, and the sacraments. A de-emphasis on church hierarchy and the idea that no mediator was needed for the individual to talk to God were principles held by all Puritans. But the Quakers rejected even baptism and communion, which are mandated by Scripture. They also believed in the "inner light," God's direct revelation to each individual, and thought that through the "inner light" everyone had the ability to overcome sin, whether they had heard the Gospel or not. In stark contrast to most Puritans, the Quakers thought human nature naturally virtuous. Thus, in their view, there was really no need for formal religious institutions of any kind.

The "Friends" took pride in their drab appearance, believing outward adornment to be a frivolous distraction from the pursuit of virtuous deeds. Some of the more extreme Quakers chose to live in the nude, a sight especially distasteful to Puritans (and most other people). One Quaker woman entered the church in Newbury, Massachusetts, stark naked and strolled down the aisle shouting insults at the minister. After her arrest, she explained that she was trying to illustrate the nakedness of Puritan religious practices.

William Penn's political philosophy was almost as radical as his Quaker religious views. With the "inner light" guiding people's behavior, not only were churches not needed, government was not needed either. *Laissez-faire* in faith, politics, and economics pretty well described the governing principles of his colony, Pennsylvania, founded in 1681. Penn hoped to lead by example rather than force. Pennsylvania had virtually no government at all until 1756, when the Quakers finally relinquished control, or rather non-control, over the colony. Because of his faith in the inherent virtue of human nature, he believed that people, if presented with reasoned arguments, and if treated fairly, would lead good lives. In the Quaker view, force and compulsion were never options. The pursuit of this principle to its extreme led both to the success and demise of William Penn's Holy Experiment. Where the Quakers were successful, they had a profound influence on American political thought; but they failed ultimately to confront the reality of man's character, irreparably flawed and at times vicious. And this accounts for their virtual elimination as a religious, political, or cultural force in America.

Penn immediately began advertising the colony to his fellow Quakers, not only in England, but in other parts of Europe as well. In 1682, he issued a pamphlet, entitled *Some Account of the Province of Pennsylvania,* outlining the benefits of emigrating to his colony. He offered complete religious liberty and easy access to land. A 5,000-acre country estate, with a city lot in Philadelphia tossed in, would cost 100 pounds. If you could not afford that, you could rent a 200-acre farm from Penn for a penny an acre.

Also in 1682, Penn wrote his famous constitution for the colony, called the Charter of Liberties, guaranteeing more freedoms than any previous constitution in history. Penn was actually reluctant to prescribe any political form at all, but he was convinced that "any government is free to the people under it (whatever be the frame) where the laws rule."

Although the Quakers comprised the official religion of the colony, Penn stressed that no religion would be compulsory. Settlers poured into the colony, not only from England, but from Ireland, Scotland, Wales, and Germany. Five hundred Dutch and Swedes already lived in Philadelphia when Penn arrived. But their settlement, formerly New Sweden, had disintegrated under Indian attack and the rigors of the frontier. Penn's colony welcomed foreign immigrants-thus institutionalizing an important American tradition. Led by Francis Daniel, the German Quakers settled Germantown. Lutherans, Huguenots, Mennonites, and Catholics also made the pilgrimage to Penn's colony on the promise of religious liberty. In the first year 3,000 settlers arrived, and by 1684 there were 2,500 living in Philadelphia. By 1689, Pennsylvania's population had swollen to 12,000. According to Andrew Hamilton, a Pennsylvania lawyer writing in 1739, the remarkable prosperity of the colony, far out-pacing its neighbors, could be attributed to "the constitution of Mr. Penn," which Mr. Penn himself described as "not so governmentish."

As a result of Penn's live-and-let-live approach to colonial rule, the tax burden in Pennsylvania was extremely light. It included a minimal duty on liquor, an export duty on furs, and a small sales tax. Moreover, on the few occasions when Penn proposed a tax increase, he was inevitably voted down by the Quaker-dominated council. When Penn returned to England in 1684 to promote his colony, he turned over full responsibility of government to the council. In keeping with the Quaker approach, a meeting of the council was not called from October 1684 to the end of March 1685. There were no meetings between November of 1686 and March 1687, and virtually none again for another year and a half. Pennsylvania during this four-year period had virtually no government at all.

The minimal taxes that existed were rarely collected. When William Dyer arrived from England in 1685 to collect the King's customs, he was ignored for the most part, and was shocked to find that no one paid any attention to the Royal Navigation Acts. Back in England, William Penn began to worry that his proprietary charter might be revoked by the Crown if his colonists did not comply with British law. He appointed as deputy governor of Pennsylvania John Blackwell, a tough English bureaucrat, who was Anglican and not Quaker, a vital qualification for any government administrator. Blackwell's travails with the Quakers in Pennsylvania have been recounted in amusing fashion by libertarian historian Murray Rothbard in his history of colonial America, *Conceived in Liberty,* the high-points of which I include here.

When Blackwell arrived in December of 1688, he had difficulty finding the offices of the government, and found the council room empty, littered with unread documents, and covered with dust. Instead of an escort greeting him upon his arrival in Pennsylvania, Blackwell was jeered at by the neighborhood children.

Council President Thomas Lloyd, a Quaker, passively resisted Blackwell's administration. Lloyd announced that Blackwell's orders could not be carried out unless they were officially stamped by the Council's Great Seal, which Lloyd kept solely for his own use. Lloyd then refused to stamp any of Blackwell's documents. Hence, government remained at a grinding standstill, to Blackwell's increased frustration. Blackwell found the state treasury so bankrupt that he was unable to hire a messenger for the purpose of calling a council meeting. Of 12 Blackwell justice of the peace appointments, four flatly refused to serve.

On April 2, 1689, Blackwell began impeachment proceedings against Council President Thomas Lloyd, charging him with about a dozen crimes and misdemeanors. Blackwell argued that because William Penn was the proprietary owner of the territory, Penn's commands were absolute; and therefore, as Penn's agent, Blackwell's orders were absolute as well. Blackwell's harangue did not impress the council.

In a heated rage at Quaker insolence, Blackwell at one point waved his sword in the air and threatened to run through anyone who protested his decrees. He then began summarily dismissing particularly uncooperative councilmen, at which point the remaining members also headed for home. It became clear to Blackwell that he had no hope of bringing order to the colony of Pennsylvania, and he resigned. "I now only wait for the hour of my deliverance," he wrote to Penn in 1689. "These people have not the principles of government amongst them."

While empathizing with poor Blackwell, Penn ultimately sided with the council, reappointing the entire board. He apologized for his mistake in selecting Blackwell as his administrator. He reminded them, though, that Thomas Lloyd had been offered the position, but refused to serve, and that he could not find a single "Friend" who wanted the post. "I have thought fit," wrote Penn, "to throw all into your hands, that you may all see the confidence I have in you."

It was back to business as usual in Pennsylvania. The council rarely met, and the colony enjoyed tremendous prosperity. During the 30-year period between 1680 and 1710, for example, the population of Pennsylvania increased by some 24-fold, actually surpassing the number of New York inhabitants. New York's population during this same period only doubled, a poor showing in comparison to other colonies. New York's less auspicious economic development can be traced to the manorial system implemented by the initial Dutch settlements. The feudal land holding structure remained in New York even after the British pushed the Dutch out of the Hudson River territory, and this greatly impeded the progress of the colony.

By 1700, Philadelphia, less than 20 years in existence, had outstripped New York as a cultural center and was challenging Boston for the top spot. Philadelphia was the second colonial town to have a printing press, and the third to publish a newspaper. It had the best hospitals, following in the Quaker tradition of compassion. Because of the book collection of James Logan, a scientist and classical scholar, Philadelphia's library placed second only to Cotton Mather's in Massachusetts.

Pennsylvania foreshadowed the ideals of the American Revolution. It was the first large state to permit citizens of various nationalities and religious faiths to enjoy equal protection under the laws. The success of Penn's colony greatly interested the classical liberal philosophers of the 18th and 19th centuries - Mill, Hume, Adam Smith, Madison, Hamilton, and Jefferson.[1] It had proved under real life conditions that society could go a long way towards total *laissez-faire* before conditions began to decay into anarchy. Philadelphia with virtually no government came very close to achieving its ideal as the "City of Brotherly Love." It was a vision of America to be, and would provide a fitting location for the signing of the U.S. Constitution in the fall of 1787.

Despite the fact that Pennsylvania under the non-rule of the Quakers was a great success in terms of its economic progress, number of settlers, and cultural advancement, King William grew peeved at Pennsylvania's state of anarchy, its refusal to abide by the Royal Navigation Acts, and its total uselessness as a fighting force against French incursions in the West. He revoked William Penn's proprietary ownership, and made Pennsylvania a Crown colony over the Quaker leader's bit ter objections.

The King, however, restored Penn's charter in 1694, after Penn promised to levy taxes to support King William's war against the French, raise a militia, and obey the Navigation Acts. James Logan, in a letter to Penn, foresaw that the pacifism of the Quakers was raising serious moral problems, especially when the Indians began routinely slaughtering settlers on Pennsylvania's western frontier:

---

1. Classical liberalism of the 18th century favored individual liberty and bore no resemblance to modern liberalism, which is statist.

> I always used the best argument I could, and . .
> . I pleaded that we were a peaceable people, had wholly
> renounced war, and the spirit of it . . . When I pleaded
> this, I really spoke my sentiments; but this will not
> answer the English government, nor the methods of this
> reign. Their answer is, that should we lose our lives only,
> it would be little to the Crown, seeing 'tis our doing, but
> others are involved with us.

Both France and Spain had huge stakes in North America and were in continuous wars with Britain over control of territory and trade. This meant that they were also at war with Pennsylvania, whether the Quakers wanted to acknowledge this or not. The settlers on the western frontier, mostly nonQuaker Germans, were growing increasingly alarmed at the lack of protection. They thought it the most fundamental duty of the legislator to defend his people, regardless of private religious scruples.

In 1755, the Delaware Indians, urged by the French, initiated a series of bloody massacres. The French hoped to prevent the purchase of territory by the Pennsylvanians from the Six Indian Nations, and convinced the Delawares that their way of life was threatened by the colony's westward expansion. The Quakers were shocked by attacks from a tribe they thought was friendly. At first, according to Daniel Boorstin's account, in his book *The Colonial Experience,* the council in Philadelphia responded by denying that the attacks had occurred. Once the facts were undeniable, it argued that unfair treatment of the Indians must have provoked the massacres. The survival of the colony was threatened because of the Quakers' false assumptions about the virtue of human nature. Aside from the reality of such motives as greed and a lust for power, sometimes honest disagreements are irreconcilable. Reason, good arguments, and compromise cannot, by themselves, guarantee security.

The Quaker legislators disagreed. They refused to appropriate any funds for defense, even after the horrific bloodbath of 1756. Instead of an armed regiment, the Quaker assembly created a commission to make sure the settlers were treating the Indians fairly. This provided little comfort for the frontiersmen seeing their wives raped and butchered, their children scalped, their crops destroyed, and their homes burned to the ground.

The Quakers remained unimpressed, even when desperate German settlers rioted in the streets of Philadelphia demanding action on the part of the assembly. Less concerned with the responsibilities of government than whether the laws they passed violated their religious beliefs, Quaker intransigence grew even more rigid as the evidence continued to mount refuting the notion that the Delawares were a peace-loving tribe.

Penn's colony came under intense political pressure in England. The social respectability that the Quakers in London had achieved had dissipated, as news of the border massacres reached Europe. The London "Friends" urged the Pennsylvania Quakers to give up government so that they could avoid some blame for the bloodletting by the Indians, and the embarrassing military conquests by the French. On June 4, 1756, six leading Quaker assemblymen handed in their resignations.

The political winner in all this was Benjamin Franklin, famous for his common-sense philosophy and practical methods. He had issued a pamphlet in 1747 entitled *Plain Truth,* providing a platform for a new political party. Franklin made a powerful case against pacifism in government, and so gained the enthusiastic support of the non-Quaker population of Pennsylvania and, perhaps more importantly, the ruling establishment in England. "The enemy, no doubt, have been told, that the people of Pennsylvania are Quakers, and against all defense, from a principle of conscience," he wrote. "To refuse defending one's self, or one's country, is so unusual a thing among mankind, that possibly they may not believe it, till by experience they find they can come higher and higher up our rivers, seize our vessels, land and plunder our plantations and villages, and retire with the booty unmolested."

In 1756, Franklin asserted in more strident terms his concern for the fate of the settlers on the frontier who were "continually butchered," concluding: "I do not believe we shall ever have firm peace with the Indians till we have well drubbed them." With the Quaker departure from government, Franklin and his followers dominated Pennsylvania politics into the American Revolution.

The Quakers were further disgraced when it became apparent that Quaker opposition to violence translated into their refusal to fight for American independence. In addition to being ridiculed as cowards (unfairly), they were subjected to charges of treason. At this point, the Quakers withdrew almost completely from public life, and concentrated their energies inward, towards further purifying their individual consciences. It is a curious fact that as the rigid dogmas of the Puritans of Massachusetts softened during the 18th century to accommodate the world outside their communities, as Boorstin's book notes, the doctrinaire pacifism of the Quakers grew inore intense in unyielding defiance to the realities of daily experience. For this reason, continued Quaker influence in the world has virtually disappeared.

Despite the ultimate impracticality of the Quaker tradition, without it the American Revolution probably would have been quite different. It would have been very difficult to explain exactly what it was Americans were fighting for if the Quakers had not in fact implemented William Penn's political philosophy: specifically, that government has no right to use force against individuals to serve the purposes of the community. There would have been no experience of such a society to point to without Pennsylvania. Quaker rule provided the needed historical precedent. They were adverse to using force to an extreme. But it was the radical nature of the Quaker conception of government that led to the new political theory that would emerge between 1776 and 1787.

Even with his death in 1718, and the abdication of Quaker rule in 1756, William Penn's philosophy continued to hold sway over the colony. His Charter of Privileges remained until 1776 when, as a state that had declared its independence from England, it formed its own government. The Pennsylvania Constitution was the most democratic of all the colonies, mandating annual elections, and requiring the retirement of legislators after four terms in office, thus subjecting officials to their own laws. The governor, who never had much power anyway, was completely eliminated, giving all authority to the legislature. Moreover, every bill passed by the General Assembly would have to be printed for consideration by the people at large before it could become law in the next legislative session. The Pennsyl vania Constitution completely obliterated privilege, government grants, and chartered monopoly.

In Pennsylvania the most radical ideas about politics and constitutional authority expressed in the Revolution found a voice. The Quakers and their successors in public life questioned assumptions about the principles of government that were taken for granted everywhere else. This colony, more than any other, had first-hand experience of life without monarchy, oligarchy, feudal, or authoritarian rule of any kind. It almost worked. With a few modifications to take into account the unpleasant reality of man's nature, it would work.

CHAPTER FOURTEEN

TWO PREACHERS AND THE GREAT AWAKENING

New England's founding fathers-Bradford, Winthrop, Hooker, and Cotton - had come to America on a mission that was primarily theological in nature. But by the start of the 18th century there had developed a feeling in New England that Winthrop's original "City on a Hill" had lost its former glory, that New Englanders had become too comfortable and cornplacent and had forgotten why they had come to America in the first place. New England had run up against the same problem that a family business confronts when the third and fourth generations take the helm. Would they continue the legacy of the first two generations, or would they coast on past efforts and eventually run the business into the ground? To some Puritans, it appeared that New Englanders had become fat in their prosperity, took their many blessings for granted, and had spent the spiritual capital their ancestors had brought to Massachusetts in the 1620s and 30s.

The most obvious symptom of Massachusetts' loss of purpose was the adoption of the so-called Half-Way Covenant in 1662 by a synod of Congregationalist clergy, the object of which was to expand church membership. Previously, only the obviously regenerate souls, those who had a demonstrable conversion experience - a "new birth" - could be church members and have their children baptized. But under the Half-Way Covenant, adults who did not have a clearly discernible "work of the Spirit" could have their children baptized as well, so long as they professed an intellectual belief in the basic tenets of Reformed Christianity. They could not take part in the Lord's Supper or vote on church matters, but they were welcomed as partial members of the congregation and honest *"seekers"* after salvation.

This trend would be further extended in 1700 by the Reverend Solomon Stoddard, pastor of the church of Northampton, Massachusetts, who permitted all those who professed a belief in the "historical truth" of Christianity to partake in the Lord's Supper even if they were not clearly part of the "elect." He argued that it was impossible for any human to discern the sheep from the goats with certainty and that it was therefore best to let God decide. Once the unregenerate were admitted to the church, Stoddard thought, it would be possible to bring about the necessary new birth with a steady stream of compelling preaching. Stoddard was himself an excellent preacher and his church prospered tremendously under the new system. Parish after parish adopted the "Stoddard Way," and it wasn't long before almost everyone had forgotten that the Lord's Supper had once been denied to the unregenerate.

Stoddard also began making subtle changes in the structure of the church. He regarded the Congregational Way as too loose. Instead of lay rule, he shifted his church to elder rule. The Mathers-Increase and Cotton-bitterly attacked the Stoddard system, calling him the "Congregational Pope." Stoddard's ecclesiastical empire, though, would be Presbyterian rather than Roman. He envisioned congregations subsisting under a larger structure, which would be administered by synods of ministers and church representatives. Of Congregational lay rule, he would say: "We have no reason to think that Christ would entrust the government of His church with men so incapable to govern." It took a half century for this biblical pharaoh to build his kingdom, but at the end of his life he had managed to sweep the congregations of Springfield, Longmeadow, Deerfield, Hadley, Westfield, Suffield, and others along the banks of the Connecticut River, under his dominion, with Northampton as the ecclesiastical capital. He called it the Hampshire Association, which was given legal status by adoption of the *Saybrook Platform.* Congregationalism in Massachusetts and Connecticut was being gradually obliterated under Stoddard in favor of a more authoritarian Presbyterian polity.

It was Stoddard's enormous popularity that enabled him to acquire so much power. He was a Harvard graduate and had written seminal theological tracts. His sermons were the most carefully crafted and eloquent in the region. But Stoddard was making the same error that Catholics and Anglicans had made by trying to pull all Christians under one roof, rather than permitting a thousand flowers to bloom. He was corrupting the federal principle so central to the Congregational Church polity. But because he was so powerful a presence, so revered by his flock, and so effective in his ministry, very few-with the exception of throwbacks such as the Mathers - thought the "Stoddard Way" a mistake.

With expansion of organization came a necessary relaxation of standards. Indeed, Stoddard opened the doors of his church to just about anyone, except the openly scandalous. He had forgotten that the source of strength of the old Congregational Way was the absence of nominal Christians. By permitting the unconverted to partake in the Lord's Supper alongside the newly born, he shattered the entire idea of the covenant and with it the internal unity of the local congregation. The result was an inevitable erosion of the pure Christian spirit that can exist only within a body of believers who are assured of where they stand with regard to salvation. Under the Stoddard system, every congregation would have to carry with it dead weight. One can sympathize with the trend. For one always wants to be hospitable, as well as rule over a huge and prosperous organization. But compromise and the subsequent tarnishing of the pristine purity of the original mission was the price.

Stoddard's open-door church policy has generally been

saluted by historians as democratic and liberalizing. But, in fact, it was the opposite. Stoddard was New England's greatest autocrat. He laid the foundation for the imposition of a national church (along Presbyterian lines), which was precisely what the first Pilgrim settlers sought to escape.

Cotton Mather opposed passionately the usurping of the authority of the autonomous local church in 1701 and the subsequent bureaucratization of Christianity. In his great New England epic, *Magnalia Christi Americana,* Mather lamented the Stoddardian corruption of the Puritan dream, recalling the flight to America "from the depravations of Europe, to the American strand." He called the "first age" a "golden age," and said "to return to that will make a man a Protestant, and, I might add, a Puritan."

Mather saw that the institutionalization of Christianity was deadening the spiritual lives of a people. His concerns foreshadowed the emergence of Jonathan Edwards, who also saw the need to revive New England's Christian mission and reaffirm the principles of Reformed Protestant Christianity. Edwards was a key figure in American history, because it was his ministry that sparked the Great Awakening in the 1740s. He was the greatest American theologian and an excellent preacher. His mind and spiritual fervor helped permanently alter the face of American Christianity, and in many important ways repealed the legacy of Solomon Stoddard, which is made all the more interesting by the fact that Edwards was Stoddard's grandson. Edwards' sermons and preaching exploded the institutional shackles man has always sought to impose on the Holy Spirit.

Jonathan Edwards was the son of Timothy Edwards, a Harvard graduate and pastor of the parish of East Windsor, Connecticut. Jonathan's mother was Esther Stoddard, the second child of Reverend Solomon Stoddard. Esther lived until she was 98, and so was able to see the spiritual earthquake her brilliant son would help bring about in the history of America. The incidents that have made Jonathan Edwards such a legend began at a very young age. He was 11 or 12 when he wrote his famous 1,000-word essay on flying spiders in which he discussed a basis for their classification and presented a theory of equilibrium explaining their ability to navigate in the air. He also hypothesized that their webs were spun from a liquid substance. At age 12, he wrote an essay on colors, in which it was clear that he had studied Newton's *Opticks*. But his primary interest from the start was God. As a child he fasted frequently and often went on long solitary walks in the forest where he prayed and meditated on the Almighty. His interest in science was merely a means to apprehend more profound eternal truths.

In those days, science had not yet turned against Christianity. Isaac Newton (1642-1727), one of the greatest scientific minds in the history of the West, spent much of his time trying to elucidate biblical prophecy. For him, science was an inquiry into the laws of God. Faith and knowledge, he believed, illuminate each other so profoundly that their relationship cannot be overemphasized. Theological references are scattered throughout Newton's works, and he wrote many tracts that were strictly devotional. Wherever one looks there is order and beauty in the universe, and this he thought was a cogent proof of God's existence and love for man. From a very early age, this was Jonathan Edwards' view as well. For him, the study of insects, animals, and plants was a way to obtain a glimpse of God's infinite creative powers. At age 13, Edwards entered Yale College. There he continued his study of Newton, and wrote his "Notes on Natural Science." There was little doubt that Edwards could have become one of America's greatest scientists if he had chosen that path. But he chose instead to follow his family heritage, and became a minister of the Gospel.

The key to Edwards' life and thought was his conversion at the age of 17. Such an assertion sounds strange to modern ears, since Jonathan Edwards from his earliest conscious days was pious to an extreme. According to his *Personal Narrative,* his new birth was the culmination of a long struggle that began during an illness that lasted many months. God seemed to be shaking the young sinner over the pit of hell. In vain, he said, he tried to throw off his evil ways and vowed to take on day and night more rigorous exercises in piety-to no avail. The despair continued for weeks and even months. But then, all at once, he felt at peace and had "a new sense of things." He could not explain the experience he felt, except that it was strangely unexpected. All the religious duties and somber rituals of prayer and devotion that he had engaged in since childhood now seemed only nominal religious expressions and had nothing whatsoever to do with true faith. No matter how hard he tried, he always found himself backsliding into sin; for he had been relying on his own futile efforts and had not placed his trust in God's power to lift him out of that fiery pit. As Edwards described it, he came to this realization when he came upon these words in Paul's letter to Timothy: "Now to the King eternal, immortal, invisible, the only God, be honor and glory forever and ever" (1 Tim. 1:17).

Edwards had read these words hundreds of times before, and certainly had an intellectual grasp of their meaning. But now they seemed to open a window into eternity that he had never seen before. He was filled immediately and unexpectedly with a sensation so unusual that he had no adequate words to explain what he felt. He suddenly burst out into songs and exclamations. He longed "to be wrapt up to Him in Heaven, and be as it were swallowed up in Him forever." He had a fresh understanding of redemption, of God's love and the price Christ paid on the cross for man's evil ways. He was overwhelmed by "an inward, sweet sense of these things." He felt, as he described it, "a calm, sweet abstraction of soul from all concerns of this world; and a kind of vision, or fix'd ideas and imaginations, of being alone in the mountains, or some solitary wilderness, far from mankind, sweetly conversing with Christ, and wrapt and swallowed up by God. The sense I had of divine things would all of a sudden, as it were, kindle up a sweet burning in my heart and ardor of my soul, that I knew not how to express." Edwards had been born again. The importance of this event went beyond the implications it had for his personal life; it formed the cornerstone of his theology.

After serving for a year as minister in a Scotch Presbyterian Church in New York, he returned to Yale for a time to teach. He then accepted an invitation to assist his aging grandfather, Solomon Stoddard, as minister of the church at Northampton. When Stoddard died at age 87, Edwards was elected pastor. He was only 24 years old. From there he began his relentless assault on the source of corruption of the original "errand into the wilderness." That source, he believed, was Arminianism, a "heresy" that is found in most large hierarchical religious establishments, and most acutely in the Roman and Anglican Churches. Paradoxically, Edwards' attack was also aimed, albeit indirectly, against the legacy of his grandfather, which Edwards believed had been built in part on the Arminian error.

Arminius was a Dutch Calvinist whose teachings were condemned by the Calvinist Synod of Dort in 1619. Even though Arminius believed in salvation by faith, his name came to be synonymous in Puritan minds with the belief in salvation by works. Arminius accepted the doctrine of election, but opposed orthodox Calvinism's doctrine of predestination. Man, he believed, was free to chose or reject Christ. Strict Calvinists, believing God's grace is irresistible, rejected Arminianism, be cause to suggest that man chooses God, and not the other way around, seemed to them to be the height of arrogance. This is a crude summary of the actual Arminian dispute, which focused on complicated distinctions regarding the nature of the human will, too involved to go into here. What is important, for our purposes, is what Arminius stood for in the mind of the New Englander. One Puritan wit, when asked what Arminians held, answered: "All the best benefices in England." Such devotional exercises as praying the rosary, paying bishops for indulgences, sprinkling holy water on people and building impressive cathedrals were, in the New England view, natural extensions of Arminianism to a position that one earned his entrance into Heaven.

National churches are especially susceptible to giving priority to works over faith because their major concern is the behavior of the people. When the church becomes an agency of the government, its priority becomes the fostering of good citizenship. From the point of view of the state, one's private relationship with the Almighty is of only secondary importance to outward expressions of reverence. The last thing officials of any government or church bureaucracy want is a sudden outburst of religious enthusiasm. For this reason, defenders of national church establishments favored Christian apologetics based on logic rather than emotional conversion. The major aim of the national church is to be as inclusive as possible, and so cannot demand that all its members have a dramatic St. Augustine-style conversion. The most it can require is an intellectual affirmation of the doctrinal essentials.

John Tillotson, who became Archbishop of Canterbury following the Revolution of 1688, exemplified the compromising spirit of Anglicanism. His sermons were edifying, but not demanding. He appealed to the lazy and worldly impulse in Anglican Christianity, and attacked religious enthusiasts for their unseemly behavior. There is nothing in the Gospel, said Tillotson, "that is either unsuitable to our reason, or prejudicial to our interest . . . nothing but what is easy to be understood, and is easy to be practiced by an honest and willing mind." Anglicans discouraged too much speculation, stressed the "golden rule" as a way to live, and looked askance at mysticism. Good deeds took precedence over the personal relationship between Christ and the individual. One can sympathize with the sentiment of a man like Archbishop Tillotson who desired business as usual, and who saw the sudden and violent conversion as dangerous to social order. In Edwards' view, however, this Arminian Anglican spirit of reasonable compromise and focus on outward religious forms had subverted the original Puritan spirit, and had done so in the form of Stoddardism.

One symptom of the Arminian disease that had started to infect New England was the obsession with regulations. Those who missed church service could expect to spend time in the stocks. There were laws against swearing, profane language, and drunkenness. These laws may have been practical from the standpoint of keeping order in the community. Indeed, New Englanders were model citizens. According to a report by Joseph Bennett, an English visitor in 1740, "it is a rare thing to meet with any drunken people, or to hear an oath sworn in the streets"; and in a tour of the local courts to see what crimes people were committing he saw "not a single criminal." But these encouraging social facts, in Edwards' view, had nothing to do with the individual sinner's salvation, or with his precarious walk on the precipice that separates him from safety and hell. Man will not be saved by laws, regulations, and institutions; nor will he be saved by good behavior. The Protestant position and Edwards' position was that he will be "saved by faith alone." Indeed, New England continued to acknowledge this fact out wardly, continued to use the language of their forefathers' original covenant and employed the same watchwords. But there seemed, in Edwards' view, little-felt inward comprehension.

On the surface, the Bible commonwealth of New England still appeared to be extremely pious. But Edwards maintained that New England was Christian in form only, and had lost sight of the substance of the faith. The churches had become spiritually hollow. The aims of Protestant Reformation, as he saw it, had to be reasserted, pushed farther than they had before. Jonathan Edwards devoted himself to this project with singularity of mind and purpose. He sought to take New England not back to Calvin or Luther, but all the way back to the Sermon on the Mount.

To his Northampton congregation he stressed the limitless power of God, pointing to both the terror of His infinite anger with sin and the infinite benevolence of His mercy. Edwards chose his words carefully, juxtaposing themes of joy and love with fear and wrath. This interplay of feelings helped bring out emotion in his listeners. It took time before people began to respond to Edwards' message. For seven years the Northampton congregation seemed fixed in their Arminian complacency, as Edwards' sermons produced little visible impact. But then, suddenly, the people began to stir. Citizens along the Connecticut River heard of Edwards and streamed into his church, filled the pews and crowded the aisles. His most famous sermon was delivered on July 8, 1741, entitled "Sinners in the Hands of an Angry God." The image he used to illustrate the sinner's predicament was the spider:

"The God that holds you over the pit of Hell, much as one holds a spider, or some loathsome insect, over the fire, abhors you, and is dreadfully provoked; his wrath towards you burns like fire; he looks upon you as worthy of nothing else, but to be cast into the fire . . . You have offended him more than ever a stubborn rebel did his prince: and yet it is nothing but his hand that holds you from falling into the fire every moment: it is ascribed to nothing else that you did not go to Hell last night; that you were suffered to awake again in this world after you closed your eyes to sleep; and there is no other reason to be given why you have not dropped into Hell, since you have sat here in the house of God, provoking his pure eyes by your sinful wicked manner of attending His solemn worship: yea, there is nothing else that is to be given as a reason why you do not this very moment drop down into Hell."

Edwards' aim was to jolt his listeners with concrete pictures (rather than lecture them with arguments) into seeing their total dependency on their Creator; most people of Northampton were, of course, well aware of the theological rationale of God's covenant with man; but the old Calvinist language had become stale, worn out. Edwards wanted his congregation not merely to acknowledge the dogma intellectually, but also to experience the reality of damnation through their senses. He sought to alert-and even terrify-his people into recognizing man's complete depravity and helplessness:

"Look over your past life... How manifold have been the abominations . . . How have you not only attended to the worship, but have in the meantime been feasting your lusts, and wallowing your self in abominable uncleanness... What wicked carriage have some of you been guilty of towards your parents!... Have you not even harbored ill-will and malice towards them?... Have you not often disobeyed your parents and refused to be subject to them? . . . What revenge and malice have you been guilty of towards your neighbors! . . . What lying some of you have been guilty of."

Edwards was not being self-righteous here. He was merely making the biblical point that "all have sinned and fall short of the glory of God" (Romans 3:23). All of us, including Edwards, are guilty and, therefore, unworthy of admission to God's kingdom. He also understood that genuine conversion involved, first, the breaking down of the sinner's pride to the point at which he saw very clearly why he deserved damnation. "What must I do to be saved?" was the cry he hoped to elicit from his flock, at which point Edwards would point to the Scriptures for answers. "For by grace you have been saved through faith; and that not of your-selves, it is the gift of God; not as the result of works, that no one should boast" (Eph. 2:8,9). "For God so loved the world, that He gave His only begotten Son, that whoever *believes* in Him *should not perish,* but have eternal hfe. For God did not send the Son into the world to judge the world; but that the world should be saved through Him. He who believes in Him is not judged... "(John 3:16-18, italics mine).

"It would be righteous in God forever to cast you off, and destroy you," said Edwards, "yet it would also be just in God to save you, in and through Christ." Edwards would take the sinner to the brink of despair, and then at the last moment relieve him of his anxiety and rush him to the pinnacle of ecstasy. The "gift of grace" is free; our only obligation is to accept it. This was Edwards' happy news. Angels, Edwards assured his listeners, would carry the faithful to the throne of God. Both Christ and the Father would welcome the saved soul into the heavenly family, and Jesus would lead a chorus of saints singing His praises. Such were the images Edwards employed, and the impact was momentous.

Edwards wrote about what happened in his congregation in *A Faithful Narrative on the Surprising Work of God in the Conversion of Many Hundred Souls in Northampton.* Without warning, Edwards reported, "the Spirit of God began extraordinarily to... work amongst us. There were, very suddenly, one after another, five or six persons who were, to all appearance, savingly converted, and some of them wrought upon in a very remarkable manner." Edwards wrote of the startling conversion of one woman "who had been one of the greatest company keepers in town." The entire congregation, he reported, was often "in tears while the Word was preached." Edwards' own home replaced the local tavern as the favorite gathering place. Those who experienced the new birth, he said, "partook of that shower of divine blessing that God rained down here and went home rejoicing." Most encouraging, in Edwards' view, was that revival did not seem to be limited to Northampton: "About the same time it began to break forth in the west part of Suffield... It next appeared in Sunderland . . . Deerfield . . . Hatfield West Springfield... Longmeadow... Westfield... Northfield... In every place God brought his saving blessings." Edwards' *Faithful Narrative* rocked the Protestant world, both in America and Europe. The Great Awakening in religion had begun, and it would unleash forces that would have a lasting impact on American theology, church-life, and politics.

The essence of the revival was feverish emotion, the antithesis of man-made theological constructs and ordered church life. It took power away from theologians and church mediators, and left the naked sinner to confront the awesome power and majesty of God on his own - as alone as he would be on Judgment Day. No longer could the sinner take comfort in the rituals of the church, but needed to experience directly the new birth.

The Great Awakening in religion was such a colossal force in America because the colonists were Protestants to begin with, most of them radical dissenters. The experience of revival intensified the dissenting Protestant bias that already existed in America against the corporate church organization. Americans were always predisposed to further battering down institutional barriers that tended to impede God's access to the individual heart. Conversion, not the sacraments, saved the sinner. God, not a bishop, was the only one who could grant absolution. The personal relationship between man and Maker was what counted. To focus on anything else-whether theological abstractions or religious exercises - was a dangerous diversion.

It is difficult for today's readers to fully comprehend the power of the Great Awakening in 18th-century America, in part because religious passion is no longer so central a component of mainstream American life. If we could see television footage of the events that took place across the American countryside during the Great Awakening, first sparked by Jonathan Edwards and carried on by other revivalist preachers, the combination of the civil rights movement, campus riots, and rock festivals of the 1960s would appear mild by comparison.

Ironically, the man who came to symbolize the revival was an Anglican from England named George Whitefield. He was a friend of both John and Charles Wesley, the founders of Methodism. Mter taking a degree at Oxford in 1736, he attracted an enormous following in England for his spectacular preaching on the new birth. He offended many ministers by attacking them for their lack of ardor, and was subsequently barred from most mainline pulpits. So he started preaching in open fields, and this became his trademark.

Whitefield, "the boy preacher," arrived in America in 1738 at age 19. He carried on and amplified the work started by Edwards. Whitefield was America's first traveling evangelist. He preached in hundreds of towns and villages. Edwards had the original mind and was by far the more profound thinker. But

Whitefield had the voice, which, without the assistance of electronic devices, could be heard clearly by 30,000 people. One especially spellbinding sermon was delivered from the courthouse steps of Philadelphia. The mob filled Market Street and stretched down Second Street. The people of Philadelphia craned their necks out windows to hear him lambast the clergy of the standing-orders, calling them unconverted and strangers to Christ.

"Father Abraham," Whitefield asked, "Whom have you in Heaven? Any Episcopalians?"

"No!"

"Any Presbyterians?"

"No!"

"Any Independents or Seceders, New Sides or Old Sides, any Methodists?"

"No! No! No!"

"Whom have you there, then, Father Abraham?"

"We don't know those names here! All who have come are *Christians-believers* in Christ, men who have overcome by the blood of the Lamb and the word of his testimony."[1]

"Oh, is that the case? Then God help me, God help us all, to forget having names and become *Christians* in deed and in truth." He waved his arms, made violent gestures, shouted and danced to the delight of the gathering throngs, who had grown weary of the highbrow, heavily annotated and gentlemanly styles of preachers from Harvard and Yale. During a Whitefield sermon, people would shriek, roll on the ground, dissolve into tears or run wild with religious ecstasy. Even the agnostic Scottish philosopher David Hume once said of Whitefield that it was worth traveling 20 miles to hear him. Skeptic Benjamin Franklin provided the following account of a Whitefield sermon that he attended in Philadelphia:

"I happened soon afterwards to attend one of his sermons, in the course of which I perceived he intended to finish with a collection, so I silently resolved that he should get nothing from me. I had in my pocket a handful of copper money, three or four silver

---

1. Revelation 12:11

dollars, and five in gold. As he proceeded, I began to soften and concluded to give the copper; another stroke of his oratory made me ashamed and determined me to give the silver. He finished so admirably that I emptied my pocket into the collection dish, gold and all."

Franklin wrote about "the extraordinary influence of Whitefield's oratory on his hearers. It was wonderful to see the change soon made in the manners of our inhabitants," he said. "It seemed as if all the world was growing religious, so that one could not walk through the town in an evening without hearing psalms sung in different families of every street." "It's all God," said Whitefield in characteristic humility. Franklin then offered to publish Whitefield's sermons for wide distribution.

Upon Whitefield's arrival in Connecticut, a local farmer provided this account of his own reaction to the news that the spectacular English evangelist was coming to Middletown: "I was in my field at work. I dropped my tool that I had in my hand and ran home and ran through the house and bade my wife to get ready to go."

Knowing they had to travel 12 miles in one hour, the farmer saddled his horse and ran much of the way alongside while his wife rode. As he approached he saw a dark cloud on the horizon, which he first thought was fog, but then found it to be dust created by thousands of his neighbors stampeding across the countryside to hear Whitefield preach in an open pasture. After listening to the eloquent sermon, the farmer concluded: "And my hearing him preach gave me a heart wound; by God's blessing, my old foundation was broken up, and I saw my righteousness would not save me."

Whitefleld often attacked the various religious establishments which were presenting an unknown and unfelt Christ, charging that "a dead ministry will always make a dead people." When he traveled to Charleston he ran headlong into the Anglican establishment, where he faced off with Alexander Garden, the commissary to the Bishop of London. It was unheard of in that region that a traveling preacher could come into the jurisdiction of the Church of England and compete for souls. After lambasting Garden for laxity and failing to tell his parishioners about grace, Whitefield was barred from the province, and warned that if ever he returned he risked excommunication from the Anglican Church. The charges that were eventually brought against him did not at all deter Whitefield from preaching. He continued to undermine Anglican authority, as well as that of other mainline Protestant denominations.

His travels through New England were among his most dramatic. Benjamin Coleman reported that after his appearance at Harvard in 1740 the students were "full of God." According to the Reverend Thomas Prince, four weeks of Whitefield's torrent cleansed Boston. He then rode across Massachusetts, preaching at Concord, Marlborough, Sudbury, and Leicester, to the gathering throngs who, he said, "were sweetly melted." He even went to Northampton and stayed at the home of the great Jonathan Edwards, who gladly opened his pulpit to the traveling evangelist. "Dear Mr. Edwards wept during almost the whole time of the exercise," Whitefield reported in his journal. In all, he made 13 trips to America, during which he spent more than two years on ships. With Edwards, he believed that the New World had been selected by God to complete His divine mission. The Prophet Isaiah had spoken of stirrings that would occur in some remote land, which the two evangelists interpreted to mean America.

Soon other revivalist preachers imitated Whitefield's example and descended with zeal upon the various standing-order ministers, who were often distressed at the threat posed by the Awakeners to the social fabric. The revival crossed denominational boundaries and put constant pressure on established religious and governing institutions. No minister and no official was immune from verbal assaults by these "New Light" preachers. This had a leveling effect on privileged position, and as such was a powerful democratic force. Anyone could have his say. No single person, priest, class of people, or institution could be considered the sole oracle of truth. Revival and aristocracy were incompatible. Who said one needed a license or a college degree to preach the Gospel? Certainly not Jesus. Like politicians and businessmen, ministers, too, would have to compete in the marketplace.

William Tennent and a group of young ministers from Pennsylvania and New Jersey concluded that too much works-oriented Arminian thought had crept into the curriculum of Harvard and Yale. So Tennent, a close friend of Whitefield, took his followers and established Log College, which trained ministers in the fervent style of the revival. Log College was renamed the College of New Jersey, and then later again renamed Princeton, of which Jonathan Edwards became president. After William Tennent died in 1746, his son Gilbert and his associates, "burning and shining lights," as Whitefield called them, kept revival going throughout the countryside with their fiery preaching until the American Revolution.

Eleazar Wheelock was another brilliant evangelist in the Whitefield tradition and a close friend of Edwards. He attacked the lame preaching of the "Old Light" clergy with piercing invective, and in 1769 moved to Hanover, New Hampshire, to minister to the Indians. There he established Dartmouth College with the assistance of a grant from the Earl of Dartmouth, who still lived in England. Brown was founded by Baptist "New Light" preachers in 1764; Rutgers was established by itinerants of the Dutch Reformed movement in 1766. Upon Whitefield's suggestion, Franklin helped found the University of Pennsylvania, which in 1914 unveiled a monument to the powerful preacher, calling Whitefield the "inspirer and original trustee." Thus, some of the most prestigious institutions of higher-learning in America were spawned by the 18th-century revival in religion. As Whitefield put it: "Learning without piety will only render you more capable of promoting the Kingdom of the Devil."

In 1755, Separate Baptists from Connecticut traveled to North Carolina and began rolling, singing, and shouting. They denounced the Anglican clergy, endured occasional floggings and imprisonment for their efforts, but rapidly gained a following. Their influence spread into Virginia, the stronghold of the planter aristocracy. It was from this movement that Southern Christianity began to take its characteristic form. Among Whitefield's most ardent followers were black slaves; the black Gospel music so popular today came out of this revivahst tradition, started by the Great Awakening. During the 1770s the Anglican Church still held sway in Virginia, but was tottering as John Wesley's Methodists became the cutting edge in evangelism, denouncing in shrill terms planter society for spiritual complacency, Arminian theology, extravagant living, and the sin of slave-owning.

The Great Awakening was not explicitly a political movement, but it had many important political implications. It meshed well with the American trend toward democracy, and complemented the Whig political tradition of Locke, Sydney, Montesquieu, and Blackstone, who were suspicious of all governing establishments. The alliance that emerged between these extreme Protestants and the radical Whig libertarians was analogous to Cromwell's co-option of the supporters of Par liamentary supremacy in 17th-century England to triumph over royal authority. The drama of England's Puritan Revolution was about to be replayed in the colonies. Only this time, the Whig/dissenting-Protestant alliance would achieve a complete victory.

For somewhat different reasons, the Awakeners and the American Whigs were critical of all large human establishments, whether religious or political: the former because of the deadening effect religious institutions can have on faith and morals; the latter because of the deadening effect governing institutions have on the human spirit of creativity and industry. There was no contradiction between revival theology and Whig political philosophy. In fact, the two movements complemented each other beautifully. Within this interplay of libertarian political theory and fervent, some would say fanatical, brand of Christianity we begin to see the emerging characteristics of a distinctly American mind.

The key to both movements was in recognition of the sanctity of the individual. It was the individual's response to God's call that was important, not the propping up of dead religious structures; it was the state interests that were subordinate to individual rights, not individual rights that were subordinate to the state's interests. Figures such as Thomas Jefferson and Benjamin Franklin had history and experience as their starting points; while preachers like Jonathan Edwards and George Whitefield began with Scripture and the Holy Spirit. But both political and religious movements sought to break away from established institutions, challenge time-honored customs, and make the individual central to both the temporal and spiritual order.

When George Whitefield came to the New World for the last time in 1770, even the Episcopal churches welcomed him, as denominational barriers no longer mattered so much in America. But the sense of unity that pervaded the colonies had nothing to do with religious complacency. Quite the contrary. The true spirit of Christ had dissolved sectarian differences. America considered itself to be a nation of Christians, pure and simple, as Whitefield noted with satisfaction. "Pulpits, hearts and affections," he said, were opened to him and any preacher of whatever denomination who had a true Christian message to share. There was no longer serious discord among the various sects as there was in Europe. America still yearned for the comfort and assurance found in the Christian faith. "Congregations are larger than ever," Whitefield noted, and the crowds for him were especially huge. "His popularity exceeded all that I ever knew," reported a New England pastor. During this period, Whitefield observed, "Never was the Word received with greater eagerness than it is now."

"Works? Works? A man get to Heaven by works? I would sooner think of climbing to the moon on a rope of sand!" Whitefield told an immense gathering at Exeter, on September 29, 1770. He spoke for two hours that afternoon, and then collapsed from exhaustion. The next day George Whitefield breathed his last, less than five years before an anonymous colonist fired "the shot heard round the world."

CHAPTER FIFTEEN

THE MAKING OF AN AMERICAN REVOLUTIONARY

Three major factors caused the American Revolution: a dissident Protestant tradition that established a *de facto* independent, self-governing commonwealth in New England; heavy-handed, shortsighted, and incredibly inept British policy; and the emergence of George Washington, a vestryman in Virginia's Anglican Church who brought discipline and decorum to a wild and disorganized band of predominantly radical Protestant-Separatists. The ideology for revolution had been expounded for 150 years in New England's pursuits, had been secularized to some extent by such Whig political theorists as John Locke and William Blackstone, and had been given fresh religious impetus by Jonathan Edwards, George Whitefield, and the "New Light" preachers of the Great Awakening who brought the ideology of revolution to the Southern colonies. America's religious institutions, for the most part, had long ago declared their *de facto* independence. The people of New England were ripe for rebellion.

By the middle of the 18th century, what they needed was a pretext, and a leader. That leader arrived on a white horse. George Washington was 6 feet 3 inches tall and weighed 220 pounds; massive proportions for those times. He was the indispensable man; one who brought coherence, leadership, and symbolism to the cause of liberty and self-government. He was 43 years old when he assumed command of the Continental Army in Cambridge, Massachusetts, but had already had a remarkable military career.

Born on February 22, 1732, at Wakefield Plantation in Westmoreland County, Virginia, George Washington was the son of Augustine Washington and his second wife, Mary Ball. He had a modest upbringing. An inventory made of his family's possessions when he was 11 shows the Washingtons' proudest possessions being: 1 soup spoon, 18 small spoons, 7 tea spoons, a watch, and a sword. George's formal schooling went only through the elementary grades. His father died when he was 11. The farm became run down, and George had to take on many of his father's duties. His half-brother, Lawrence, 14 years George's senior, was a regular in the British Army and, in the absence of a father, became a role model for our future hero. Lawrence, though, died of tuberculosis in 1752.

At an early age, George became a great horseman, and at age 17 he set himself up as a surveyor of the Blue Ridge Mountains. During these early years, he gained knowledge of the ways of the wilderness and of how to get along with the Indians. At age 18, he made his first land purchases 59 acres on Bullskin Creek, a part of the Shenandoah. Washington's mother worked hard to raise him a committed Christian, and admonished him before he left home as a young soldier: "Remember that God is our only sure trust." "My son," she added, "neglect not the duty of secret prayer." Young Washington was a diligent and earnest reader of the Scriptures, which he always kept near his bed at night.

Washington joined Virginia's volunteer militia, and by age 20 achieved the rank of major. This was not considered terribly significant, since the volunteer militia resembled more a political club than a fighting force. Nevertheless, to those who knew him it was immediately clear that Washington was a born leader and that he had the air of manifest destiny about him.

Washington came to the public's notice for his exploits

during the French and Indian War, known also as the Seven Years War between Britain and France. It might also be considered the first world war. The conflict between Britain and France spanned the globe, from Europe to the Philippines. But Washington had little interest in geopolitics. His country was Virginia. His concerns were local He did, however, want the French Army out of Virginia. So did Governor Dinwiddie, who employed young Washington to deliver a message of ultimatum to the French to leave the Ohio Valley, a British possession.

Washington departed for the French stronghold in November 1753 with a small party, including his guide and life-long friend Christopher Gist. This 1,000-mile journey through the wilderness in the dead of winter made Washington a local hero. Along the way he encountered numerous Indian leaders, many of whom were wreaking havoc on the white settlers along the Virginia frontier. Through skillful diplomacy, he survived meetings with Shingiss, the king of the Delawares; the chief of the Oneidas; and Half-King, chief of the Senecas. The weather was terrible, and Washington had difficulty even finding the French encampments. He finally reached Fort Le Boeuf on December 12, 1753, at one point walking with Gist 200 miles on foot through trackless forests and freezing rivers. When Washington returned, Governor Dinwiddie was so amazed that he published a narrative of Washington's journey, which was widely read, not only in Virginia, but throughout the colonies and even in England. At age 21, Washington was the most celebrated hero in Virginia.

So impressed was Governor Dinwiddie with the young major that he put Washington in command of an attack on the French Fort Necessity, which had assumed control of the Ohio Valley. The battle turned out to be a complete fiasco, as the heavily out-gunned and out-manned Washington lost a third of his men. It was a horrible defeat for the British, and was the trigger for the extremely bloody French and Indian War. Nevertheless, Washington had gained valuable battle experience: "I heard the bullets whistle," he wrote in a letter, "and believe me, there is something charming in the sound."

The Virginia militia was disbanded, however, upon the arrival of British regulars, leaving Washington without a military post. In 1755, Major General Edward Braddock arrived in Alexandria with two regiments. Braddock was contemptuous of the colonials, and did not want any part of them in his army. He had heard, however, that George Washington knew more than anyone about the wilderness in the Virginia region, and decided his expertise might be of use. The British military was a well-oiled machine, and Braddock's men were part of an elite corps. Superbly equipped and supplied, they could move and wheel with perfect precision in any direction. Braddock's mission was to take the French Fort Duquesne, located at the fork of the Ohio River.

But Washington saw immediately that the British approach was inappropriate for the American wilderness. He warned Braddock that the Indians had their own ways, and that heavy artillery and rows of riflemen clad in red, though suitable for the wide open battlefields of Europe, were doomed in the American forests. Braddock paid no attention to Washington, seeing him as an upstart colonial who had no sophisticated understanding of the world of empire-building.

British progress toward Fort Duquesne was incredibly slow, because engineers had to construct roads on which to transport the heavy guns. Washington informed Braddock that this was absurd. Not only would the British be cut to ribbons in an Indian ambush, but they would not reach the French fort before winter. His warnings fell on deaf ears. Braddock proceeded according to plan, and Washington, suddenly seriously ill, probably with dysentery, was left behind.

Despite his illness, the young warrior concluded that he did not want to miss this chance to repay the French for what they had done to him at Fort Necessity. Washington hitched up a wagon and, barely able to sit up, caught Braddock, who had decided, after all, to take Washington's advice and pick up the pace. July 9, 1755, would, however, prove to be one of the bloodiest days in Anglo-American history.

Washington, still in terrible pain, managed to mount a horse and join Braddock's assault on Fort Duquesne. But as the British forces proceeded through the woods and entered a clearing, shots suddenly rang out, followed by a series of blood-curdling war whoops. One thousand warriors had come from all over the region to assist the French. British soldiers began dropping in bloody heaps. Washington pleaded with Braddock to allow him to lead, to no effect. Unnerved by the Indian screams, British soldiers panicked in the face of an invisible enemy. Braddock was shot off his horse, and Washington seized the opportunity to lead the desperate British regulars in an orderly retreat. Twice Washington's horse was shot out from under him, and twice he mounted a new one. Four bullets tore through his clothes, but miraculously he remained unscathed. Washington moved unflinchingly through the shower of lead to collect hundreds of wounded soldiers, including Braddock, and loaded them into wagons. Fortunately for him, the Indians were too busy scalping and torturing to pursue Washington's wagons, or they could have butchered every single man in Braddock's force. But the damage was done. Of 1,459 British soldiers, 977 were killed or wounded. Incredibly, providentiaHy for the fate of our nation, Washington's body had not been touched, though his clothes had been shredded by gunfire.

The wounded Braddock ordered Washington to ride 40 miles through the night to get reinforcements. He tore through the woods, encountering incredible scenes, horrible beyond description, piles of mangled flesh and earth soaked with blood. The forest was so dense and dark that at times Washington had to dismount and crawl on his hands and knees to find a path. Still sick with fever, his resilient constitution summoned the strength to carry him to his destination. But when he told British forces what had occurred, they were too terrified to march. Braddock died of his wounds.

The expedition was a clear catastrophe for the British, but

not for Washington. The veteran regulars marveled at his bravery, and his reputation spread throughout the colonies. "I was saved," said Washington, by "the miraculous care of Providence that protected me beyond human expectation." The story of his valor, loading the wounded into wagons without regard to his personal safety, became legendary. Benjamin Franklin of Pennsylvania praised young Washington publicly for his bravery and cool head in a time of such grave disaster. One preacher told his congregation that surely God had spared this young soldier's life for some great future purpose. The Braddock defeat was a Pearl Harbor for the British, but on that day the world took notice of the birth of the Washington legend.

The British decided to pull their forces out of the region, leaving Virginia's inhabitants to fend for themselves. It was a decision, no doubt, that planted a seed of doubt in Washington's mind about the benefits of remaining a part of the empire. Washington did not care about power politics. His love for Virginia, not imperial interests, was his reason for fighting the French and Indians. The British departure left a power vacuum, and the Indian attacks on frontier homes grew ferocious. The Virginia Assembly voted to reconstitute the militia, and to make Washington Commander in Chief of Virginia forces. While Washington was headquartered in Winchester, terrifying reports of burnings, scalpings, death, and mayhem poured into the young commander's offices. "The supplication and the tears," Washington lamented, "melt me into such deadly sorrow that I solemnly declare, if I know my own mind, I could offer myself a willing sacrifice to the butchering enemy, provided that would contribute to the people's ease . . . If bleeding, dying'. would glut their insatiate revenge, I would be a willing offering to savage fury, and die by inches to save a people."

To make matters worse, Washington came down with tuberculosis, which actually turned out to be a blessing, because it immunized him from the worst killer of the American Revolution The Army doctor James Craik believed that "the fate of your friends and country are in a manner dependent upon your recovery." Craik had given up hope. But, just as Washington appeared about to die of "violent pleuritic pains," he suddenly, and inexplicably, got well.

Meanwhile, William Pitt, the great empire-builder, had taken over as Prime Minister. He saw England's future as being tied to North America. Pitt decided to withdraw British forces from the European continent, and concentrate them almost exclusively in the American frontier. He would keep the French occupied in Europe by subsidizing his Prussian allies. Brigadier General John Forbes arrived with a force three times the size of Braddock's. Forbes had the foresight to recognize Washington's experience and made him a brigadier general. They would launch another attack on Fort Duquesne, and Washington would lead the advance brigade.

During the expedition, however, Washington's troops got split up. Edgy after the Braddock affair, his men panicked and began firing wildly at every movement, having confused each other for the enemy. But Washington, cool as always, saw immediately what had happened. He rode out in the midst of the crossfire and with his sword knocked his soldiers' rifles upward so that the bullets rocketed harmlessly into the air. Fourteen men were killed and 26 wounded. But, again, Washington emerged untouched, despite the fact that he was the most exposed.

The rest of the tale is an anti-climax because the French, upon hearing about the size of Forbes' approaching force, abandoned the fort and burned it to the ground. The location was renamed Pittsburgh, after the British Prime Minister. The Indians were no longer so interested in fighting for French causes, and Pitt's army and navy in short order defeated the French forces everywhere on the continent: Pennsylvania, New York, Quiberon Bay, Quebec. In 1763, the Treaty of Paris was signed, marking the end of France as a power in North America.

But the Washington legend seemed etched forever, not just in the minds of Virginians, but also in the memories of the Indians who fought against him. Fifteen years after the war, according to an account in George Bancroft's *Histoiy of the United States,* Washington and Craik were exploring the forests on the banks of the Ohio River when they encountered a band of Indians. They immediately recognized the war hero, and invited the two white men back to camp to powwow with the chief. As it turned out, the tribe had fought on the side of the French, and the chief remembered Washington's exploits at the battle of Fort Duquesne.

"I am chief and ruler over all my tribes," he told Washington. "My influence extends to the waters of the great lakes, and to the far blue mountains. I have traveled a long and weary path, that I might see the young warrior of the great battle. It was on the day when the white man's blood mixed with the streams of our forest that I first beheld this chief," he said, pointing to Washington. "I called to my young men and said, 'Mark yon tall and daring warrior? He is not of the redcoat tribe-he hath an Indian's wisdom, and his warriors fight as we do-himself alone is exposed. Quick, let your aim be certain, and he dies.' Our rifles were leveled, rifles which, but for him, knew not how to miss... 'Twas all in vain; a power far mightier than we shielded him from harm. He cannot die in battle . . . The Great Spirit protects that man, and guides his destinies. He will become chief of nations, and a people yet unborn will hail him the founder of a mighty nation."

But after the French and Indian War, Washington had no appetite for more military glory. The Virginia frontier seemed safe for the time being. He decided to go home and nurture a prosperous marriage to Martha Dandridge Custis, to whom he was engaged before the Forbes expedition. Martha was a widow with two small children when she met the great soldier. Washington believed his marriage to her was the event of his life. Martha was not a talker or an intellectual. She was, said Washington, "a quiet wife, a quiet soul," and most "conducive to happiness." Until America's war with Britain, he would devote his energies to becoming a large-scale planter.

CHAPTER SIXTEEN

THE MAKING OF AN
AMERICAN IDEOLOGY

Tension between England and her colonies, particularly the New England colonies, went all the way back to their founding, as we have seen, and this conflict was largely religious in nature. Nevertheless, for a century and a half, America saw the benefits of remaining in some loose affiliation with the empire as outweighing any advantage of complete separation. In addition to the religious conflict, however, England and the colonies, especially those in New England, had evolved different conceptions of government. The Puritans, which included Congregationalists, Baptists, and other dissenting Protestant groups, had put into practice the compact theory, dating back to the founding of Plymouth under the Mayflower Compact. Massachusetts, Connecticut, and Rhode Island were established by people voluntarily covenanting together to form a "civil body politic." Under the covenant conception, government's legitimate and proper function was to protect the inalienable rights of man, as granted by God, such as the rights to life, liberty, and property. Indeed, this is the philosophy of government set forth in America's Declaration of Independence. Under the American form of government, which is really an extension and secularization of the New England conception, government receives its authority only from the consent of the governed as expressed in the covenant, compact, or constitution.

That government's authority derived from the "consent of

the governed" was a notion some Englishmen could accept -in theory. But to permit the people to actually dissolve and establish governments at will sounded utopian and anarchistic. London could accept much of Locke's social compact, but not the part about rulers serving at the whim of the ruled. The lesson of the Puritan and Glorious Revolutions, to most British, was that only under the most dire circumstances could the people dissolve an existing regime. Moreover, the American colonists were second-class citizens within the British empire. If pressed, officials in London would have conceded that the rights of Englishmen extended to the people of North America, but they did not actually believe this. The colonists were British subjects, not citizens, and British policy reflected this perspective. The colonies, in England's view, were Crown possessions. Even though Americans had been governing themselves for most of their colonial history, the sovereign political authority still rested with London.

Thus a conflict was inevitable, particularly when England became serious about administering its empire, annulled the authority of the colonial governments, and in their place appointed governors who would report directly to London. Though the colonies retained assemblies elected by the local population, the direction that English policy was heading was unmistakable. Consolidation of the empire in North America took place over a long period of time, by degrees. So while there was often much tension and unhappiness over English policy, London's behavior never seemed to warrant full scale rebellion - not, that is, until 1776.

The conclusion of the French and Indian War produced an outpouring of patriotic fervor in the colonies. The Americans felt proud of their contributions to victory, began to think of themselves as a nation in their own right, and had their own war hero, that gallant man on a white horse from Virginia. The colonists began to talk of their own glorious future as Americans, with barely a reference to Britain. One Massachusetts doctor, Nathaniel Ames, asked if it made sense for an entire continent of more than

2 million people to be subordinate to a set of small islands off the French coast. Moreover, the British throughout the French and Indian War had treated the colonial militia with disrespect and had abandoned the American theater when it no longer suited their purposes to remain there, thus leaving the colonists to confront the savagery of the French and Indians on their own.

There was also the entire matter of trade. To London, the colonies were useful only so far as they were profitable The colonies were enmeshed in Britain's commercial mercantile system, which was designed to finance Britain's war machine. The arrangement was essentially as follows: the colonies were to provide raw materials that British industry would turn into finished products that could then be sold back to the colonies. England looked with favor upon colonies that fit into the system. Virginia was London's favorite colony. It produced tobacco and other agricultural products that did not compete with British industry and that could be loaded onto British vessels and exported all over the world for substantial profit. In addition, Virginia did not have advanced industry, and so bought many products from the old country: clothes, linens, shoes, and the like.

New England, however, was not satisfactory from England's perspective. The Puritans discovered that it was far cheaper to produce finished products at home than to pay the cost of importing them from England. Moreover, the Puritan products were often superior to those of British industries, which had grown somewhat fat and lazy under the protection of monopoly trade laws. The Puritans were building and sailing their own ships that were faster and better than the British ships, and they had no qualms about moving into British markets. In response, Parliament began to pass a patchwork of irksome laws, directed at New England, such as the Molasses Act of 1733, which interrupted the Puritan rum business by placing a stiff tariff on molasses from the French and Spanish West Indies. The law was calculated to punish three long-time enemies of the Crown: the French, the Spanish, and the Puritans. But the Puritan mer-

chants simply ignored the law, smuggling the molasses past customs officials and trading for it in the under-ground market.
Massachusetts also had its own money - the "pine-tree" shilling-
which was honored in the colonies to the endless irritation of the
British authorities.

From the days of its founding, New England wanted no
part of the British system, had no desire to finance its empire,
and above all wanted no part of the Anglican Church. The Crown
was constantly threatening to install bishops in the colonies to
administer their churches according to acceptable English ways.
The Society for the Propagation of the Gospel in Foreign Parts,
originally established in 1701 by the Anglican Church for the purpose of converting the Indians, had become, by the middle of the
18th century, an instrument for bringing America's Protestant
dissidents into communion with the English Church.
Congregational, Presbyterian, and Baptist ministers would
respond to every rumor of London imposing bishops on them with
flurries of impassioned sermons, scathing editorials in such papers
as *The Boston Gazette,* and shrill pamphlets denouncing the proposal. When the Reverend Jonathan Boucher, an Anglican rector
from Annapolis, returned to England in 1775, he said the issue
of bishops was the backbone of the revolutionary cause. According
to historian Arthur L. Cross, "The efforts of the Episcopalians to
push their plan [to install bishops in America] was at least one
of the causes tending to accentuate the growing alienation between
Great Britain and her colonial subjects beyond the seas which
prepared the ground for revolution soon to follow." And it was in
New England that the sentiment for revolution was most fervent.
The ministers and civil leaders of the towns along the Eastern
Seaboard made it clear very early that they did not want taxes
and they did not want bishops.

The Reverend Jonathan Mayhew, a Harvard graduate and
pastor at Boston's West Church, was passionate in his warnings
of the danger the prospect of bishops presented to the colonists.
Bishops, said Mayhew, were instruments for "establishing tyran-

nies over the bodies and souls of men." Since an Anglican bishop in those days was merely an extension of the arm of the London government - "different branches of the same plan of power," as Mayhew put it - it is easy to see how this issue triggered thought on the entire issue of when rebellion against civil authority is justified. In his famous sermon, *A Discourse Concerning Unlimitted Submission,* which he delivered at West Church in January 1750, Mayhew maintained that the people are bound by Scripture to obey only just authorities. His sermon was an answer to those who cite Romans 13:1-3 as an argument for unquestioned, passive obedience to the government. It is "blasphemy," he said "to call tyrants and oppressors God's ministers. . .

"It is unquestionably the duty of children to submit to their parents; and of servants to their masters. But no one asserts that it is their duty to obey and submit to them in all supposable cases; or universally a sin to resist them. Now does this tend to subvert the just authority of parents and masters? Or to introduce confusion and anarchy into private families? No. How then does the same principle tend to unhinge the government of that larger family, the body politic? We know, in general, that children and servants are obliged to obey their parents and masters respectively. We know also, with equal certainty, that they are not obliged to submit to them in all things, without exception; but may, in some cases, reasonably, and therefore in nocently, resist them."

Mayhew's sermon was published and widely circulated in pamphlet form. There was a Lockean ring to his words. But he was mainly concerned with bringing his politics in line with principles in Scripture: "What unprejudiced man can think that God made ALL to be thus subservient to the lawless pleasure and frenzy of ONE, so that it shall always be a sin to resist him! Nothing but the most plain and express revelation from heaven could make a sober impartial man believe such a monstrous, unaccountable doctrine, and, indeed, the thing itself appears so shocking- so out of all proportion, that it may be questioned whether all the miracles that ever were wrought could make it credible, that this doctrine really came from God. At present, there is not the least syllable of Scripture which gives any countenance to it."

In the pamphlet version of his sermon, it is evident that Mayhew came under some criticism for bringing politics so blatantly into the pulpit; he attached a preface explaining his rationale for doing so: "It is hoped that but few will think the subject an improper one to be discoursed on in the pulpit under a notion that this is preaching politics instead of Christ. However, to remove all prejudices of this sort, I beg it may be remembered that All Scripture is profitable for doctrine, for reproof, for correction, for instruction in righteousness (2 Tim. 3:16). Why then should not those parts of Scripture which relate to civil government be examined and explained from the desk... Civil tyranny is usually small in its beginning, like 'the drop of a bucket,' till at length, like a mighty torrent, or the raging waves of the sea, it bears down on all before it, and deluges whole countries and empires."

Mayhew is considered by many to be a prophet of the American Revolution. Most Americans were in fact still quite happy to be in the empire at this time. But Mayhew in 1750 had fired the first volley, and his sermon set forth both the inteHectual and Scriptural justification for viewing British policy with jaundiced eye, and for beginning to think about possible rebellion. Though he was much criticized for his inflammatory rhetoric by some, his words rang true with many others, especially in 1762, when Parliament voted to station 10,000 British troops in the colonies. The British said the troops were necessary to provide adequate protection for the people of North America. Their real purpose, however, was to enforce existing trade laws, in particular the Sugar Act. The Archbishop of Canterbury added fuel to the fire in 1763 when he issued a formal recommendation to the King to begin appointing colonial bishops. Over these issues James Otis and Samuel Adams made names for themselves and launched their careers as revolutionaries.

James Otis, a prosperous Boston lawyer, fired another shot

across the bow of England's colonial mercantile policy when he objected to British customs officials being granted authority, with so-called writs of assistance, to enter people's homes, ships, or shops at any time to search for smuggled goods. Writs of assistance were unlike search warrants, which require justification for a search as well as a list of specific items being sought.

Otis resigned his post as the king's advocate general in 1761 to argue against the writs on principles of the laws of God and nature. His speech before the Court, presided over by the newly appointed Lieutenant Governor of Massachusetts, Thomas Hutchinson, took Mayhew's sermons another step toward the codification of a coherent revolutionary ideology. "A man who is quiet and orderly is as secure in his house as a prince in his castle," said Otis, arguing that "should an Act of Parliament be against any of His [God's] natural laws . . . their declaration would be contrary to eternal truth, equity and justice, and consequently void." The views of the "English government towards the colonies and the views of the colonies towards the British government," he said, are "directly in opposition to each other." He warned England to "give up its pretensions" of complete dominion over the colonies, or there would be a violent "collision." A young John Adams, who was in the audience, said "Otis was a flame of fire,; . . the seeds of patriots and heroes were then and there sown.

Otis later extended his arguments at a town meeting in Boston and published them in a pamphlet entitled *Rights of the British Colonies Asserted and Proved.* Though Otis profusely quoted John Locke throughout his treatise, he took issue with the notion that government is an arbitrary contrivance of men, dependent, as Locke suggested, upon a compact between men. Certainly, said Otis, there must be a compact, but for a compact to "have any solid foundation," it must be planted "in the unchangeable will of God, the author of nature, whose laws never vary." Government is "most evidently founded on the necessities of our nature. It is by no means an arbitrary thing, depending merely on compact of human will for existence. We come into the world forlorn and helpless; and if left alone and to ourselves at any one period in our lives, we should soon die in want, despair or distraction . . We have a King, who neither slumbers nor sleeps, but eternally watches for our good; whose rain falls on the just and unjust".1 Locke actually believed this as well and would have found no fault with Otis's assertions. But Otis wanted to make crystal clear to British authorities the identity of America's true King.

Otis warned, "Tyranny of all kinds is to be abhorred, whether it be in the hands of one, or of the few, or of the many . . . The power of God Almighty is the only power that can properly and strictly be called supreme and absolute. In order of nature immediately under Him comes the power of simple democracy, or the power of the whole over the whole. Subordinate to both these are all other political powers."

Otis articulated the case for diffusion rather than concentration of power in the hands of one or a few men: "It is the greatest idolatry, begotten by flattery, on the body of pride that could induce one to think that a single mortal should be able to hold so great a power, if ever so well inclined. Hence the origin of deifying princes: It was from the trick of gulling the vulgar into a belief that their tyrants were omniscient; and that it was therefore right that they should be considered omnipotent."

The purpose of government, said Otis, must be the protection of life, liberty, and property: "There is no one act which a government can have a right to make that does not tend to the advancement of the security, tranquility and prosperity of the people. If life, liberty and property could be enjoyed in as great perfection in solitude, as in society, there would be no need of government." Quite clearly Otis would not consider compelling people through taxation to finance Social Security, Medicare, food stamps, welfare, or Urban Development Block Grants, to be a legitimate government function. "Government is founded on the necessities of human nature and ultimately on the will of God, the author of nature." But, said Otis, "it is left to every man as he

---

5. Jesus claims to be God: John 8:58, 10:27-30; 14:9.

comes of age to choose what society he will continue to belong to. Nay if one has a mind to turn hermit, and after he has been born, nursed, and brought up in the arms of society, and acquired the habits and passions of social life, is willing to run the risk of starving alone, which is generally unavoidable in a state of hermitage, who shall hinder him? I know of no human law, founded on the law of nature, to restrain him from separating himself from all species if he can find it in his heart to leave them.. . The grand political problem in all ages has been to invent the best combination or distribution of the supreme powers of legislation and execution. Those states have made the greatest figure, and have been most durable in which those powers have not only been separated from each other, but placed each in more hands than one, or a few." The Romans, said Otis, "never had a proper balance between the senate and the people, and the want of this is generally agreed by the few who know anything of the matter to have been the cause of their fall."

Otis' pamphlet was a sensation. It was printed in *The Boston Gazette* as well as in London. The Massachusetts legislative assembly adopted some of the most poignant excerpts in a resolution protesting arbitrary taxation imposed by the Sugar Act. Some in Parliament and the King's Court must have thought Otis' words to be wild ranting. England had forgotten the principles of government that had been won over the course of two Revolutions: the Puritan Revolution that established the supremacy of God's fixed laws over all government, even the king; and the Glorious Revolution of 1688 that established Parliament as the supreme legislative authority and codified a body of inalienable rights and privileges held by the people.

But England, by the middle of the 18th century, had grown corrupt during its period of unparalleled prosperity and military grandeur, and did little more than pay lip service to the great principles of liberty and justice enshrined in the Declaration of Rights. To the average American, Britain was nothing more than a policeman, an arbitrary and capricious one at that, whose only apparent function was to present the colonials with a growing list of prohibitions. Otis's pamphlet could not have been published at a worse time for the British, who had just passed the Revenue Act of 1764 and were putting the finishing touches on the notorious Stamp Act of 1765. For as Otis had said: "The sum of my argument is that civil government is of God... [and] that no parts of His Majesty's dominions can be taxed without consent."

The Revenue Act, in addition to taxing sugar, levied duties on wine, silk, linen, leather, and coffee. Though these were primarily luxury items, many colonists relied on them as currency to exchange for life's necessities. The Stamp Act of 1765, which levied duties on tea and glass, raised the greatest uproar yet. Also taxed were newspapers and all legal documents, including land deeds, college diplomas, liquor licenses, and dona tions to churches, schools, and colleges. Worst of all, every tax-able document had to be printed on special stamped paper sold by official distributors certifying the tax had been paid. The incredibly cumbersome government machinery needed to implement the law was almost beyond belief.

"If the colonist is taxed without his consent," warned one New York newspaper, "he will perhaps seek change." As Richard Henry Lee of Virginia put it: "The ways of Heaven are inscrutable"; concluding: "This step of the mother country, though intended to secure our dependence, may produce a fatal resentment and be subversive of that end." Meanwhile, James Otis was making speeches all over Massachusetts, calling on the people to oppose the tyrannical laws, especially the Stamp Act. "One single act of Parliament," he said, "we find has set people a thinking in six months more than they had done in their whole lives before."

"Otis everywhere appeared the principal," wrote the Governor of Massachusetts, Francis Bernard in 1766, alarmed at the unruly behavior of the colonists, who in every town along the Eastern Seaboard had begun rioting, terrorizing customs officials and burning the dreaded stamp paper. Otis, lamented Governor Bernard, "was the chief director, chamber council, counsellor at the bar, popular haranguer and assembly orator . . . .I desire not to revive the disputes concerning the Stamp Act; I wish they were buried beyond the reach of memory."

Otis's brilliant oratory inspired Samuel Adams to help mobilize the Sons of Liberty, which was to become the central organizing vehicle for the American Revolution. Adams and Otis were masters of political agitation, organizing leaders of churches as well as street gangs. On August 14, 1765, some Patriots hanged an effigy of newly appointed stamp paper distributor Andrew Oliver. Dangling next to Oliver was a boot with a devil crawling out of it. A squad of law enforcement officers arrived to arrest the rioters, but fled in fright when they saw the size of the mob. The crowd took the effigy down, proceeded to the stamp office, destroyed it, and then marched to Oliver's house. Oliver had long since departed to a royal fort in Boston Harbor. The mob was not interested in bloodshed, but frightened some of Oliver's friends when they beheaded Oliver's effigy and set it on fire.

Patriot rabble threatened customs officials everywhere, sometimes forcing them to eat the stamp paper. In New York, Lieutenant Governor Colden took refuge on a British ship after a mob broke into his house and forced the people there to burn the stamp paper. When an Anglican cleric in New York used a sermon to advocate loyalty to the King, Patriot William Livingston retorted: "The people are the Lord's anointed. Though named 'mob' and 'rabble,' the people are the darlings of Providence." "Power is a sad thing," proclaimed the Presbyterians of Philadelphia. "Our mother should remember we are children, not slaves." "When all Israel saw that the king did not listen to them," said Congregationalists in the North, "the people answered the king, saying: 'What portion do we have in David? We have no inheritance in the son of Jesse; to your tents, O Israel! Now look after your own house, David!'" (1 Kings 12:16).

Such was the feeling throughout the colonies. So spontaneous and widespread was the outpouring of sentiment against the Stamp Act that Otis and Adams actually found their primary task was to control the protests, lest they become violent and undermine the cause of liberty they were meant to defend. Indeed, says historian Samuel Eliot Morison, "no blood was shed anywhere" by the rioters during the Stamp Act crisis.

Samuel Adams was a Calvinist "of the strictest sect," says historian George Bancroft. He was a member of Boston's Congregational church. Evening and morning in his house was a place of prayer and, says Bancroft, "no one more revered the Sabbath. He was a tender husband, an affectionate parent the walls of his modest mansion never witnessed anything inconsistent with the discipline of a man whose desire for his birthplace was that 'Boston might become a Christian Sparta.'" Inspired by Adams's and Otis's example, Sons of Liberty organizations sprouted in virtually every major town in every colony. Many were led by people who would prove to be the most luminous leaders in American history. Before Virginia's assembly, Patrick Henry in May 1765 made a famous speech- "Caesar had his Brutus, Charles I his Cromwell" - which inspired a vitriolic set of resolves by the Virginia assembly condemning the Stamp Act taxes.

Adams, Otis, and their followers saw an opportunity to demonstrate to the British a united colonial opposition. Upon their urging, Massachusetts sent a circular letter in June 1765, inviting all the colonies to send delegates to a Congress, which would convene in October in New York City. Twenty-seven representatives from nine colonies responded, demonstrating that the Americans were capable of united action when pressed. In attendance at the gathering, known as the Stamp Act Congress, were such luminaries as John Dickinson of Pennsylvania; Thomas Lynch, Christopher Gradsden, and John Rutledge of the Carolinas; Daniel Dulany of Maryland; Eliphalet Dyer and William Samuel Johnson of Connecticut; Robert and Philip Livingston of New York. A delegate from Delaware, Caesar Rodney, declared it "an assembly of the greatest ability I ever saw.

The Congress passed a set of resolutions demanding that

Parliament repeal the Stamp Act immediately, asserting the right to trial by a july of one's peers and that only their own representatives in their own legislatures had the right to levy taxes on the colonies. This was a fateful day for British rule, because from that moment on the colonies would work in concert to defy British claims to legislative authority over North America.

The Sons of Liberty of Providence, Rhode Island, sent circular letters to all the colonies, saying: "We shall be ready at all times not only to vindicate ourselves. . . from lawless might, but as occasion may require to give aid to the other colonies for the rescuing them from every attempt against their liberties." And in December 1765, delegates of the Connecticut Sons met with New York Sons to form a mutual defense agreement, pledging to "match with the utmost dispatch . . . with their whole force if required . . to the relief of those that shall, are, or may be in danger from the Stamp Act." Boycotts of English goods were organized. American merchant ships sailed with unstamped cargos. And from the pulpit in Boston, Mayhew preached: "The Gospel promises liberty and permits resistance."

It did not much matter that Parliament repealed the Stamp Act in March 1766 as unenforceable. For the Sons of Liberty had demonstrated their ability to organize a rebellion and had caused the fall of the ministry of Richard Grenville, who had come under political fire in England for his inept handling of colonial policy. After the Stamp Act repeal, the Reverend Jonathan Mayhew wrote a letter to Otis, which suggested structuring their political organization according to the Congregational Church model. "You have heard," he wrote, "about the communion of churches; while I was thinking of this in my bed, the great use and importance of a communion of colonies appeared to me in strong light. Would it not be decorous for our assembly to send circulars to all the rest, expressing a desire to cement union among ourselves? A good foundation for this has been laid by the Congress at New York; never losing sight of it may be a means of perpetuating our liberties."

It is a shame that Mayhew died shortly thereafter. For no one better understood that the future of America's success lay in the idea of small federated republics patterned after the primitive churches in the New Testament, and governed according to laws that have the consent of the people. America would be a nation of decentralized authority and voluntary associations; or, as far as these radical Protestant Patriots were concerned, there would be no human authorities whatsoever.

Not long after the repeal of the Stamp Act, Charles Townsend, the ambitious Chancellor of the Exchequer (Britain's version of Treasury Secretary) chastised Parliament: "Fear! Cowards! Dare not tax America! I dare tax America!" Townsend was pompous, vain, and conceited. He was, said Edmund Burke, "a statesman who has left nothing but errors to account for his fame." He was contemptuous of the colonists, but he was eloquent in speech. His orations in the House of Commons often lasted more than an hour. "I would govern the Americans . . . I would restrain their trade and their manufactures as subor dinate to the mother country," he declared. "I dare tax America! I will! I will!" And tax America he did.

Passed in June 1767, the Townsend Act imposed stiff duties on all English products entering the colonies: tea, paper, glass, and other materials. Moreover, Townsend proclaimed, these taxes would be enforced with rigor. Violators would be tried without a jury by judges who received their pay from the duties collected. An especially odious feature of the Townsend duties was that revenue collected financed the administration of the colonies, paying the salaries of soldiers, policemen, judges, and governors. In other words, a major aim of the law was to force the colonists to pay for their jailers.

One effect of the Townsend duties was to cause an American depression. Just prior to the passing of this act, Parliament had enacted the Declaratory Act, which rejected the colonial position that Parliament's powers were in any way limited with regard to the administration of America, stating: Parliament had "full power and authority to make laws and statutes of sufficient force and validity to bind the colonies and people of America, subjects of the Crown of Great Britain, in all cases whatsoever."

As usual, it was the people of Boston who took the lead in expressing resentment, and re-instituting boycotts of English products. "The die is thrown," cried one Boston Patriot. "We will form an immediate combination to eat nothing, drink nothing, wear nothing imported from Great Britain... Our strength consists in union; let us above all be of one heart and one mind; let us call on our sister colonies to join with us in asserting our rights." The Sons of Liberty's information and organizational apparatus once again cranked into full gear and launched a vigorous campaign to win support for their boycott. *The Boston Gazette,* under the editorship of Sons of Liberty member Benjamin Edes, filled its pages with screeching broadsides against the taxes.

The New York Gazette, ordinarily more circumspect in tone, published an article by William Livingston, significant because Livingston was from a powerful, aristocratic family, which under normal circumstances would not be expected to mix with the rabble-rousing Protestant dissidents of New England. Livingston wrote: "Courage Americans . . . the finger of God points out a mighty empire to your sons. The savages of wilderness were never expelled to make room for idolaters and slaves. The land we possess is a gift of Heaven to our fathers. Divine Providence seems to have decreed it to our latest posterity. The day dawns in which the foundation of this mighty empire is to be laid by the establishment of a regular *American Constitution.* All that has hitherto been done seem to be little besides this collection of materials for the construction of this glorious fabric. 'Tis time to put them together . . . Our growth is so vast," said Livingston, "that before seven years roll over our heads the first stone must be laid-Peace or war: famine or plenty; poverty or affluence . . . What an era this is to America; and how loud the call to violence and activity!"

The Puritan merchants, artisans, craftsmen, and preachers

of New England needed to persuade men of substance of the justice of their cause. Men such as Livingston had much to lose from revolution. That he had virtually advocated war against Great Britain meant America was on the brink of explosion.

John Dickinson of Pennsylvania joined in the chorus. A prosperous lawyer and gentleman farmer who was married to a rich Quaker, Dickinson during the winter of 1767-68 wrote a series of letters, modestly titled "A Farmer's Letters to the Inhabitants of the British Colonies." Published in newspapers throughout the colonies, Dickinson's essays were among the best expositions of colonial rights that had yet appeared.

"Our vigilance and our union are success and safety. Our negligence and our division are distress and death," he wrote. "Let us consider ourselves as men - freemen - Christian freemen - separated from the world, and firmly bound together by the same rights, interests and dangers.

"Let these truths be indelibly impressed on our minds-that we cannot be happy without being free - that we cannot be free without being secure in our property, if without our consent others may, as by right, take it away - that taxes imposed on us by Parliament do thus take it away - that duties laid for the sole purpose of raising money are taxes - that attempts to lay such duties should be instantly and firmly opposed - that this opposition can never be effectual unless it is the united effort of these provinces...

"The belief in these truths, I verily think, my countrymen, is indispensably necessary to your happiness. I beseech you, therefore, teach them diligently to your children, and talk of them when you sit in your houses, and when you walk by the way, and when you lie down, and when you rise up

The "prosperity [of the colonies] does not depend on ministerial favors doled out to particular provinces. They form one political body, of which each colony is a member. Their happiness is founded on their constitution, and is to be promoted by preserving that constitution[2] in unabated vigor, throughout every

---

2. England's Declaration of Rights and the chartered constituition of each respective colony.

part. A spot, a speck of decay, however small the limb on which it appears, and however remote it may seem from the vitals, should be alarming...

"Let us take care of our rights, and we therein take care of our prosperity." For "slavery is ever preceded by sleep . . . If we are not affected by any reverence for the memory of our ancestors who transmitted to us that freedom in which they had been blessed-if we are not animated by any regard for posterity, to whom, by the most sacred obligations, we are bound to deliver down the invaluable inheritance, then indeed any minister, or any tool of a minister, or any creature of a tool of a minister, or any lower instrument of administration, if lower there be, is a personage whom it may be dangerous to offend.

"Whatever kind of minister he is that attempts to innovate a single iota in the privileges of these colonies, him I hope you will undauntedly oppose. . . On such emergencies you may surely, without presumption, believe that Almighty God Himself will look down upon your righteous contest with gracious approbation. You will be a band of brothers, cemented by the dearest ties, and strengthened with inconceivable supplies of force and constancy, by that sympathetic ardor, which animates good men, confederated in a single cause... You are assigned by Divine Providence in the appointed order of things, the protectors of unborn ages, whose fate depends on your virtue."

Liberty and virtue, in Dickinson's mind, were indissolubly connected. When states lose their liberty, he said, "this calamity is generally owing to the decay of virtue."

Widely published, Dickinson's letters had momentous impact. English politicians studied every sentence and waited with nervous anticipation for each of the 12 epistles to appear in order to gauge the mood of the colonies. It was clear that the Americans were not accepting the taxes with aplomb. "My Lord," wrote Massachusetts Governor Bernard to the English authorities, "this is not a fictitious argument, but a real one." As eloquently as any, Dickinson had provided more intellectual and moral ammunition for liberty.

But Samuel Adams understood that activists are motivated more by emotion than logic. A master agitator, he invented
symbols and organized street theater to keep the masses involved.
There was dancing around the Liberty Tree, which was a large
elm in Boston Common. Effigies of unpopular customs officials and
tax collectors were hung and burned. He and James Otis asked
John Dickinson, who had proven himself so eloquent in prose, to
compose an American freedom song to be sung at demonstrations.
Dickinson obliged, and this is what he produced:

> Come join hand in hand, brave Americans all;
> And rouse your bold hearts at fair Liberty's call.
> No tyrannous acts shall suppress your just claim;
> Or stain with dishonor America's name.
>
> (chorus) In freedom we're born and in freedom we'll live;
> Our purses are ready, Steady, Friends, steady.
> Not as slaves, but as freemen our money we'll
> give.
>
> Then join in hand brave Americans all;
> By uniting we stand, by dividing we fall.
> To die we can bear, but to serve we disdain.
> For shame is to freemen more dreadful than pain.

CHAPTER SEVENTEEN

"GIVE ME LIBERTY, OR GIVE ME DEATH"

At the age of 31, John Hancock, Boston's wealthiest merchant, was the most wanted man in America by British authorities. He was the chief financier of the Sons of Liberty. He paid for their leaflets and banners, as well as for food and drink for demonstrations at the Liberty Tree. In British eyes he was dangerous.

The new Commissioners of the Customs, Joseph Harrison and Benjamin Hallowell, seized on an opportunity to arrest Hancock, who was sailing around Boston Harbor in his sloop *Liberty* in open defiance of British authority. Hancock was charged, falsely, with smugghng. He was, however, rescued by a Boston mob, who managed to catch Harrison and Hallowell and beat them to battered pulps. Poor Harrison was dragged through the streets by his hair. Adams and Otis were alarmed by the mob's brutal behavior, and worked frantically to bring the crowd under control. Harrison and Hallowell were released, and promptly retired from customs enforcement. The British authorities subsequently abandoned their case against Hancock, as they saw the throngs gather in the streets. At this point General Thomas Gage began to figure prominently in American affairs. He would be the future commander of the British cause against America. The British government, he wrote from New York, "cannot act with too much vigor" against the Patriots of Massachusetts. Let's 'squash this spirit at a blow," said Gage, who sent two regiments of redcoats to Boston.

"If an army should be sent to reduce us to slavery, we will put our lives in our hands and cry to the Judge of the earth," editorialized *The Boston Gazette,* in response to the news. "Behold how they come to cast us out of this possession which Thou hast given us to inherit. Help us Lord, our God, for we rest on Thee."

On March 5, 1770, Parliament repealed the Townsend taxes as ineffective - the same day that a very nasty confrontation took place between English redcoats and Boston civilians. There was continuous tension between the townspeople and the occupying military. "Lobsterbacks" was a favorite insult directed at the redcoats, who were constantly the targets of thrown rocks, sticks, and snowballs.

On the evening of March 5, a gang of youths gathered around the customs office and began hurling snowballs and ice at a guard. Words were shouted back and forth, when about 20 soldiers arrived to protect their beleaguered colleague. A violent scuffle took place, and suddenly a soldier named Montgomery, who had been hit with a club, fired a round from his musket. The shot missed, but another soldier, named Kilroy, shot his gun and put a gaping hole in the chest of Sam Gray. Other shots rang out and two bullets hit and killed Crispus Attucks, a large black man. More shots were fired, and when the smoke cleared three townspeople lay dead in the street; two others were fatally wounded.

Massachusetts would never forget this episode, which came to be known as the Boston Massacre, a label probably invented by Samuel Adams to describe what he called the brutal slaying of peaceful citizens by the agents of tyranny. The halls of America raged with shrill screams for justice, and the Sons of Liberty circulated a deluge of literature on the incident, con demning Britain's occupation of Boston and the "licentious" behavior of its troops. The army was forced to withdraw from Boston in the face of mounting active resistance. As Massachusetts Governor Thomas Hutchinson put it: "Government is at an end and in the hands of the people."

A number of historians have suggested that the Boston

Massacre was a minor event, made significant by propagandists such as Samuel Adams who blew the episode out of all proportion to serve his own political purposes. Mter all, only five people were killed, hardly a massacre. That Adams took advantage of the incident as an illustration of oppressive British policy to foment discontent is not in dispute. But people were also sincerely outraged by British behavior. That troops from a foreign land would occupy a major city, in effect declare martial law, and then kill five civilians would cause a hue and cry anywhere, particu larly among a people who had a tradition of self-rule.

Indeed, William Pitt, then an aged member of the House of Lords, agreed, saying British colonial policy from the start in America was badly flawed. "I love the Americans because they love their liberty, and I love them for the noble efforts they made in the last war," Pitt told the House of Lords. "I think the idea of drawing money from them by taxes was ill-judged. Trade is your object with them, and they should be encouraged; those millions who keep you, who are the industrious hive employed, should be encouraged."

As Prime Minister, William Pitt was perhaps the most successful empire-builder of all time. His strategy, especially where America was concerned, was to permit as much autonomy as possible for the colonies, and to protect them with British military might. Pitt understood that happy colonists are good for Britain and, indeed, good for civilization. He believed they ought to be trading partners, not serfs to be exploited. British policy, in his view, should focus on making the sea lanes safe for trade so all could prosper, rather than rousing the populace against Parliament by shooting civilians for throwing snowballs. William Pitt was revered at least as much in America as in England. But Pitt was old, had lost influence, and England was under a new administration, that of Lord North, George III's henchman. North believed in crushing colonial industrial competition, and then teaching the Americans a lesson when they objected.

In 1772, Samuel Adams announced at a Boston town

meeting the formation of a Committee of Correspondence, which would supplement the activities of the Sons of Liberty. Essential to revolt was establishing lines of communication, which could bring order and effectiveness to what, until then, had been primarily spontaneous mob uprisings. Each colony was to circulate news to the committees of the other colonies. These committees proved remarkably effective in binding the revolutionary leaders together in a common cause, and helped form the nucleus of a shadow government. Boston initiated the first committee, under the leadership of Adams, Otis, Hancock, and 18 others, and passed a resolution stating that the aim of the Correspondence Committee was to defend "the rights of colonists, and of this province in particular, as men, as Christians, and as subjects; to communicate and publish the same to the several towns in this province and the world as to the sense of this town ... also requesting each town a free communication of their sentiments on this subject."

The series of events leading to independence began with the financial disintegration of the East India Tea Company, which was suffering from amazingly inept and corrupt management as well as the boycott organized by the Sons of Liberty, which cut off the American market. The dissolution of the East India Tea Company (a government monopoly) would be a serious blow to England's fiscal situation, which had grown shaky because of the burdens of running an empire.

England sought to remedy the situation by putting America's tea companies out of business with a tea tax, a remnant of the Townsend duties, from which the East India Company would be exempt. Thus the East India Company could easily undercut American tea company prices. As usual, the law was designed to hit the Eastern Seaboard hardest, where tea was a most important export. From the newspapers, pulpits, and printing presses came screams of anguish. The Committees of Correspondence immediately began circulating literature denouncing the "illegal monopoly."

If Parliament can ruin our tea industry, why could it not legislate other monopolies and assume control of all our industries, eventually putting England in a position of being able to determine when we could eat? Such were the concerns expressed in the streams of editorials, broadsides, and leaflets. The Tea Act helped merchants to see the long-term threat to American liberties posed by acquiescing to even a single law that was not in the general interest of all the people.

On November 3, 1773, Sons of Liberty members met at the Liberty Tree, and then with a crowd of 500 marched on agents of the East India Company. "The people are greatly affronted," said Patriot leader Joseph Warren. "Out with them!" the mob yelled, and in every city mobs shouted the same refrain: "Out with them! Out with them!" Delaware River pilots were warned by notices circulated by the Committees of Correspondence that anyone transporting tea into Philadelphia would be "tarred and feathered." The colonies, however, all looked to Massachusetts for leadership and courage. A Philadelphia letter, printed in Boston, said, "All we fear is that you will shrink at Boston. May God give you virtue enough to save the liberties of your country." Boston did not shrink in fear. Indeed, "Massachusetts Bay has raised a higher spirit than I have ever seen before," wrote Governor Hutchinson.

On December 16, 8,000 people assembled at the Old South Church in Boston. A leaflet circulated by the Committee of Correspondence had called people to action, announcing: "Friends! Brethren! Countrymen! that worst of plagues, the detested TEA . . . is now arrived in this harbor. The hour of destruction or manly opposition to the machinations of tyranny stares you in the face." "This meeting," said Samuel Adams, "can do nothing more than save the country," and the war whoops and shouting "became tremendous," according to one account. The city was bold and united in its contempt for British authority, and it was resolved at the meeting that no British tea would ever make it to shore.

The story is well known. That evening, a mob, disguised as Indians, banded together in parties of 50, rowed out to where three ships were anchored, boarded them, seized the tea and tossed it into the ocean. Thousands of pounds worth of the hated commodity were destroyed.

The Boston Tea Party was a new milestone in America's journey toward independence. It was not like the disorganized rioting that brought on the Boston Massacre. The tea party was carefully orchestrated by Adams and his fellow Patriots. No blood was shed, but the ideological point had been made: there would be no taxation without representation. John Adams was out of town for the occasion, but recorded his feelings about the evening in his journal: "Last night," he wrote, "three cargos of Bohea Tea were emptied into the sea. This is the most magnificent moment of all. There is a dignity, a majesty, a sublimity, in this last effort of the Patriots that I greatly admire . . . This destruction of the tea is so bold, so daring, so firm, intrepid and inflexible, and it must have so important consequences, and so lasting, that I can't but consider it as an epoch of history."

Once again, William Pitt urged restraint: "I fear the bond between us and America will be cut off forever. Devoted England will then have seen her best days, which nothing can restore again." And Edmund Burke, in his famous speech, admonished the House of Commons to "revert to your old principles" and "leave America, if she has taxable matter in her, to tax herself. . . Leave the Americans as they anciently stood . . . Let the memory of all actions in contradiction to that good old mode, on both sides, be extinguished forever. Be content to bind America by laws of trade . . . Do not burden them with taxes; you were not used to do so from the beginning." But King George III was enraged, and ignored the wise counsel of Burke and Pitt.

Parliament passed, and King George signed, a series of bills that came to be known as the "Intolerable Acts," the most severe of which was the Boston Port Bill, which closed Boston Harbor to all commercial ships through naval blockade. In addition, the Quartering Act enabled British troops to commandeer civilian homes, food, and possessions for their own purposes. Also passed was the Massachusetts Government Act, which made council positions Crown appointments, rather than elected by the local population. Judges on the colony's Supreme Court would also be appointed by the King. Meetings could be held only with the governor's permission and juries were to be selected by the governor, thus ensuring composition favorable to British aims. *As if* this was not enough, Parliament asserted the right to abolish at will all rights and liberties protected in the Massachusetts charter. Other ominous laws were also passed during this period, but these were bad enough.

Additional troops were dispatched to see that the laws were enforced, bringing the total in Boston to six regiments. The closing of Boston's port to commercial ships raised the greatest indignation, because it was clear that the intent was to starve the colony into submission. To quote the Whig statesman Edmund Burke again: "The rending of the means of subsistence of a whole city upon the King's private pleasure . . . was without precedent, and of a most dangerous example."

The British military controlled Boston, but the Committees of Correspondence dominated the countryside. Committees of Correspondence formed in virtually every New England town, and had control of almost all the local organs of government. They dominated the town assemblies and pulpits, and controlled the newspapers. Fiery sermons from Presbyterians, Congregationalists, and Baptists roused the people to action. By the fall of 1774, the Committees of Correspondence had isolated the British authorities in Boston, and Massachusetts was virtually self-governing.

The same spirit manifested itself in other New England colonies. The Connecticut assembly appointed a day for humiliation and prayer, and resolved to begin amassing stores of ammunition. Providence, Rhode Island, recommended the assembling of an intercontinental congress to determine actions to be taken against the British, as did New York, which formed a Committee of Correspondence, and on May 16, 1774 issued a handbill with the following call to action: "In a word, let all our merchants unite as one man; let them strive against this division in this crisis of jeopardy; let them show themselves worthy of that divine appellation, 'the fathers of their country.' And let not the ministers of the Gospel neglect their duty; let them remember the example of the Apostles, who embraced every opportunity to testify to their zeal for the civil and religious liberties of mankind; and while they teach men to consider their oppressors as 'the rod of God in anger, and the staff of his indignation,' let them not fail to excite and encourage them to hope of His interposition in their behalf, while they humble themselves by fasting and prayer, and are in use of all proper means for deliverance."

Southern journals abounded with accounts of the success of Massachusetts in opposing the Port Act. Virginia, in a resolution drafted by Thomas Jefferson, appointed June 1, the date the Port Act was to take effect, a "day of fasting and prayer," and asked that all the oppressed people of America "invoke the divine interposition" to give the American people "one heart and one mind" to oppose all transgressions against American rights.

From all over British America, supplies of relief poured into Massachusetts. Virginia sent 8,600 bushels of wheat and corn and George Washington immediately donated 50 pounds (about $5,000 in 1988), his initial contribution to the cause. "We take pleasure in transmitting to you . . . a few cattle, with a small sum of money," said a letter from Durham, New Hampshire. Patriots in every town walked door to-door to collect offerings for the beleaguered victims of the Port Act. We are "ready to march in the van and sprinkle the American altars with our hearts and blood," the town of Brooklyn, Connecticut, in a letter drafted by Israel Putnam, told the people of Boston. "You are held up as a spectacle to the whole world. All Christendom is longing to see the event of the American contest." And Boston showed its appreciation in a circular letter, directed in particular to the people of New

Jersey, dated August 22, 1774: "The Christian sympathy and generosity of our friends through the continent cannot fail to inspire the inhabitants of this town with patience, resignation, and firmness, while we trust in the Supreme Ruler of the universe, that He will graciously hear our cries, and in His time free us from our present bondage, and make us rejoice in His great salvation."

All the committees favored a Continental Congress, which convened in Philadelphia on September 5, 1774, in Carpenter's Hall. Fifty-five delegates represented 12 of the 13 colonies. Only Georgia was absent, but promised to abide by the decisions of her "sister colonies." It was the most illustrious group of American men ever to meet in one place and included: the learned lawyer John Jay from New York; William Livingston from New Jersey; John Adams and his cousin Samuel Adams from Massachusetts; Roger Sherman from Connecticut; John Dickinson from Pennsylvania; John Rutledge and Christopher Gradsden from South Carolina; the Presbyterian minister Dr. John Witherspoon of New Jersey; and from Virginia, Richard Henry Lee, Patrick Henry, and George Washington, who, said Henry, "unquestionably is the greatest man of them all." Thomas Jefferson failed in his bid to become a delegate.

The Adamses, of Puritan heritage, made a special effort to ease the minds of Episcopalians of Virginia who worried about the radical Protestants of the North. They suggested that an Episcopalian open the Congress with a prayer. The Reverend Jacob Duche, whom Samuel Adams described as a man of piety and virtue, delivered several prayers and then read the 35th Psalm:[1]

"Plead my cause, O Lord, with them that strive with me: fight against them that fight against me. Take hold of shield and buckler, and stand up for mine help. Draw out also the spear, and stop the way against them that persecute me: say unto my soul, I am thy salvation. Let them be confounded and put to shame that seek after my soul: let them be turned back and brought to confusion that devise my hurt. Let them be as chaff

---

1. Psalm 35:1-5, 17-20, 22-25, 27-28 (King James Version).

before the wind: and let the angel of the Lord chase them . . . Lord, how long wilt thou look on? Rescue my soul from their destructions . . . I will give Thee thanks in the great congregation: I will praise Thee among much people. Let not them that are mine enemies wrongfully rejoice over me: neither let them wink with the eye that hate me without a cause. For they speak not peace: But they devise deceitful matters against them that are quiet in the land . . . O Lord, be not far from me. Stir up thyself, and awake to my judgment, even unto my cause, my God and my Lord. Judge me, O Lord my God, according to thy righteousness; and let them not rejoice over me. Let them not say in their hearts . . We have swallowed him up . . . Let the Lord be magnified, which hath pleasure in the prosperity of His servant. And my tongue shall speak of thy righteousness and of thy praise all the day long."

That evening, word came that the British had commenced the bombardment of Boston. In addition, the great rider Paul Revere had galloped into Philadelphia with the news that a convention of the towns around Boston had passed the sensational Suffolk Resolves, written by Joseph Warren, which began: "Whereas the power but not the justice, the vengeance but not the wisdom of Great Britain, which of old persecuted, scourged, and exiled our fugitive parents from their native shores, now pursues us, their guiltless children, with unrelenting severity: And whereas this, then savage and uncultivated desert was purchased by the toil and treasure, or acquired by the blood and valor of these our venerable progenitors; to us that bequeathed the dear bought inheritance, to our care and protection that consigned it, and the most sacred obligation are upon us to transmit this glorious purchase, unfettered by power, unclogged with shackles, to our innocent and beloved offspring. On the for titude, on the wisdom and on the exertions of this important day, is suspended the fate of this new world, and of unborn millions."

In addition to declaring the Intolerable Acts unconstitutional and void, Suffolk County, which includes Boston, resolved to make Massachusetts a free state, recommended economic sanctions against the British, and advised the formation of an armed militia, led by officers who have been "judged of sufficient capacity for that purpose, and who have evidenced themselves the inflexible friends to the rights of the people." But, the resolves were careful to warn against following the lead of colonial enthusiasts, rioters, and "unthinking persons to commit outrage upon private property; we would heartily recommend to all persons of this community not to engage in routs, riots, or licen tious attacks upon the properties of any person whatsoever, as being subversive of all order and government; but a steady, manly, uniform, and persevering opposition, to convince our enemies, that in a contest so important, in a cause so solemn, our conduct shall be as to merit the approbation of the wise, and the admiration of the brave and free of every age and every country."

Joseph Warren and the people of Massachusetts understood that in a revolution that is trying to make constitutional points on the protection of liberties, private property must be sacrosanct. It is on private property that all other freedoms rest. For if the government can seize one's home, money, or possessions, the individual has no means of resisting the whims of kings, ministers, courtiers, or other agents of the state. And what point is there in overthrowing a tyrannical government if the result is that mobs of rioters commit the same crimes? Warren in Massachusetts and the Continental Congress in Philadelphia had the difficult task of raising the people's indignation against the King and his government, while simultaneously keeping that indignation in check so that society would not degenerate into chaos. The Suffolk Resolves went a long way toward solving this problem by agreeing to submit to the authority of the Continental Congress. Thus a giant step had been taken in the creation of a new nation, as the delegates in Philadelphia voted overwhelmingly to approve the Suffolk Resolves.

On October 14, the Continental Congress issued a Declaration of Rights, similar to the English Declaration in that it enumerated specific colonial grievances against the Crown and Parliament. "Whereas, since the close of the last war, the British Parliament, claiming a power, of right, to bind the people of America by statutes in all cases whatsoever," the Declaration began, and went on to proclaim the Intolerable Acts as "impolitic, unjust, cruel, as well as unconstitutional, and most dangerous and destructive of American rights." It also complained of the dissolving of American assemblies "when they attempted to deliberate on grievances," denounced the imposition of taxes without the consent of the colonies, and expressed opposition to "the extended jurisdiction of the courts of admiralty." We, said the Declaration, "are entitled to life, liberty and property," and "have never ceded any sovereign power whatever." As a consequence of England's tyrannical behavior, the Continental Congress has taken the necessary steps to defend America's "religion, laws, and liberties."

On October 20, 52 delegates formed an Association of the United Colonies under these words: "We do for ourselves, and the inhabitants of the several colonies whom we represent, firmly agree and associate under the sacred ties of virtue, honor, and love of country." They considered this to be a compact for the defense of American freedoms, "a league of the continent, which first expressed the sovereign will of a free nation in America." The Puritan influence in this document was clear, as the delegates pledged themselves to "encourage frugality, economy and industry, and . . . discountenance and discourage every species and extravagance and dissipation, especially all horse-racing and all kinds of gaming, cock-fighting, exhibition of shews, plays, and other expensive diversions and entertainments." But these prohibitions were also practical. The nation was effectively at war, was in a life and death struggle with the greatest empire on earth. Success would depend on the ability of the American people to keep their attentions fixed on the task at hand. The delegates understood very well that liberty has a price, that a people which is immodest, extravagant, and frivolous will not remain free for long.

When word of the Suffolk Resolves and of the proceedings of the Continental Congress reached England, the attorney general immediately denounced the conclaves as treasonous. But William Pitt in the House of Lords and Edmund Burke in the House of Commons thought differently and advised an immediate policy of reconciliation with the colonies. Although their words fell upon deaf ears, their speeches are so powerful and so prophetic that any account of this period must contain some of the more poignant excerpts.

Pitt, the elder statesman, spoke in dramatic fashion before Parliament in January 1775. He praised the "papers transmitted to us from America," for their "decency, firmness and wisdom . . In all my reading and observation - and it has been my favorite study - I have read Thucydides, and have studied and admired the master states of the world - that for solidity of reasoning, force of sagacity, and wisdom of conclusion, under such complication of difficult circumstances, no nation or body of men can stand in preference to the general Congress at Philadelphia." The people of America, "who prefer poverty with liberty to gilded chains and sordid affluence," will "die in defense of their rights as men." America, Pitt said, had allied itself with "God and nature" on principles that are immutable, eternal -fixed as the firmament in heaven." Pitt asked England to swallow its pride: "With a dignity becoming your exalted situation, make the first advances to concord, to peace and happiness." All attempts to establish a tyranny over such a people had failed. There is "not time to be lost . . . Nay, while I am now speaking the decisive blow may be struck."

Pitt's speech was perhaps superceded in eloquence when the great writer, orator, and statesman Edmund Burke, one month later, delivered his most famous address on reconciliation with the colonies. Burke spoke of the folly of Britain trying to subject a distant continent of almost three million colonists by force.

"Those who wield the thunder of the state may have more

confidence in the efficacy of arms," he said. In reality, though, force is "a feeble instrument for preserving a people so numerous, so active, so growing, so spirited as this . . . It may subdue for a moment; but it does not remove the necessity of subduing again: and a nation is not governed which is perpetually to be conquered." Moreover, said Burke, "Terror is not always the effect of force, and an armament is not a victory. If you do not succeed, you are without resource: for conciliation failing, force remains; but, force failing, no further hope of reconciliation is left . . . A fierce spirit of liberty has grown up. It has grown with the growth of people in your colonies, and increased with the increase of their wealth.. . Perhaps a more smooth and accommodating spirit of freedom in them would be more acceptable to us. Perhaps ideas of liberty might be desired more reconcilable with an arbitrary and boundless authority. Perhaps we might wish the colonists to be persuaded that their liberty is more secure when held in a trust for them by us. . . than with any part of it in their own hands." Not likely, concluded Burke: for "an Englishman is the unfittest person on earth to argue another Englishman into slavery." The question, he said, "is not whether you have a right to render your people miserable, but whether it is not in your interest to make them happy."

But Burke spoke to empty benches. Parliament passed the Restraining Act forbidding the four colonies of New England from trading with any other nation but England. Four more regiments were then dispatched to Boston under the command of General Gage, who was instructed to hunt down the leaders of the Massachusetts rebellion and arrest them as traitors.

On March 23, 1775, Patrick Henry stood up in Virginia's House of Burgess and sounded an American battle cry: "There is no room for hope," he said. "If we wish to be free, we must fight! An appeal to arms and to the God of Hosts is all that is left us!. . . Three million people, armed with the holy cause of liberty and in such a country, are invincible by any force which our enemy can send against us. We shall not fight alone. God presides over the destinies of nations, and will raise up friends for us. The battle is not to the strong alone; it is to the vigilant, the active, the brave. . . Is life so dear, or peace so sweet as to be purchased at the price of chains and slavery? Forbid it Almighty God! I know not what course others may take, but as for me, give me liberty or give me death!"

The American War for Independence had begun.

CHAPTER EIGHTEEN

WHEN IN THE COURSE OF HUMAN EVENTS . . .

Under the presidency of John Hancock, the Provincial Continental Congress of Massachusetts, based in Concord, began to make preparations for war. It appointed its own treasurer to collect taxes and a Committee of Public Safety to train militia and store munitions. Informed by spies of the arms and ammunition being collected in Concord, about 18 miles from Boston, General Gage decided that Concord, the seat of New England's revolutionary government, would be an excellent place to administer a sound thrashing to the rebels. The Patriots were planning to adjourn on April 15 in order to send delegates to the Second Continental Congress, scheduled to convene in May 1775. So Gage knew he had to strike quickly.

Gage launched a night raid on April 18 in an attempt to surprise the Patriots while they slept. In all, about 1,800 British regulars would be dispatched along various routes, out of a total Boston garrison of 3,500. This was to be a major attack. But Joseph Warren, the Patriot spy-chief based in Boston, learned the specifics of the operation by 10 o'clock and promptly dispatched Paul Revere to alert the countryside in the most celebrated ride in American history. Two of Revere's fellow spies warned Patriots by hanging a lantern in the tower of Christ Church - the agreed upon signal of an impending British raid. At one point, Revere was spotted by two British officers who gave chase, but were easily outdistanced by the famed Patriot horseman. "The British are coming! The British are coming!" he yelled as he passed every home. Samuel Adams and John Hancock were in Lexington, staying at the home of the Reverend Jonas Clarke. The Provincial Congress had adjourned and they were on their way to Philadelphia. Revere galloped up to Clarke's house. "The British are coming!" he yelled. Adams and Hancock awoke, and Revere disappeared into the night to alert the residents of Concord. By daybreak, Minutemen were on the march as far distant as New Hampshire and Connecticut.

At Lexington, about 100 militia gathered on the Lexington common. The air was chilly and damp. As dawn broke, a farmer arrived to say that the redcoats were two miles away. It wasn't long before faint lines of British soldiers came into view, barely visible in the expanding light. It was an advance guard led by Major John Pitcairn. The church bells sounded the alarm. The redcoats continued their advance. Captain Jonas Parker saw that his band of farmers would be easily overwhelmed, and so ordered them to disband and wait for reinforcements-yet someone fired; no one knows who. But the shooting rapidly became general. "Fire, fire, fire!" screamed one junior redcoat officer. The militia shot back. The British returned the volley, wounding Jonas Parker and killing Isaac Muzzy. Jonathan Harrington was shot in the chest. As the wounded Parker tried to raise his musket to let off a last shot, he was run through with a bayonet. When the smoke cleared 10 Minutemen lay dead and nine more were badly wounded. Jonathan Harrington's wife was seen sobbing over the body of her dead husband. The entire battle of Lexington had lasted less than 15 minutes.

Major Pitcairn waited to be joined by Lieutenant Colonel Francis Smith's forces, fully confident that the day ahead would be an easy one. The scene at Concord, however, would be very different. Revere and his riders had alerted the entire region, and every New England town and village had sent militia. The main battle took place on Concord's North Bridge where three

British companies encountered about 1,000 Patriot militia, whose ranks were rapidly swelling with every passing minute. Emerson immortalized the confrontation in his famous poem:

. . .the embattled farmers stood,

And fired the shot heard round the world.

A nervous British commander ordered his men to withdraw. The Americans opened fire on the rear of the British company. Four officers were hit, along with a number of soldiers, and an orderly retreat rapidly degenerated into a panicked, every-man-for-himself sprint. But the Minutemen, who knew the terrain, took a shortcut and blocked the British withdrawal. Moreover, militia seemed to be coming from every direction, taking shots at the redcoats from behind stone walls, barns, hedges, and trees.

The entire British force made a mad dash back to Boston. Some threw their guns away in order to lighten the load. Others dropped from sheer exhaustion. One British soldier described his own experience: "I never broke my fast for 48 hours, for we carried no provisions. I had my hat shot off my head three times. Two balls went through my coat and carried away my bayonet from my side."

The Patriots had soundly thrashed a British force of 1,800 men, who were the best trained and most experienced in the imperial army. In all, the British suffered some 273 casualties. By contrast, 49 Americans were killed, and 41 wounded. The numbers were not especially large. But the British had never suffered a defeat more humiliating. Following the Lexington and Concord episode, Lord Hugh Percy wrote of the Minutemen: "Whoever looks upon them as an irregular mob will find himself much mistaken."

In the weeks that followed, Patriot militia poured into Cambridge and the towns surrounding Boston. The British General Gage estimated that he was surrounded by some 15,000 New England Minutemen and an untold number of Patriot sympathizers. The Patriots began to build fortifications on Breed's Hill (not Bunker Hill) on the Charlestown Peninsula across the Charles River from Boston. This was a strategic location, because it enabled Patriot forces to monitor British troop move ments and shell British naval vessels.

On the night of June 16, General Gage ordered a massive frontal assault on Breed's Hill. He knew the importance of the battle. New England had gained confidence from the skirmish at Concord, and Patriot volunteers were streaming into Boston's surrounding towns by the thousands. Gage dispatched British General William Howe, with 2,200 men, as his field commander; Gage himself would oversee the shelling of Patriot fortifications from British ships. Howe's first attempted assault up Breed's Hill failed, leaving his entire front rank destroyed. Howe ordered a second charge. It too was repelled. Howe did, however, take the Hill on the third charge, but at enormous expense. Militiaman Amos Farnsworth wrote a moving account of the battle in his journal:

"Having fired away all [our ammunition and having no reinforcements . . . we were overpowered by numbers and obliged to leave . . . I did not leave the entrenchment until the enemy got in. I then retreated ten or fifteen rods. Then I received a wound in my right arm, the ball going through a little below my elbow, breaking the little sheilbone. Another ball struck my back, taking a piece of skin about as big as a penny. But I got to Cambridge that night. .. O, the goodness of God in preserving my life, although they fell on my right hand and on my left! O may this act of deliverance of Thine, O God, lead me never to distrust Thee; but may I ever trust in Thee and put my confidence in no arm of flesh."

The British had taken the Hill, but it was a Pyrrhic victory. As General Henry Clinton remarked, "another such would have ruined us." The British had lost 1,150 men out of 2,500 engaged, while the Americans lost 400, out of 1,500 who fought. General Howe had watched the scene in horror. One British regular described the battle from his perspective: "As we approached, an incessant stream of fire poured from rebel lines. It seemed a continuous sheet of fire for barely 30 minutes." The Battle of Bunker Hill, as it came to be called, was a military and symbolic disaster for the British because it signaled that New England could defend itself; instilled all the North American colonies with a feeling of unity and patriotic pride; and gave the illustrious men deliberating at the Second Continental Congress in Philadelphia the courage to take up arms.

As one militiaman wrote a few months later: "The whole series of divine dispensations, from the infant days of our fathers in America are big with importance in her favor, and point to something great and good. If we look 'round the world, and view the nations with their various connections, interests and dependencies, we shall see innumerable causes at work in favor of this growing country. Nature and Art seem to labor, and as it were, travail in birth to bring forth some glorious events that will astonish mankind and form a bright era in the annals of time."

In other words, more than economics and duties on tea were at stake here. The major reason these men took up the fight against the great British empire was their steadfast belief that they were an intricate part of God's plan. Religious conviction gave them the strength needed to persevere in the seven-year war for American independence.

New England's fierce spirit of independence, derived chiefly from its dissenting Protestant heritage, was responsible for pressing events forward. "It must not be forgotten," writes historian Alice Baldwin in her book *The New England Clergy and the American Revolution,* " ... that the source of greatest authority and the one most commonly used was the Bible," which to the New Englander, was "a sacred book, infallible, God's will for man." Of necessity, writes Baldwin, "it colored his political thinking. His conception of God, of God's law, and of God's relation to man determined to a large extent his conception of human law and of man's relation to his fellows. If his ideas of government were in part derived from other sources, they were strengthened and sanctioned by Holy Writ." As John Adams noted, "Honor and obedience to good rulers and spirited opposition to bad ones" was a central tenet of the New England Way.

Burke, in his 1775 speech on "reconciliation with the colonies," predicted that America's pervasive dissenting Protestant creed would prove an insurmountable barrier to London asserting its will over the colonies. "Everyone knows," said Burke, "that the Roman Catholic religion is at least co-equal with most of the governments where it prevails, that it has generally gone hand in hand with them, and received great favor and every kind of support from authority. The Church of England, too, was formed from her cradle under the nursing care of regular government. But the dissenting interests have sprung up in direct opposition to the ordinary powers of the world, and could justify that opposition only on a strong claim to natural liberty. Their very existence depended on the powerful and unremitted assertion of that claim. All Protestantism, even the most cold and passive, is a sort of dissent. But the religion most prevalent in our northern colonies is a refinement on the principle of resistance: it is the dissidence of dissent, and the Protestantism of the Protestant religion."

Thus, when the Second Continental Congress gathered on May 10, 1775, the War for Independence was already well under way on the Eastern Seaboard. Many of the delegates had hoped to restore harmony between America and the mother country, but to do so would be to desert the Patriot Army, which had succeeded in blockading General Gage's forces. There was also the amazing news that two small bands of irregular troops, one led by Benedict Arnold and commissioned by Massachusetts, and the other group (83 Green Mountain Boys) led by the frontiersman Ethan Allen, had captured the British Fort Ticonderoga in early May. This victory provided the colonies with strategic control of an important route between Canada and New York. Moreover, John Hancock had arrived from the seat of war in order to preside as President of the Congress. Meanwhile, news came in that the British planned to strengthen the army, rebuild the navy, and devote all of England's attention and power to suppressing the revolt around Boston. No longer could this be a mere conference of delegates. The Second Continental Congress had to transform itself into an actual governing body with executive war powers. It voted to issue paper money and to meet British encroachments with force. What was needed, however, was a leader, someone who could transform a part-time militia of farmers, merchants, and preachers into a disciplined army.

John Adams proposed George Washington as the obvious choice. Washington was still remembered and revered for his exploits 20 years earlier in the French and Indian War. He was also a Southerner, and thus could help cement a union between North and South. Many Southerners, especially Episcopalians, viewed the conflict as essentially regional, involving New England's religious zealots and mother England. Washington's nomination broadened the war and the cause to include all the colonies.

But Washington was the reluctant warrior, and had slipped out of the convention hall, hoping his name would be overlooked. Twenty years earlier, he might have welcomed the opportunity for military glory. But he was happy in private life. When he heard that he might be made Commander in Chief of the Continental Army, he urged his friends at the Congress to block the move. On June 15, he was unanimously selected to lead America into war. He said he would accept the command only on the condition that Congress appoint and fund chaplains for his troops, which Congress promptly did. He then accepted this "momentous duty," but warned his fellow countrymen: "With utmost sincerity, I do not think myself equal to the command I am honored with." He refused financial compensation. The New England Patriots eagerly awaited the arrival of the legend.

Washington was an Anglican, a member of the established English Church, and was, in fact, a vestryman. But he was also revered by the strictest of New England Congregationalists. In many respects, he was the ultimate Protestant hero. He had many of the qualities of Oliver Cromwell, John Winthrop, and WiHiam Bradford, the great Protestant figures of Anglo-American history. Washington epitomized the Protestant virtues of self-discipline, of will triumphing over the passions. Washington, as a youth, had a violent temper. But as an adult, he never lost self-control, fearing that, if he did, he might easily kill someone, so powerful was his frame. Washington had a preference for repub-lican (really Protestant) simplicity. "Modesty marks every line and feature on his face," wrote Abigail Adams of Washington. He was a Protestant, though, who had been shaped by Virginia's cul-ture, and reflected many of the Anglican virtues without its vices. He was definitely a committed and believing Christian, but not a wild-eyed Separatist like Roger Williams. Unlike a George Whitefield or Jonathan Edwards, he preferred a more private religious life. He cared perhaps more about duty than theology, about living the Christian life than speculation. Washington does not seem to have had the kind of emotional, almost violent, con-version experience the Puritans believed so important. It was his composure, his equanimity in the face of setbacks, his self-less commitment to public service - all of which are archetype Protestant virtues -for which Americans admire him most.

Historians have avoided discussing Washington's religious life, in part because of bias and in part because Washington him-self did not discuss it much. He believed in the necessity of a public religion, in the general acceptance of basic biblical tenets. "It is impossible to govern rightly without God and the Bible," he said. But he also believed that faith was primarily a matter between the individual and his Maker, which in itself is a very Protestant belief. Jesus tells us: "But you, when you pray, go into your inner room, and when you have shut your door, pray to your Father who is in secret, and your Father who sees in secret will repay you" (Matt. 6:6).

That Washington was a devout Christian can be seen by looking at his private prayer book, 24 pages in length and writ-ten

in his own handwriting. He titled the little book *Daily Sacrifice*.
He called his first entry, very simply, "Sunday Morning," which
reads as follows:

> Almighty God, and most merciful Father, who
> didst command the children of Israel to offer a daily sac-
> rifice to Thee, that thereby they might glorify and praise
> Thee for Thy protection both night and day . . . I beseech
> Thee, my sins, remove them from Thy presence, as far
> as the east is from the west, and accept of me for the
> merits of Thy Son Jesus Christ . . . Let my heart, there-
> fore, gracious God, be so affected with the glory and
> majesty of (Thine honor) that I may not do mine own
> works, but wait on Thee . . . As Thou wouldst hear me
> calling upon Thee in my prayers, so give me grace to hear
> Thee calling on me in Thy word, that it may be wisdom,
> righteousness, reconciliation and peace to the saving of my
> soul in the day of the Lord Jesus.

In his Sunday evening entry, he wrote the following:

> O most glorious God, in Jesus Christ . I acknowl-
> edge and confess my faults, in the weak and imperfect
> performance of the duties of this day. I have called on
> Thee for pardon and forgiveness of sins, but so coldly and
> carelessly that my prayers are become my sin and stand
> in need of pardon. I have heard Thy holy word, but with
> such deadness of spirit that I have been an unprofitable
> and forgetful hearer . . . Let me live according to those
> holy rules which Thou hast this day prescribed in Thy
> holy word . . . Direct me to the true object, Jesus Christ
> the way, the truth and the life. Bless, O Lord, all the
> people of this land.

His other morning and evening prayers, each assigned a
specific day, contained such invocations as: "Direct my thoughts,

words and work, wash away my sins in the immaculate Blood of the Lamb"; "daily frame me more and more in the likeness of Thy Son Jesus Christ"; "look down from Heaven in pity and compassion upon me Thy servant, who humbly prostrate myself before Thee, sensible of Thy mercy"; and "be merciful to all those afflicted with Thy cross or calamity, bless all my friends, forgive my enemies and accept my thanksgiving this evening for all the mercies and favors afforded me." To Washington, God was not merely some distant celestial clock-maker indifferently watching His creation wind down. He was a personal God, who died on the Cross for sinners (such as Washington). Washington's God cared about people, watched over the faithful, and played an active role in world events. America's greatest hero and first President was no deist, but a devout, Bible-believing Christian. "I am but dust," Washington wrote, "and remit my transgressions, negligences and ignorances, and cover them all with the absolute obedience of Thy dear Son... Thou gavest Thy Son to die for me; and Thou hast given me assurance of salvation, upon my repentance and sincerely endeavoring to conform my life to His holy precepts and example."

When Washington took command of the Continental Army at Cambridge on July 2, he immediately sent out an order forbidding "profane swearing, cursing and drunkenness. And in like manner," the order stated, "he [Washington] requires and expects of all officers and soldiers, not engaged in actual duty, a punctual attendance of Divine services, to implore the blessing of Heaven upon the means used for our safety and defense."

Washington was pleased that the 15,000 men encamped around Boston were eager to fight, but was appalled by their utter lack of discipline. Washington stayed at the home of the Reverend William Emerson, from where he issued the day's orders following mandatory morning prayers. One of those orders reiterated the requirement that all officers and soldiers attend divine service and added that a national fast day of July 20 would be "religiously observed by the forces under his command, exactly in the manner directed by the Continental Congress." Moreover, said Washington's order, "it is expected that all those who go to worship do take their arms, ammunition and accoutrements, and are prepared for immediate action if called upon." Governor Jonathan Trumbull of Connecticut, a defector to the Patriot cause, welcomed Washington's arrival in a letter: "Now, therefore, be strong and very courageous," wrote Trumbull. "May the God of the armies of Israel shower down the blessings of his Divine Providence on you; give you wisdom and fortitude; cover your head in the day of battle and danger; add success; convince your enemies of their mistaken measures . . . " On December 3, 1775, George Washington raised the new American flag on a hill near Boston. It contained 13 stripes, signifying the union of the 13 colonies. The British Union Jack was displayed in the upper left hand corner, but would be replaced with stars in June 1777.

In February 1776, Washington spoke publicly, for the first time, of possibly severing all political ties with Britain. "If nothing. .. could satisfy a tyrant and his diabolical ministry, we are determined to shake off all connections with a state so unjust and unnatural," he told the Continental Congress. Around this time Washington saw an opportunity to deliver a major military defeat to the British by taking Dorchester Heights, a bluff overlooking British-held Boston, much like Breed's Hill. From Dorchester Heights, the Patriots could shell the British. The problem was, Washington had no cannons or sufficient powder with which to bombard Boston once the Patriots occupied the hill.

It then occurred to Washington that heavy artillery had been captured by Ethan Allen and Benedict Arnold at Fort Ticonderoga. Henry Knox, a chubby bookseller from Boston who would become Washington's artillery commander, oversaw the transport of some 50 cannons and heavy guns to Cambridge. The task was extremely difficult. Knox moved them hundreds of miles up and down hills and across rivers on sleds. One cannon fell through the ice, but Knox through enormous effort and ingenuity retrieved the piece. The completion of this almost impossible but vital job, without once complaining, made the 250-pound Knox Washington's favorite officer.

During the night of March 4,1776, Washington moved 3,000 men to the base of Dorchester Heights, a very risky operation because the location was in full view of British forces. But, suddenly, a low mist rolled in, in perfect time to conceal Patriot movements, while at the same time leaving the top of the hill perfectly clear, fully lighted by a bright moon, thus aiding the Patriots who were building fortifications. Boston and the red coats remained shrouded in fog throughout the night, and so could not see what was happening. In addition, a breeze blew noises made by Patriot engineers away from British ears. As the Reverend William Gordon put it, "everyone knew his place and business." At three in the morning, work was completed. The 3,000 builders departed, and 3,000 fresh soldiers moved in. At dawn, the British looked upon the Patriot fortifications with amazement. Captain Charles Stuart wrote that the guns appeared "like magic." Another officer put the blame on "the genie belonging to Aladdin's wonderful lamp." The rebels have "done more in one night than my whole army would have done in months," said British General William Howe.

Howe desperately wanted to attack Dorchester Heights, now teeming with soldiers and cannons. He made hasty preparations, but, according to historian J. T. Flexner, "the sky suddenly blackened with what soldiers on both sides considered the most awesome storm they had ever seen." The winds were of hurricane strength, making a British attack impossible. Americans continued to work through the storm, and, when the sky cleared, Patriot fortifications were such as to convince Howe that an attack on Dorchester would be suicidal. Two weeks later, the Patriots fortified and armed Nobs Hill, making Boston untenable for the British. Completely humiliated, Howe elected to evacuate. The Patriots heard that Howe planned to burn Boston to the ground before he left. Washington informed Howe that he could depart unmolested so long as the city remained unharmed. With help from the weather, Washington was able to retake Boston without shedding any blood. He called the storm "a remark-able inter- position of Providence." And Timothy Newell, a Boston selectman, agreed, writing in a journal entry of March 17: "Thus was this unhappy distressed town through a manifest interposition of Divine Providence relieved from a set of men whose unparalleled wickedness, profanity, debauchery and cruelty is inexpressible." When Washington's troops marched into Boston, amid much cheering and fanfare, they saw that the Old South Church had been desecrated, turned into a riding school for British cavalry. This underscored the conviction of many Patriots that they were fighting not only for political freedom; they were also fighting for God.

The signing of the Declaration of Independence on July 4, 1776, was really just an official ratification of what had already occurred. On May 10, town meetings all over Massachusetts had already declared independence. Five days later, Virginia declared independence. Moreover, the British ministry had decided to hire German mercenaries to use against the colonists, in part because the war was so unpopular among the general population in England. Whigs in Parliament-such as Pitt and Burke-were aghast at the use of Prussian mercenaries. Not only had George III and his Tory supporters in Parliament ignored every reasoned plea by the colonists to allow them to govern themselves, but he had hired foreigners, whose values were directly opposed to liberty, to do England's fighting.

While the war continued to escalate, a number of inde- pendent governments began to take shape in the various colonies. The royal governors were virtually powerless even by the time of Lexington and Concord. But after hostilities commenced, the Committees of Correspondence had gone a long way toward estab- lishing their own governments, with executive powers, including the authority to tax and recruit soldiers. With the loyalty of the population moving to the Patriots, the authority of the royal government was rapidly fading. Governor Martin of North Carolina fled to a British warship, and others soon followed. Governor Trumbull of Connecticut switched sides, and was given a leadership position in the Revolution. Massachusetts reestablished its government according to the old charter. Soon other states were busy writing their own constitutions.

Long before the signing of the Declaration of Independence, the colonies had passed the point of no return. George III would not accept reunification under the terms demanded by the colonists, which included complete autonomy within the empire. "What profit is there in that?" was England's question. The answer was, "plenty," but the King and his ministers were too shortsighted to understand that freedom is beneficial to everyone. Many in the Continental Congress were very apprehensive about total separation and pushed for reconciliation. But events had overtaken such sentiments.

Thomas Paine's famous pamphlet *Common Sense,* published in 1776, made the case for independence even plainer: "Society in every state is a blessing, but government, even in its best state, is but a necessary evil; in its worst state an intolerable one." "Everything that is right or reasonable pleads for separation. The blood of the slain, the weeping voice of nature cries, 'TIS TIME TO PART. Even the great distance at which the Almighty hath placed England and America is strong and natural proof that the authority of the one over the other was never the design of Heaven."

In its first three months, Paine's pamphlet sold 120,000 copies. Read and reread copies, frayed and tattered, were passed from hand to hand. An estimated 1 miflion Americans had read it by the time the Declaration of Independence had been signed. Paine himself was no model human being. He was drunk much of the time, careless in financial matters, and disrespectful of authority to an extreme. But his tract was a brilliant piece of agitprop: "O Ye that love mankind," Paine rhapsodized. "Ye that dare oppose not only the tyranny but the tyrant, stand forth!

Every spot of the Old World is overrun with oppression. Freedom hath been hunted 'round the globe. Asia and Africa have long expelled her. Europe regards her like a stranger, and England hath given her warning to depart. O receive the fugitive, and prepare in time an asylum for mankind!" Paine, the man, had many flaws. But he had written the most successful political pamphlet in history.

On June 7, 1776, Virginia's Richard Henry Lee finally proposed a motion that the United Colonies declare themselves free and independent states. John Adams seconded the motion. And on June 11, Congress appointed a committee of five to prepare the formal declaration: Benjamin Franklin, Roger Sherman, John Adams, Robert Livingston, and Thomas Jefferson. Because Jefferson was the best writer, he wrote the first draft. Alterations, though, were made by Adams, Franklin, and the Congress.

The Declaration of Independence contained nothing new:

"We hold these truths to be self-evident, that all men are created equal, that they are endowed by their Creator with certain unalienable rights, that among these are life, liberty, and the pursuit of happiness: that to secure these rights, governments are instituted among men. . . " These ideas had been expounded in thousands of sermons throughout America. For as the Apostle Paul told the Galatians: "The Jerusalem above is free; she is our mother . . . So then, brethren, we are not children of a bondwoman, but of the free woman" (vv. 4:26,31). The power of the Declaration was that it was *not* novel. It was a political document that sought to build a political consensus by demonstrating that the British government had egregiously threatened the liberty, morality, and religion all Americans cherished. The colonists were supposed to read this document and immediately agree.

Not surprisingly, then, the document was heavily laden with religious references, though not so blatantly as to cause division between the various Christian sects. Government, they believed, was an instrument of God, established for the protection of the individual (His most valued creation) from men with evil aspirations. The Reverend Phillips Payson, in a sermon before the House of Representatives of Massachusetts Bay in May 1778, articulated this point well: "The qualities of a good ruler," he said, "may be estimated from the nature of a free government. Power being a delegation, and all delegated power being in its nature subordinate and limited, hence rulers are but trustees, and government a trust. . . A state and its inhabitants thus circumstanced in respect to government, principle, morals, capacity, union and rulers, make up the most striking portrait, the liveliest emblem of the Jerusalem that is above."

The purpose of government, according to the Reverend Payson, was to duplicate on earth (so much as man's fallen nature would permit) the condition of liberty that exists in Heaven. As the Reverend Jonathan Mayhew put it in his autobiography: "Having learnt from the Holy Scriptures that wise, brave and virtuous men were always friends to liberty - that God gave the Israelites a king in His anger, because they had not the sense and virtue enough to like a free commonwealth[1] - and 'where the Spirit of the Lord is there is liberty'[2] - this made me conclude that freedom was a great blessing." Indeed, this is exactly the view presented in the Declaration of Independence. A careful examination of the Declaration reveak its strong biblical roots. In chapter eight of Deuteronomy, one of the books in the Old Testament most frequently quoted by American colonists, we read the following admonition: "Therefore, you shall keep the commandments of the Lord your God, to walk in His ways and to fear Him. For the Lord your God is bringing you into a good land, a land of brooks of water, of fountains and springs, flowing forth in valleys and hills; a land of wheat and barley, of vines and fig trees and pomegranates, a land of olive oil and honey; a land where you shall eat food without scarcity, in which you shall not lack anything... "(vv. 6-9).

The Americans saw themselves in just such a land. They viewed themselves as the new Israelites and George III as the modern-day pharaoh. In the minds of the colonists, it was their

1. 1 Samuel 8:1-22.
2. 2 Corinthians 3:17.

Christian responsibility to separate themselves from the corrupt
British government. "Do not be bound together with unbelievers,"
Paul warned the Christians at Corinth. "For what partnership
have righteousness and lawlessness, or what fellowship has light
with darkness?" (2 Cor. 6:14). In obedience to this command, the
Declaration states, in one of the most majestic phrases ever written
by a human hand: "When in the course of human events, it
becomes necessary for one people to dissolve the political bands
which have connected them with another, and to assume among
the powers of the earth the separate and equal station to which the
laws of nature and of nature's God entitle them, a decent respect
to the opinions of mankind requires that they should declare the
causes which impel them to the separation."

We find, in the Old Testament, God leading His people,
the Israelites, out of bondage, just as Bradford, Winthrop, and
their Christian followers had fled the Stuart tyranny. Pharaoh's
yoke inhibited the Israelites from keeping God's commandments,
just as the Puritans believed the English Church was an imped-
iment to the true Christian faith. In a long catalogue of abuses,
the Declaration made a case for why the Americans could no
longer live under such a corrupt, dissolute, and tyrannical regime:

"The history of the present king of Great Britain is a history of repeated injuries and usurpations, all having in direct object the establishment of an abs&ute tyranny over these states. .
.   He has refused his assent to laws, the most wholesome
and necessary for the public good... He has dissolved representative houses repeatedly . . . He has refused for a long time,
after such dissolutions, to cause others to be elected . . . He has
obstructed the administration of justice. . . He has made judges
dependent on his will alone . . . He has erected a multitude of
new offices, and sent hither a swarm of officers to harass our
people, and eat out their substance. He has kept among us, in
times of peace, standing armies, without the consent of our legislatures. He has affected to render the military independent of'
and superior to, the civil power. He has combined with others to

subject us to a jurisdiction foreign to our constitution and unac-knowledged by our laws. . . He has abdicated government here, by declaring us out of his protection and waging war against us. He has plundered our seas, ravaged our coasts, burnt our towns, and destroyed the lives of our people. He is at this time trans-porting large armies of foreign mercenaries to complete the work of death, desolation and tyranny, already begun with circumstan-ces of cruelty and perfidy scarcely paralleled in the most bar-barous ages, and totally unworthy the head of a civilized nation. . .In every stage of these oppressions we have petitioned for redress in the most humble terms: Our repeated petitions have been answered only by repeated injuries. A prince whose character is thus marked by every act which may define a tyrant is unfit to be the ruler of a free people. . ."

In the American mind, England's government had be come a tyranny and her church a harlot. Dissolution of all political ties between the two nations was not only justified, it was mandated by the laws of nature and nature's God: "We therefore, the Representatives of the United States of America, in General Congress assembled, appealing to the Supreme Judge of the world for the rectitude of our intentions. . . solemnly publish and declare that these united colonies are, and of right ought to be, free and independent states . . . And for the support of this Declaration, with a firm reliance on the protection of Divine Providence, we mutually pledge to each other our lives, our for-tunes and our sacred honor."

"Supreme Judge of the world," "the protection of Divine Providence," and "sacred honor" were not empty phrases in the minds of the signers. Jefferson and the U.S. Congress were very much concerned that their cause was right with God. "I tremble for my country when I reflect that God is just: that His justice cannot sleep forever," said Jefferson. These Americans had read how God, after freeing Israel from bondage in Egypt, punished them for failing to keep His laws. Chapter eight of the Book of Deuteronomy concludes with the following warning, appropriate for free people in all ages:

"When you have eaten and are satisfied, you shall bless the Lord your God for the good land which He has given you. Beware lest you forget the Lord your God, by not keeping His commandments and His ordinances and His statutes which I am commanding you today; lest, when you have eaten and are satisfied, and have built good homes and have lived in them, and when your herds and your flocks multiply, and your silver and gold multiply, and all you have multiplies, then your heart becomes proud, and you forget the Lord your God who brought you out from the land of Egypt, out of the house of slavery. He led you through the great and terrible wilderness, with its fiery serpents and scorpions and thirsty ground where there was no water; He brought water for you out of the rock of flint. In the wilderness He fed you manna which your fathers did not know, that He might humble you and that He might test you, to do good for you in the end. Otherwise, you may say in your heart, 'My power and the strength of my hand made me this wealth.' But you shall remember the Lord your God, for it is He who is giving you power to make wealth, that He may confirm His covenant which He swore to your fathers, as it is this day . . . if you ever forget the Lord your God, and go after other gods and serve them and worship them, I testify against you today that you shall surely perish. Like the nations the Lord makes to perish before you, so you shall perish; because you would not listen to the voice of the Lord your God" (vv. 10-20).

The Americans were very familiar with the plight of the Israelites, who failed to keep God's laws even though they were His favored people. The Declaration continuously calls on God, the "Creator," the "Supreme Judge of the World," to approve of their separation. We fled from Pharaoh, the colonists seemed to be saying, but what happens when Pharaoh follows? God answered that question in the Old Testament at the Red Sea, when He destroyed Egypt's army. The Americans responded with revolution. They knew they too would need miracles such as occurred at the Red Sea if they were to have any hope of freeing themselves from George III and his imperial army. The Americans had already seen one such miracle at Dorchester Heights, and there would be others.

It is very useful to lay out the Book of Deuteronomy, particularly chapter eight, alongside a copy of the Declaration of Independence. The parallels and the obvious connection between the two documents are startling. America was very concerned about the righteousness of its cause, not only in the eyes of the rest of the world, but also, and more importantly, in the eyes of God. Abraham Keteltas, a Presbyterian minister, told his Newburyport congregation in 1777 that the War for Independence had become "the cause of truth against error and falsehood the cause of pure and undefiled religion against bigotry, superstition and human inventions . . . In short, it is the cause of Heaven against Hell - of the kind Parent of the Universe against the Prince of Darkness and the destroyer of the human race." Another Presbyterian, Robert Smith, spoke of "the cause of America as the cause of Christ."

The Declaration is also filled with Locke's language, as well as his political ideas. As such, many historians have called it a product of the Enlightenment, because some have tried to claim Locke as a pillar of the Enlightenment. But Locke's ideas, as we have seen, are biblically based. His background and education were dissenting Protestant. He was himself a devout Christian. Locke's notions about government have their foundation in the Scriptures. The Declaration has been called a revolutionary document. But its power came from its affirmation of truths long established. This point was made well in a popular song of the American Revolution:

> Let tyrants shake their iron rod,
> And slavery clank her galling chains.
> We fear them not, we trust in God.
> New England's God forever reigns.

CHAPTER NINETEEN

BLOODY FOOTPRINTS IN THE SNOW

During the summer of 1776, the largest expeditionary force of the 18th century, 32,000 British troops (9,000 of whom were German mercenaries) gathered on Staten Island under the command of William Howe. The British plan was to take New York and thereby cut off troublesome New England from the other colonies. It was the classic strategy of divide and conquer. Congress gave Washington the assignment of defending New York. With 18,000 men, he was heavily outnumbered. Moveover, most of his troops consisted of militia, enrolled only for short terms, and as such were unreliable. Washington moved his army to Long Island and fortified Brooklyn Heights in the hope of closing the East River.

Washington expected Howe to attack from Staten Island. But Howe had deftly moved his troops in boats to Long Island, from which he could attack to the south and east. Washington, having gathered a force at Manhattan, left command of Brooklyn to Major General John Sullivan. Foolishly, Sullivan moved his troops out of their fortifications to an open plain to the south. The British seized on this opportunity to launch their attack. Howe had the Americans exactly where he wanted them, in an open field where the British had the clear advantage. The New England militia panicked in the face of overwhelming firepower, and the result was 1,000 Americans dead and 1,000 more taken prisoner, including General Sullivan. Washington watched through field glasses from Manhattan Island in disbelief as Howe's forces surrounded 8,000 Patriot troops in Brooklyn, and was about to tighten the noose. He had the Continental Army at his mercy, pinned against the East River. It appeared that the American Revolution was about to conclude in abrupt fashion. Only a miracle could save the American cause, something akin to the parting of the Red Sea.

The miracle came in two parts. First, Howe hesitated. No one knows why. Perhaps he wanted reinforcements; perhaps he felt he needed better information on Patriot troop strength. In his mind, time seemed to be on the British side. Better to move slowly and precisely than hastily and risk making costly errors. But when Howe was ready to move, a violent storm erupted, making it impossible for the British fleet to sail into the necessary position on the East River, thus causing more delays. This gave Washington time to organize a rescue from Manhattan Island. He collected every vessel he could find: fishing boats, row boats, rafts, anything that would float.

Then a replay of Dorchester Heights occurred. As historian John Fiske reports, "The Americans had been remarkably favored by the sudden rise of a fog which covered the East River." Every man who kept a journal described the phenomenon. "At this time a very dense fog began to rise," wrote Major Ben Talimadge. "It seemed to settle in a particular manner over both encampments. I recollect this peculiar providential occurrence perfectly well, and so very dense was the atmosphere that I could scarcely discern a man six yards distant."

This enabled Washington to rescue his 8,000 troops, in addition to moving artillery, horses, and wagons across the river on the flotilla, completely unseen by Howe. The evacuation took 13 hours, after which the fog lifted. To Howe's astonishment, the entire Continental Army had vanished, as if into thin air. If Howe had captured Washington's forces, as he should have, the American cause would have died on Brooklyn Heights.

Washington suffered another defeat at White Plains on

October 28. Howe then began mobilizing to take the American capital of Philadelphia. So far, about all Washington had been able to do was survive. By Christmas, Patriot morale was probably at its lowest ebb. Washington was short of supplies, had almost no gunpowder; most of his militia had temporary commissions and were continuously leaving to tend to matters on their farms. Congress was becoming impatient, and Washington had a disgruntled general in his midst, Charles Lee, who believed he should be the Commander in Chief. Lee had been spending much energy running down Washington's reputation behind his back with members of Congress. Howe had only to cross the Delaware River, and Philadelphia would be his. Washington badly needed a victory.

He got that victory in a brilliant coup in Trenton, New Jersey, on Christmas night, when he made his fabled crossing of the half-frozen Delaware River. The Patriot forces had to endure a terrible storm. But, once again, the operation could not have succeeded without help from the weather. The storm actually was a godsend. The British forces encamped in Trenton, mainly German mercenaries, did not believe any army could function under such conditions and so ignored reports that Washington was planning an attack. In sub-freezing and blizzard conditions, Washington packed onto a fleet of 40-feet long boats 2,400 troops, in addition to horses, artillery, ammunition, and supplies. Soldiers who got wet found themselves encased in frozen clothing; floating ice chunks in the river threatened to smash the boats; and progress was slow. Washington hoped to attack at night. But it became clear that it would be broad daylight by the time they reached enemy encampments.

When the final march actually began, the storm was at its worst. Two Americans dropped and froze to death during the march. But the blizzard and howling winds also concealed American troop movements, allowing Washington to take the enemy encampments by surprise. The battle was actually an anti-climax in comparison to the horrific conditions of the journey. The German (Hessian) mercenary forces were surprised and completely overwhelmed. Henry Knox's artillery lit up the streets. Blinded by the snow and unable even to discern from which direction Patriot shots were being fired, 1,500 Hessians surrendered. In addition, Washington captured six brass cannons and 1,200 small arms. Total American casualties: two men had frozen to death on the march, and three more were wounded during the battle. This was a staggering victory for Washington, and greatly boosted American spirits.

A week later, Washington repeated the feat, this time in the Battle of Princeton. He crossed the Delaware again and was almost trapped by Lord Cornwallis' forces. In well-ordered fashion, the British formed their customary battle lines and were about to slice the Patriots to ribbons. Washington, seeing confusion among his ranks, galloped to the front in an attempt to steady the nerves of his wavering recruits. On his huge white horse, with his 6-foot 3-inch frame, he was a conspicuous target. He stopped only 30 yards from the first British line, and directed his men to take aim. Miraculously, he survived the first volley. As historian J. T. Flexner recounts the episode: "When the two forces came in range, both fired; Washington was between them. An aide, Colonel Richard Fitzgerald, covered his face with his hat to keep from seeing the Commander in Chief killed. When Fitzgerald lowered the hat, he saw many men dead and dying, but the General was sitting untouched on his horse."

The British lines retreated to Princeton, where one regiment barricaded itself in Nassau Hall. After a few cannon balls were fired from Knox's field pieces, the British surrendered. It was the first time American forces had defeated lines of redcoats in a face-to-face battle on open territory.

Meanwhile, far to the north, Benedict Arnold had brilliantly foiled British attempts to retake Fort Ticonderoga. He had thrown together a flotilla of boats, small vessels, and rafts, and battled British ships as brilliantly on the lake as he fought in the forest. Arnold was relentless, fearless, and brilliant in guerrilla warfare, and proved definitively that the British could not win a war in the interior of the American continent. The best England could hope for was the holding of the major ports and cities. He repeatedly ambushed General Burgoyne's army at every turn with a growing army of New England militia. On October 17, 1777, General Burgoyne offered to surrender in Saratoga, promising that he and his 6,000 troops would go home to England and never again return to American soil. Arnold was badly wounded in one battle and his superior, General Horatio Gates, claimed and received credit for the victory. No doubt, this got Arnold thinking that his skills would be better appreciated by the British King than the American Congress.

Arnold would later betray his country, which was tragic because he may have been America's best warrior. His defection to the British side was the worst wound George Washington ever received. Arnold was very similar to Judas in that he appeared to be the strongest and most loyal soldier (apostle). Treason is especially tragic because it usually involves the very people we love and trust most. It was a decision he would later regret. On his deathbed in England, Arnold's final request was to be buried in an American uniform.

Howe easily captured Philadelphia, but this was really a Pyrrhic victory. America was not like Europe, heavily dependent on its cities. If Paris or London fell to an invading army, this would signal the end for France or England. But America was a vast continent; its composition was rural. Ninety-three percent of the population lived on farms. Philadelphia, the capital, was still little more than a large town by European standards. To lose ports and cities to British occupation was bad symbolically for the American cause, but by no means disastrous militarily. This was a guerrilla war, a contest of wills, a fact the British never fully understood.

Valley Forge has come to represent, through the ages, the price America was willing to pay for freedom. Washington chose the site to quarter his army during the ferocious winter of 1777-

78 because it was only 15 miles from British occupied Philadelphia and easily defensible. Like the Pilgrims and Puritans of the first settlements, the Patriots would have to endure their starving time. The Continental Congress, stationed in York, Pennsylvania, had been ineffective at procuring supplies and troops from the states and had been financing the war mostly by printing large quantities of paper money. This caused rampant inflation, at times as much as 50 percent a day. Washington's army was in dreadful straits. Pay for soldiers was five months behind. The able-bodied succeeded in building 700 makeshift huts in the first four weeks. But, during those four weeks without shelter, the Americans encountered the worst weather of the winter. One in four died of exposure or fever during that period and the ensuing months when the men were without proper clothing. Bloody footprints were left in the snow from soldiers who had no shoes.

America's greatest enemy was not the British, or lack of desire on the part of the militia, it was a vacillating Congress which often could not make up its mind about how it wanted to proceed with the war. There was still substantial sectarian feeling among Southerners about the predominantly New England composition of the Army's rank and file. "Was this a New England- or an American-war for independence?" some asked. "What kind of disaster had Separatist Protestant opinions in flicted on our poor people?" others wondered. Alexander Graydon of Philadelphia noted in his journal that New Englanders were viewed with contempt by the more aristocratic and episcopal Southerners. But Washington, a Southerner him-self, had a different opinion of them. Of the New Englanders he wrote: "It is painful for me to hear such illiberal reflections upon the eastern states. . .I have always and always shall say that I do not believe any of the states produce better men, or persons capable of making better soldiers . . . no people fly to arms readier than they do, or come better equipped, or with more regularity into the field than they do."

But government, meaning Congress, was almost as inept then as it is today. After much debate and sectarian squabbling,

Congress finally sent a committee to inspect conditions and was shocked at what it saw. Dr. Albigence Waldo wrote of the situation in his journal: "There comes a soldier, his bare feet are seen through his worn out shoes, his legs nearly naked from tattered remains of an old pair of stockings; his breeches are not sufficient to cover his nakedness, his shirt hanging in strings, his hair disheveled, his face meager. His whole appearance pictures a person forsaken and discouraged. He comes and cries with an air of wretchedness and despair: 'I am sick, my feet lame, my legs are sore, my body covered with this tormenting itch.'"

The miracle of Valley Forge was that they stayed. That Washington endured with them lifted their spirits. Washington wrote about the admiration he had for his men: "Naked and starving as they are, we cannot enough admire the incomparable patience and fidelity of these soldiers." More and more, sermons (particularly Congregationalist, Presbyterian, and Baptist) began drawing analogies between Washington and Moses. And despite the hardships, Washington found time to tend to the spiritual Hves of his men: "To the distinguished character of a Patriot," he told them, "it should be our highest glory to add the more distinguished character of Christian." And the Reverend Henry Muhlenberg had the opportunity to observe Washington's conduct from his nearby Lutheran Church: "Washington rode around among his army yesterday and admonished each and every one to fear God," Muhlenberg recounted. "This gentleman does not belong to the so-called world of society, for he respects God's word, believes in atonement through Christ, and bears himself in humility and gentleness." It appears, concluded Muhlenberg, that "the Lord God has also singularly, yea marvelously, preserved him from harm in the midst of countless perils. . and hath hitherto graciously held him in His hand as His chosen vessel."

Valley Forge seemed to serve a purpose in testing Patriot resolve. How much, really, did freedom mean to them? While the British Army basked in the high life and comfort of Philadelphia, Washington's army was becoming a hardened core of veterans.

The congressional committee sent back its report, and after more discussion and debate, supplies in February began to trickle in.

Meanwhile, important negotiations were taking place in France. Roundly trounced in the Seven Years War, France thought that if it could not own North America, at least England could be prevented from owning it. What France needed was evidence that the Patriots had a chance of winning. Benjamin Franklin was the American minister in Paris, where both he and the American cause had attained celebrity status. Burgoyne's surrender to Benedict Arnold was the evidence France needed of Patriot seriousness. A treaty of friendship and commerce, which recognized American independence, was signed on February 6. This treaty caused yet another war to break out between France and Great Britain. France then informed the Americans that a condition of peace between Paris and London was contingent on America's independence. The new alliance encouraged Congress, gave America's legislators reason for optimism, and supplies poured into Valley Forge in comparative abundance.

In addition, the American cause began to attract volunteers from foreign lands. Some were genuine idealists; others were mercenaries looking for employment. Most caused more problems than they were worth. But there were some notable exceptions, one of which was the Marquis de Lafayette from France. He arrived in 1777, before the formation of the Franco-American alliance. A true freedom fighter and only 19 years old, he made the journey on a ship equipped at his own expense. Congress made him a Major General, and he became one of the most flamboyant and effective leaders of the American cause. He was revered by the Patriot ranks, and Washington gave him an independent command. Most important, his political ties at home enabled him to convince France to devote substantial resources and firepower to the American theater. Washington saw Lafayette as akin to a son, and they became life-long friends.

Developments in France were augmented by the arrival of a Prussian volunteer, who called himself Lieutenant General

Friedrich Wilhelm Ludolf Gerhard Augustin Baron von Steuben. He claimed to have held a high rank in the army of Frederick the Great. It was discovered later that he had not held the rank; nor was he a baron. Nevertheless, he turned out to be a great drillmaster. The troops loved his sense of humor as well as his tough Prussian style. He would arrive at the training ground at 3 a.m. to make preparations for drills to begin at sunrise. He organized competitions where the losers would have to sacrifice such luxuries as tobacco and brandy. He taught the Patriots how to march, how to use bayonets, and how to function like a professional fighting force.

Meanwhile, General Howe was coming to the understanding that occupying Philadelphia meant little in this war. He and his troops had become something akin to prisoners in the city. Every time a regiment of redcoats ventured beyond town boundaries, they would be swarmed by Patriot militia coming from every direction. So unsatisfactory were developments from the British perspective that Howe was relieved of his duties and replaced by Sir Henry Clinton, whose performance proved even less satisfactory than Howe's.

Clinton moved out of Philadelphia on June 18, 1778; when he reached New York it was not on the attack, but in retreat. Many redcoats were either killed or wounded along the way. Clinton would have been finished off completely at the battle of Monmouth, New Jersey, except that Patriot General Charles Lce bungled the attack and missed an opportunity for total victory. Lee, a disagreeable braggart who spent most of his energy criticizing his Commander in Chief, was relieved of his duties by a furious Washington, who suspected him of treason. Washington's armies went on to recapture White Plains and then chased the British almost into the harbor. "After two years of maneuvering," Washington observed, "both armies are brought back to the very point they set out from." And with prospects of French military assistance, the Patriot forces had every reason to be jubilant.

One of the seldom mentioned results of the French alliance was the unprecedented prestige it brought to the Catholic Church in Patriot eyes. American Catholics had not fared well in colonial America. They had been persecuted more than any other religious group, including Quakers and Jews. But Americans began to rethink their position on the papists. Perhaps they really were "brothers in Christ." On July 4, 1779, members of the Continental Congress, on invitation from the French diplomatic mission, attended Mass at St. Mary's Catholic Church in Philadelphia. In his sermon, the Reverend Seraphin Bandol said that victory in this "glorious revolution" would come under the protection of God's providence:

"It is that God, that all powerful God who hath directed your steps when you knew not where to apply for counsel; who when you were without arms, fought for you with the sword of justice; who, when you were in adversity, poured into your hearts the spirit of courage, of wisdom and of fortitude . . . We have nothing now to apprehend but the anger of heaven, or that the measure of our guilt should exceed His mercy. Let us then prostrate ourselves at the feet of the immortal God who holds the fate of empires in His hands and raises them up at His pleasure, or breaks them down to dust. Let us conjure Him to enlighten our enemies, and to dispose their hearts to enjoy that tranquility and happiness which the revolution we now celebrate has established for a great part of the human race. Let us implore Him to conduct us by the way which His providence has marked for union at so desirable an end. Let us offer unto Him hearts imbued with sentiments of respect, consecrated by religion, by humanity, and by patriotism."

By this time, the Northeast, except for the ports, had been retaken by Patriot forces. In fact, the British had given up on the Northeast, and tried to redirect their efforts against the weaker and more thinly populated South. They did this to some effect by maintaining their ports in New York and Newport and skirting the coast with their navy, picking their locations to launch raids against coastal towns, rebel encampments and munitions stores. The British hoped they could take advantage of lingering Anglican/Tory sentiment in the South and perhaps intimidate the uncommitted to oppose independence. Indeed, there was plenty of anti-New England bigotry in lazy Anglican Virginia, Carolina, and Georgia, where the spirit of liberty was not as strong. The British conceded that New England and the middle colonies had won independence, but hoped for a Southern secession. A union of North and South, London saw, would eliminate Great Britain as a player in the American theater, while simultaneously ensuring America's position as a future world power. But London was competing against the clock, as France was poised to enter the war.

Throughout the war, Washington's problem was that he had no navy to compete with the British. The British could move men and supplies over water much faster than Washington could over land. Because of their naval supremacy, the British could hold the ports and supply their army indefinitely. The entrance of the French Navy would begin to change the balance.

The French Admiral D'Estaing arrived with a fleet off New York in July 1778. But when he saw the size of the British force, he decided that it would be imprudent to attack. He sailed up to Newport, and again decided against engaging the British Navy. He then departed without explanation for the West Indies to the great disappointment of Washington. D'Estaing would not return for more than a year, at which point he launched a dis- astrous campaign in the South. He, with about 4,500 French troops and some continental militia, failed in an effort to recapture Savannah, Georgia, which had been taken by the British. After suffering heavy casualties, D'Estaing and his fleet returned to France and the alliance again proved a disappointment.

A significant French force did not arrive until spring 1780, when the compte de Rochambeau and 5,000 troops landed in Newport, Rhode Island, which the British had abandoned in order to intensify their efforts in the South. But Rochambeau, without a navy, was ineffective from the standpoint of mounting any threat to British coastal domination. Nor was his positioning (marooned in Rhode Island) of much use in challenging Britain's major Southern offensive.

Meanwhile, British behavior during their campaign through the Carolinas in terms of looting, vandalism, and barbarism made General Sherman's bloody march through Georgia during the Civil War seem mild by comparison. A British force of 1,700, now under the command of Benedict Arnold, easily captured Virginia, which failed to mount serious opposition because of incompetent administration on the part of Governor Thomas Jefferson. Arnold harried Jefferson out of Richmond, and then proceeded to burn Virginia's tobacco crops as part of a program to destroy the state's economy.

In the summer of 1781, General Cornwallis moved his entire force from North Carolina to Yorktown, which is below Williamsburg near the tip of the Virginia peninsula. There he established a major naval base. The British then controlled every important seaport along the East Coast with the exception of Boston and Newport.

Louis XVI finally decided to get serious about the American cause and dispatched 21 battle ships under the command of the great fighting Admiral compte Francois de Grasse. It had been more than three years since the Franco-American alliance was formed. De Grasse's fleet arrived in Chesapeake Bay on August 12, 1781, and outmaneuvered the British fleet which, under the command of Graves, was forced to retreat to New York. General Cornwallis suddenly found himself cut off from the sea and surrounded by hostile ships. Meanwhile, Rochambeau and his 5,000 troops had joined Washington's army in White Plains, where they made preparations to converge on Cornwallis, who was trapped in Yorktown. Everything hinged on de Grasse's ability to keep the British fleet out of the Chesapeake Bay long enough to enable Washington and Rochambeau to finish off an isolated

Cornwallis.

Not only did de Grasse hold the line against Graves, he defeated Graves decisively. For two hours on September 5, it was "fire away." The British suffered severe casualties, and two of their ships were on the verge of sinking. The French vessels emerged relatively unscathed.

After de Grasse's victory, Cornwallis' fate was sealed. De Grasse continued his blockade of the Chesapeake Bay, cutting off all supplies and reinforcements to Cornwallis who was then left to face an allied army of some 16,000, twice the size of his own. On October 19, Cornwallis, before casualties grew too large, surrendered his entire force to Washington. Cornwallis' sword was turned over in customary fashion, the ammunition of his troops stacked in neat piles, and the British band played "The World Turned Upside Down."

Though the war, in official terms, would drag on for another two years, everyone knew that the American victory at Yorktown signaled the end. A preliminary peace treaty was signed on November 30, 1782. The final treaty, known as the Peace of Paris, was signed on September 3, 1783. Washington summed up his thoughts on the war in a letter to James McHenry: "Providence has done much for us in this contest, but we must do something for ourselves." Washington knew that the real danger lay ahead. What kind of a regime would be established? Was it really such a good idea to sever political ties with Great Britain which, despite its faults, still had the freest form of government ever established? These were the kinds of questions many Americans were asking.

On December 4, 1783, Washington called together his troops for a meeting at the Fraunces Tavern in lower Manhattan to bid them farewell. Raising a wine glass, he said: "With heart full of love and gratitude, I now take my leave of you. I most devoutly wish that your later days be as prosperous and as happy as your former ones have been glorious and honorable." Tears welled up in his eyes when he said goodbye to his favorite general, artilleryman Henry Knox. After seven years of war, Knox no

longer resembled the portly Boston bookseller who had commanded the New England militia at the Battle of Bunker Hill.
He was now a war-hardened veteran. Washington loved Knox,
be cause Knox in eight years of fighting had never once complained of the hardships. Washington embraced his officers one
by one, and then walked past a row of soldiers standing at perfect
attention. How far they had come since he first took command
in Cambridge in July 1775, when they did not know how to march
and when they often quit to go home and plant a crop. But they
had shown the world that they were an army now. For they had
driven the world's most feared war machine off of American soil.
Washington loved these men, especially the New Englanders,
who had fought most bravely under the gravest of circumstances.
He saluted them and tears streamed down their cheeks.

He then turned and passed through a mob of cheering cit-
izens to a wharf on the North River where a boat took him to the
New Jersey shore. There he mounted his horse and rode to
Annapolis, the temporary seat of the continental government, to
inform Congress that he was resigning his command. His address was a moving spectacle, and was related in a letter by James
McHenry to his fiancee Peggy Caldwell: "The spectators all wept...
The General's hand which held the address shook as he read it.
When he spoke of the officers who had composed his family, and
recommended those who had continued in it to the present
moment to the favorable notice of Congress, he was obliged to
support the paper with both hands. But when he commanded
the interests of his dearest country to Almighty God... his voice fal-
tered and sunk . . . After a pause, which was necessary for him
to recover himself, he proceeded to say in the utmost penetrating
manner, "Having now finished the work assigned to me I retire
from the great theater of action."

CHAPTER TWENTY

DIFFERENT GODS, DIFFERENT REVOLUTIONS

The American Revolution was an unprecedented event, which is why it is so vital to study it and discover why the Americans succeeded where so many others have failed. Wars of independence are constantly being waged, but few have accomplished anything more than replacing one dictator with another.

The American Revolution was different because, as Irving Kristol writes: It "was a mild and relatively bloodless revolution. A war was fought to be sure, and soldiers died in that war. But . . .there was none of the butchery which we have come to accept as a natural concomitant of revolutionary warfare. There were no revolutionary tribunals dispensing 'revolutionary justice'; there was no reign of terror; there were no bloodthirsty proclamations by the Continental Congress."

Most startilling of all was that when the gunfire ceased and the war came to a close, the end product was a constitutional republican democracy. The American people had become a truly free people. There were more opportunities for economic, political and social advancement in America than in England, where the people still had to contend with hereditary privilege and court favor. In America, titles of nobility were abolished; there were no more aristocratic shackles on private aspirations; and the possibihties for individual achievement were unprece-

dented. The guiding principle of political philosophy that prevailed in America at this time was that all was permitted so long
as it did not harm someone else.

* * *

Many modern historians have spent great energy trying
to demonstrate that the architects of the American Republic were
attempting to recreate Rome and the classical world on the
American continent. To prove this, they select quotations from
the founding fathers citing Cicero, Tacitus, and the Greek philosophers, most notably Plato and Aristotle. The point these historians are trying to make is that America became a free nation as
it moved away from Christian "superstition," and that the
American Revolution embodied the ideal of secular humanism.

It is worth looking for a moment at Greece, because Greece
was the most advanced and enlightened of pagan cultures. Secular
humanism, as it relates to the world today, had its origins with the
Greeks. It is often asserted that ancient Greece laid the foundation for democracy, which is in part true. But the lesson to be
learned from the Greek example is not that democracy is the
secret to protecting liberty, but that democracy, not anchored in a
"Higher Law," can be just as tyrannical as other forms of government. Both Socrates and Jesus, after all, were victims of the
vote.

An even casual examination of Athenian life reveals a
society run by an elite. Slaves made up one-third of the population of the city. A census taken in Athens in the fourth century B.C.
showed that only 21,000 Athenians were considered to be citizens, even though the total population numbered 431,000.
Aristotle believed that "the slave is a piece of property which is ani-
mate," and that "slavery is natural. In every department of the
natural universe," observed Aristotle, "we find the relation of ruler
and subject. These are human beings who, without possessing
reason, understand it. These are natural slaves." Aristotle concluded this discussion on "natural slaves" by saying: "Slavery is

condemned by some; but they are wrong. The natural slave benefits by subjection to his master" *(Politics,* Book I, Ch. 3-7).

Now, it is true that America tolerated slavery on its soil. But Americans, unlike the pagans, understood slavery to be counter to Christian principles. Indeed, it was the Puritan churches of New England and the revivalist ministers of the 18th and 19th centuries who became the most ardent opponents of this abominable institution of pagan origin. The subject of slavery was an explosive issue in the colonies throughout the Revolutionary War. Under the Articles of Confederation, slavery was abolished north of the Ohio River.

Christians have often behaved with cruelty toward their fellow man. The history of Christianity can be summed up as the story of men continuously and consistently disobeying God. But whereas the Christian knows when he is doing evil, Aristotle believed slavery both natural and just, and here lies the difference between the plantation owner and Nero. Southerners, such as Charles Pickney and John Rutledge of South Carolina, may have seen slavery as a "necessary evil," but it was an evil; indeed, the South was continuously on the moral defensive until slavery was eliminated from American life. But Aristotle saw slavery, not as necessary, but as wholesome and good. His moral standards were different precisely because his god was different. The contrast between America and ancient Greece is as stark as the contrast between the God of Scripture and the god of Reason.

Plato, another pillar of pagan thinking, is also a good illustration of where the human intellect, left to its own devices, will take us. Oblivious to man's fallen state, Plato laid the philosophical basis for the totalitarian slave state. He believed, as the secular humanists of today believe, that education will produce the perfect ruler: "Unless either philosophers become kings in their countries and rulers come to be inspired with a genuine desire for wisdom; unless, that is to say, political power and philosophy meet together. . . this commonwealth which we have imagined will never see the light of day and grow to its full stature."

What Plato is saying here is frightening. He believed the ideal society - which Christians know can never exist in the material world - would be built by "philosopher kings" directing the industry of others: "The philosopher, who is in constant contact with the ideal order of the world, will reproduce that order in his soul and, so far as any may, become Godlike." Such a man, thought Plato, "will take society and human character as his canvas, and begin by scraping it clean." This was Pol Pot's idea for Cambodia (to create the "New Man"), which resulted in the extermination of one-quarter of that country's population.

Aristotle and Plato were the best thinkers the pagan world produced. Indeed, they made an enormous contribution to human knowledge in that they asked crucial questions about who man is, and tried to discover the meaning of existence through logic and systematic thought. But they found few answers. Reason, unaided, could not take them far, as can be proven by examining the kinds of societies their minds produced.

That the founders often cited writers from pagan antiquity is, of course, true. But the framers considered these citations to be little more than window dressing, necessary to make their points on independence and self-government more convincing to the European elite who were heavily influenced by Enlightenment skepticism. As Alexander Hamilton put it: "No friend to order or to rational liberty can read without pain and disgust the history of the Commonwealths of Greece." "Generally speaking," said Hamilton, Greece was "a constant scene of the alternate tyranny of one part of the people over the other, or of a few usurping demagogues over the whole." Thomas Jefferson said of Plato's *Dialogues* that they were full of "sophisms, futilities, and incomprehensibilities." The Americans often gave an obligatory nod to the classical world, but they certainly did not embrace it. Harvard historian Bernard Bailyn says that "the classics of the ancient world are everywhere in the literature of the Revolution, but they are everywhere illustrative, not determinative of thought."

Another major enterprise of liberal historians has been to recast the American Revolution in the image of the French Revolution. The tendency of Thomas Jefferson and Benjamin Franklin toward deism is often cited as evidence of America's trend toward "enlightened rational humanism" during the period of America's founding. Whatever still remained of the Christian faith in America was merely a fading remnant - or so we are told.

It is very instructive, therefore, to turn for a moment to the revolution in France, whose announced aim was to duplicate the American Revolution, which had been such an obvious success. In fact, Thomas Jefferson traveled to Paris in order to assist Lafayette and his associates to draft their own Declaration of Rights. "Everyone here is trying their hands at forming a declaration of rights," Jefferson wrote in a letter to Madison, and included in his correspondence several drafts. "As you will see," Jefferson observed, "it contains the essential principles of ours accommodated as much as could be to the actual state of things here." Article Four of the French Declaration of the Rights of Man, drafted in August of 1789, for example, states that "liberty consists in the ability to do whatever does not harm another." France's Declaration abolished slavery, titles of nobility, and the remnants of feudalism and serfdom. In many respects, the French Declaration appeared superior to Jefferson's Declaration of Independence. But whereas the American Revolution ended in the establishment of a constitutional democracy, a government under law, the French Revolution ended in tyranny and government by the guillotine, followed by the rise of Napoleon. The obvious question is: What went wrong in France?

The French Declaration did not acknowledge that the source of man's rights is man's "Creator," as Jefferson had affirmed in America's Declaration of Independence. The French Declaration did not even state that rights are inherent, in-alienable, or derived from any transcendent authority. Rights for the Frenchman were granted by an "enlightened" government.

Tocqueville noted the striking contrast when he explained to his countiymen a half century later that America's experiment in liberty was firmly rooted in the fact that "in the United States the sovereign authority is religious." The French Revolution was explicitly anti-religious, and could not replicate the American example on a secular humanist foundation. Moreover, the prevailing sentiment in the American colonies was to preserve liberties they already enjoyed, to prevent the British monarchy from taking over their churches and subverting their colonial ways of life. But the driving force behind the French Revolution was a fanatical determination to tear down established ways and institutions, which the disciples of Rousseau saw as responsible for corrupting human nature.

Rousseau did not believe in original sin or private property. He hated European civilization precisely because he saw it as a product of Christianity. Rousseau stated flatly that "our souls are corrupted in proportion to the advance of arts and sciences. His society rejected all forms of Christianity, and put in its place the gospel of the "General Will." Against it no individual rights would stand, because, in Rousseau's view, the protection of individual rights stood in opposition to the sovereignty of the people. Following Rousseau's doctrines, the French executed their king, even after he had accepted their constitution.[1] From here, conditions rapidly degenerated into anarchy, with the outbreak of internal ideological war and, in the words of historian Henry May, the subsequent "executions of deviants, the lukewarm and the suspect," culminating in the Reign of Terror presided over by Robespierre. In just two years 20,000 people-considered allies of the Old Regime-were executed. France's complete break with the past and with Christianity was symbolized by the introduction of a new calendar that took 1792 as the year One, the first year of the Republic.

The revolution finally turned against itself and began to devour its own. Robespierre denounced the Encyclopedists, even though they were a symbol of Enlightenment thinking, for their compromises with the monarchy. Robespierre was himself guillotined in the summer of 1794. The French Revolution was a grim example of how people behave when they are unchecked by a sense of religious obligation.

The British statesman Edmund Burke, a Whig, saw this point clearly. After making a trip to Paris and talking with the French *philosophes,* he told Parliament as early as 1773 that their political theories could only produce tyranny. "The most horrid and cruel blow that can be offered to civil society is through atheism," Burke predicted. After the fall of the Bastille in 1789, he wrote his most famous work, *Reflections on the Revolution in France.* Burke placed the blame for France's miseries on a philosophy that denied God. Remarking on the beheading of the beautiful Marie Antoinette in 1793, Burke wrote: "The age of chivalry is gone. That of sophisters, economists, and calculators, has succeeded; and the glory of Europe is extinguished forever."

Burke, by contrast, called the American Revolution a "glorious revolution." In his speech on conciliation with the American colonies, delivered on the floor of the House of Commons on March 22, 1775, he made the case for Britain leaving America alone: "England, Sir, is a nation which I hope respects, and, formerly adored, her freedom. The colonists emigrated from you when this part of your character was most predominant; and they took this bias and direction the moment they parted from your hands. They are therefore not only devoted to liberty, but to liberty according to English ideals, and on English principles." Moreover, said Burke, "the people are Protestants; and of that kind which is most adverse to all implicit subjection of mind and opinion. This is a persuasion not only favorable to liberty, but built upon it." William Penn agreed: "If man is not governed by God," he wrote, "then he must be governed by tyrants."

Thomas Paine failed to make a distinction between the revolution in America and the one in France. He was a political agitator and ideologue, pure and simple, and was not disposed to looking closely at the facts. Paine traveled to France to help top-

---

1. In striking contrast to Oliver Cromwell and the English Puritans, who, with extreme reluctance, executed a king who steadfastly refused to curb his tyrannical behavior.

ple the monarchy there, and published *The Rights of Man.* Paine's behavior in France was rebuked by John Quincy Adams, who challenged Paine's latest political tract designed to throw fuel on the flames of the French Revolution. Adams objected principally to Paine's main premise that "whatever a whole nation chooses to do, it has the right to do," echoing Rousseau. Adams replied: "Nations, no less than individuals, are subject to the eternal and immutable laws ofjustice and morality." Paine's "doctrine," said Adams, "annihilated the security of every man for his inalienable rights, and would lead in practice to a hideous despotism, concealed under the party-colored garments of democracy."

Paine, Adams pointed out, had missed the entire point of the American Revolution, which was the assertion of rights that cannot be deprived from an individual even by a majority. Adams rejected Paine's contention that the people of Great Britain should follow the example of France and "topple down headlong" their present government on the grounds that the Anglican Church did not allow religious freedom: "Happy, thrice happy the people of America!" said Adams, "whose principles of religious liberty did not result from an indiscriminate contempt of all religion whatever, and whose equal representation in their legislative councils was founded upon equality *really existing* among them, and not among the metaphysical speculations of fanciful politicians, vainly contending against the unalterable course of events, and the established order of nature [emphasis added]."

Thomas Paine eventually learned through personal experience that the revolution in France was radically different from the one in America. He was jailed by Robespierre for protesting the execution of the King and having qualms about the direction of events. It took the intervention of Thomas Jefferson to rescue Paine from the guillotine. Prior to this, Paine had spent much of his political life crusading against Christianity, again failing to make distinctions between the true Christianity of Scripture and the often corrupt version taught by religious establishments. His relentless attacks against the hypocrisy of clergymen and religious institutions could be fully endorsed by the most fervent Separatist Puritans and Great Awakeners who lambasted the "dead faith" of the standing order churches. But Paine's attacks were of a different order, often denouncing the substance of the faith itself. "What is it the Testament teaches us? - to believe that the Almighty committed debauchery with a woman engaged to be married, and the belief of this debauchery is called faith."

It is easy to see how a demagogue such as Paine could be attracted to the cause of an extremist like Robespierre. But his experience in France seems to have altered his thinking. He began to see how the philosophy of atheism plays itself out in actual politics. His final work, *The Age of Reason* (1794-96), although very critical of Christian institutions, indicates something of a change of heart. He had become a defender of reHgious faith against atheism: "Lest in the general wreck of superstition, of false systems of government, and false theology, we lost sight of morality, of humanity, and of the theology that is true." On his deathbed he went still another step, embraced faith, and retracted any and all attacks against Christianity in *The Age of Reason:* "I would give worlds, if I had them, if *The Age of Reason* had never been published. O Lord, help me! Christ, help me! Stay with me! It is hell to be left alone." Paine, as vocal a debunker of Christianity as there was in the colonies, died believing passionately in God and hoping for a future life. He had learned the hard way the lessons of the French Revolution.

In contrast to the hatred and loathing driving the French Revolution, the American Revolution was strictly defensive. Historian Russell Kirk prefers to call it America's "War for Independence," because, says Kirk, it was actually "a revolution prevented." America's leaders had no desire to impose an alien structure on society; but instead sought to preserve life as it already existed, and to protect the liberties they had enjoyed for a century and a half. In this sense, the real revolutionaries were the British. The Crown had altered the colonial governments and imposed its own governors and place-men to carry out an obnoxious policy over the objections of the local colonial assemblies. The American Revolution succeeded because it was a conservative revolution; it sought merely to return to old ways. The radicals were not the Americans, but the British, who were attempting to uproot customary laws and traditions.

The colonists had a deep and abiding Christian respect for legitimate authority, and we see in the Declaration of Independence the extreme reluctance with which the colonists decided to revolt: "Prudence, indeed, will dictate that governments long established should not be changed for light and transient causes; and, accordingly, all experience hath shown that all mankind are more disposed to suffer, while evils are sufferable, than to right themselves by abolishing the forms to which they are accustomed. But when a long train of abuses and usurpations, pursuing invariably the same object evinces a design to reduce them under absolute despotism, it is their right, it is their duty, to throw off such a government, and provide new guards for their future security." What the Patriots stood for was the time-honored right of the colonies to manage their own affairs. That right had been usurped by a grasping British government attempting to consolidate its empire.

With the dissolution of British rule, the world expected chaos to ensue in the colonies. The British wholeheartedly believed that the Americans would soon beg for the return of rule by London, so intolerable would be conditions without government. Instead, almost before the ink was dry on the Declaration, constitutional governments were instituted among the states with very little internal disruption, even while the war against British rule raged. Ten constitutions were drafted in 1776. In the minds of the framers, it was essential that each state be free to establish its own government so that they would learn the principles of government from experience, suffering under their mistakes and reaping the rewards of their successes. "When this is done,"

Samuel Adams predicted, "the colonies will feel their independence." John Adams advised in his classic *Thoughts on
Governnzent* that the states "proceed in all established modes, to
which the people have been familiarized by habit."

The tried and tested path to which most states returned
was government rooted firmly in a traditional, Puritan understanding of human nature. All the constitutions, for example,
demonstrated suspicion of a single executive authority. Recent
experience with the British monarch had much to do with this,
but it only confirmed the long-held Puritan belief about the un-
reliability of human authority in spiritual or political matters.
The American Protestants had rejected popes and bishops, just
as Oliver Cromwell had shattered the doctrine of the divine right
of kings. If vesting ecclesiastical authority in one man, or group
of men, is dangerous, then it follows that trusting one man, or a
group of men, with unbridled political power is also a bad idea.
Dispersion of authority, separation of powers, and accountability
to the voters became central features of all the state constitutions, just as this structure had been an integral part of virtually
all the American Protestant churches. A pastor of a Protestant
church in America was accountable to his congregation, served
at the pleasure of his flock, and did not claim the same spiritual
authority as a priest in the Catholic or English Church. Similarly, the executive in American government would not have the
same powers as a European monarch.

Suspicion of power, especially if it was concentrated in one
individual, was part of the fabric of American culture, inherent
in its religious assumptions as well as its historical experience.
This is why we find in most state constitutions of the period that
the governor was stripped of the royal grandeur he had enjoyed
under British rule and was reduced to a mere figurehead.
Pennsylvania completely abolished the office. Abolished, too,
were titles of nobility and hereditary privilege -not from any
utopian socialist idea, but because privilege was counter to long-
held Puritan religious conviction. "All men are created equal,"

says the Declaration of Independence, which, of course, is a Christian concept: all men are equal in the eyes of God, and therefore should be equal under the law. The abolition of royal titles and hereditary privilege was not done out of hate and envy (as in France), but out of deep-seated religious conviction held by the vast majority of the American people.

A fixed code of law was an essential feature of every state constitution. The colonists had had an unpleasant experience under England's unwritten "flexible" constitution. Consequently, rigid restrictions were placed on government powers. Most state constitutions had bills of rights. Frequent elections to keep government close to the people was the rule, with 10 states having annual elections. A common American belief was that "where annual elections end, tyranny begins." Judges were appointed, usually by the legislature, but sometimes by the governor, to interpret the laws and settle disputes. In all the states, elected assemblies held the dominant power, but governed by the consent of the people.

Not surprisingly, the Massachusetts Constitution was widely acknowledged as superior. In drafting it, John Adams adopted John Winthrop's views of mixed government, today more commonly called "checks and balances." In fact, Adams essentially copied the charter of the old Massachusetts Bay government, as codified under Winthrop. The Massachusetts Constitution would serve as a model for the Federal Constitution. In 1780, the Massachusetts courts interpreted its bill of rights as having abolished slavery, demonstrating that Puritan New England was still on the cutting edge of the debate on what constitutes a free society. Indeed, Massachusetts held the first constitutional convention, involving representatives from all the towns, of which a two-thirds vote was required to ratify the state constitution. While in other states constitutions were written and then simply promulgated by the legislatures, Massachusetts believed a legitimate government had to be ratified by the people themselves. The Massachusetts Constitution of 1780 declared: "The body politic is formed by a voluntary association of individuals; it is a social compact, by which the whole people covenants with each citizen, and each with the whole people, that all shall be governed by certain laws for the common good." The Federal Constitutional Convention was a virtual copy of the one that took place in Massachusetts.

By the conclusion of the war, the states were functioning as 13 little republics, all formed according to the same basic pattern for an identical purpose: the protection of individual liberties. The enactment of grand schemes for transforming man into a new kind of egalitarian social animal in order to conform to a theory invented by some *philosophe* was a notion that could not have been further from the American mind. The main concern of the Continental Congress after the surrender of Cornwallis at Yorktown was to establish a stable national government that could pay its debts, mediate trade and boundary disputes between the several states and provide for the common defense. The Articles of Confederation was passed on March 1, 1781, and provided the first constitution for the operation of a national government. Actually, it did little more than ratify what the Continental Congress had already been doing since 1776. Its guiding principle was to acknowledge that there was a union, but also, at the same time, the states were to be independent and sovereign. The concept was taken from John Winthrop's New England Confederation, which was an attempt to provide an overall unity of purpose while maintaining diversity in particulars.

Much has been said to denigrate the Articles of Confederation. It certainly had serious problems, as we will see in a moment. Nevertheless, it was the best national frame of government that had ever been devised up until that time, and compiled a record of some remarkable achievements. It established a three-man Treasury Board to work out a system of paying back the tens of thousands of American citizens who had lent the Continental Congress money to finance the war. The new national government also acquired title to the vast territory north of the Ohio River. It then passed the celebrated Northwest Ordinance of 1787, which prohibited slavery in the area, and admitted as equal states regions that attained a population of 60,000.

In a way, this revolutionized the theory of empire-building. Instead of conquering new lands, the United States would make itself so attractive that new territories would voluntarily join the union. Thus, instead of 13 sovereign little republics jealously guarding their borders, the Articles of Confederation, by allowing so much local autonomy, laid the groundwork for making America a unified whole. The result was that the U.S. -though coercing no one - rapidly grew into a world power. The contrast between the growth and prosperity of the United States and the isolated and atomized republics of Latin America, which formed without the benefits of the federalist principle, is striking. For the most part, the new nation prospered under the Artides of Confederation. After the war, people were free to apply themselves steadily to agriculture and business and the economy grew swiftly. Most Americans were well fed, well clothed, and even had leisure time.

But there were difficulties. Under the Articles, the Congress had many responsibilities, but almost no authority to carry them out. It was responsible for Indian affairs and the nation's foreign policy, refereed disputes between the states, coined money, operated the postal service, and managed the Western territories. But the central government had no power to levy taxes directly on the people to finance these operations. It had to rely on requisitions from the state legislatures, which, in turn, had to get the money from the people; this in itself was no easy feat given that the Americans had just fought a war in large part over the tax issue. As a result, the Congress was almost always bankrupt.

On the other hand, the Articles of Confederation never would have been ratified at all had it given the central government the power of taxation, and for good reason. Americans understood the connection between private property and liberty. If the government can take the people's earnings at will, freedom is in jeopardy, which is exactly what was occurring when the colonies were under the authority of the Crown and Parliament. The communists certainly understand this principle, which is why their first step on the road to establishing a tyranny is to seize private property, and then redistribute it according to political loyalties. The Americans saw private ownership as a major bulwark for individual freedom, which is why they were so reluctant to permit the central government to tax it. So suspicious were Americans of central government that it took five years for the Congress to pass the Articles of Confederation, first proposed in 1776, but not ratified until 1781. The Articles of Confederation, which in essence provided for a central government without the power to tax, as inefficient as it was, was the most efficient central government Americans were willing to accept at the time. Americans were not interested in efficient government; they were interested in liberty. Given the growth of the federal government in recent decades and the enormous increase in taxes since the New Deal, the fears of these early Americans were not unfounded. Central government, even in a constitutional democracy, has proven itself very efficient at what it does best: taking people's money.

Nevertheless, most Americans were willing to tolerate a few modest changes. Ensuring a stable legal environment for the free flow of commerce was a major concern. In 1785-86, seven states were issuing their own paper money, which was considered by the legislatures legal tender in payment of debts. Many creditors were outraged because in their view the money was worthless. There were also trade wars developing between the various states, with some enacting tariffs and other trade barriers to protect assorted indigenous industries. In addition, many states had so-called 'stay laws" that made it difficult, sometimes impossible, for creditors in one state to collect debts in another. Prior to the convention in Philadelphia, there was a serious depression in large part due to the difficulty of engaging in interstate business.

In March 1785, George Washington invited the leaders of Virginia and Maryland to his home at Mount Vernon for the purpose of arriving at some agreement over navigation rights to the Potomac River and Chesapeake Bay. This led to a general discussion of commercial problems, upon which Virginia Governor John Tyler the elder, James Madison, and others proposed a national convention on the subject of commerce to meet in Annapolis in September 1786. Invitations went out to all 13 states to send delegates. But only five states bothered to attend, demonstrating the lack of consensus on the need for any additional national authority. Nevertheless, Alexander Hamilton, perhaps the staunchest nationalist of all the framers, used the occasion to propose still another convention which would convene at Philadelphia in order to make the necessary minor changes in the Articles of Confederation to solve its deficiencies.

The catalyst event leading to the famous convention was Shays' Rebellion in rural Massachusetts in the fall of 1786. Massachusetts wound up paying more of the war's expenses than any other state - as much as Virginia, New York, Pennsylvania, and Maryland combined. Because of its Puritan sense of morality, the Massachusetts legislature was determined to pay back every cent of its war debt in real money, not in bogus depreciated paper. "A bargain's a bargain and must be made good," went the old Puritan saying. To do this, taxes were raised, which fell hardest on the rural subsistence farmer, such as Daniel Shays. He and about 3,000 armed men roamed the countryside, prevented the seating of some town courts, and generally frightened the people.

The rebellion was easily crushed by the Massachusetts militia and a volunteer force with minimal bloodshed. But the episode presented the impression that a condition of general anarchy was about to break out - a truly grave threat to private property. There was a sense that government was not doing an adequate job of either maintaining law and order or protecting people's legitimate business interests. Rumors, unfounded, circulated throughout the states that Shays' Rebellion was only the beginning, that indeed a second revolution was being planned. None of this was remotely true, but the fear that it might be true propelled Congress on February 21, 1787, to approve the Madison proposal that states send delegates to Philadelphia "for the sole and express purpose of revising the Articles of Confederation," in order to "render the federal constitution adequate to the exigencies of government." Had the people been aware that the Constitutional Convention that convened in Philadelphia beginning in May 1787 was to produce an entirely new frame of government, there would have been no Constitutional Convention and no national constitution.

CHAPTER TWENTY-ONE

THE PHILADELPHIA MIRACLE

What would transpire in Philadelphia between the spring and fall of 1787 was the construction of the most successful frame of government ever devised in the history of man in terms of ensuring the liberty of the people and perpetuating their prosperity. America's written constitution is the oldest still in use, now covering 50 states instead of the original 13, and 250 million people instead of approximately 3.5 million in 1787.

A good definition of what we mean by *constitution* is "the rules and procedures under which government must operate." The purpose of a constitution is to prevent government from engaging in arbitrary and capricious behavior; to limit as much as possible human discretion; to ensure that the operations of government are uniform and fair; and to take measures that limit the natural urge of those in government to grasp power at the expense of the people the government was set up to protect. The reason the U.S. Constitution is considered so successful is that, to a greater degree than any other governing structure devised previously or since, America's government accomplished these aims.

These men were able to construct such a government because they agreed on the purpose of government. Everyone agreed that any legitimate government must have the consent of the people; but that individuals must be protected by law from the tyranny of the majority. Most importantly, everyone agreed that people by nature are selfish. And because government, of necessity, must be run by men, institutions must be designed to prevent the people in government from using the power at their disposal to benefit themselves at the expense of the country. The role of the central government must therefore be limited, an aim that is stated well in the preamble of the Constitution:

"We the people of the United States, in order to form a more perfect union, establish justice, ensure domestic tranquility, provide for the common defense, promote the general welfare, and secure the blessings of liberty to ourselves and our posterity, do ordain and establish this Constitution for the United States of America." Now the term "welfare" in this context had nothing to do with income redistribution or the modern welfare state, the taking from person A and giving to person B. Promotion of the "general welfare" to the founding fathers meant taking necessary measures to promote the good of the whole, such as protecting the environment and building roads, which benefit everyone. Modern liberals have hijacked the term "welfare" and distorted its original meaning in order to advance egalitarian economic redistribution, an idea that could not have been farther from the thoughts of America's founding fathers, who in fact took extraordinary measures to make sure that private property was protected and that people could enjoy the fruits of their labor.

The framers agreed emphatically with John Locke, who said, "The great chief end, therefore, of men uniting into commonwealths, and putting themselves under government, is the preservation of their property." Most states required that voters own 50 acres of land. It was generally believed that property owners were the most responsible citizens, and would be less likely to vote for radical, leveling measures.

"Property," said Samuel Adams, "is admitted to have an existence even in the savage state of nature. . and if property is necessary for the support of savage life, it is by no means less so in civil society. The utopian schemes of leveling, and a community of goods, are as visionary and impracticable as those which vest all property in the Crown are arbitrary, despotic, and in our government, unconstitutional."

"Government is instituted to protect property of every sort," said James Madison in 1792, a conviction many framers received directly from the Bible, as John Adams noted. "Property is surely a right of mankind as really as liberty," wrote Adams. "The moment the idea is admitted into society that property is not as sacred as the laws of God and there is not a force of law and public justice to protect it, anarchy and tyranny commence. If THOU SHALT NOT COVET, and THOU SHALT NOT STEAL, were not commandments of Heaven, they must be made inviolable precepts of every society before it can be made civilized or made free." A crucial tenet of political philosophy surrounding the creation of the American Republic, in other words, was the right to enjoy the rewards of one's own exertions; private ownership of property was considered a God-given right, inalienable and eternal. Any government that violated this right, in the view of the founding fathers, was tyrannical, despotic, evil, and therefore illegitimate. Revolt against such a regime would be justified.

The great problem of government has always been that man, with his fallen nature, must run it, and that too many men seek office in order to use the powers of the state to further their own ambitions. This appeared to be happening in the local and state governments, which were more interested in their own interests than the good of the union, under the Articles of Con federation, which is one reason the Philadelphia convention was called. "We have probably," wrote Washington, "had too good an opinion of human nature in forming our confederation." "Take mankind in general," said Hamilton, "they are vicious."

A central assumption of America's founders was original sin, meaning the corruption of man's character. Self-interest, they saw, was one of the most powerful of all human motives. If properly channeled, the desire to improve one's condition can lead to tremendous accomplishments and lift the entire community. But government, because it is in the hands of men, has the same motive. It addresses its own aims first, which usually is the accumulation of wealth and power for itself. Moreover, government, by its nature, has no qualms about sacrificing the interests of the weak and isolated individual for its own aggrandizement.

In the minds of the framers, politics was nothing more than the perpetual struggle between the passions of those in power and the rights of the people. As Thomas Gordon put it in *Cato's Letters* an influential work of the period, "Whatever is good for the people is bad for the governors." The nature of power, wrote one 18th-century American poet, is that "if at first it meets with no control [it] creeps by degrees and quickly subdues the whole."

Until the founding of the United States, power had always emerged victorious over freedom. Individual liberty directly challenges the domain of authority. It is, therefore, not in government's interest to permit freedom to flourish. Moreover, restricting choice is what government is supposed to do. Government acts as umpire, regulator, jailer, war-maker, and, sometimes, executioner. Its function is to force people to do things for which they would not otherwise volunteer, such as pay taxes, or stand in front of a firing squad. The trick is to prevent government from compelling people to do these things illegitimately. Virtually all 18th-century Americans believed that individuals have inalienable rights to life, liberty, and the protection of property, and that it is government's responsibility to protect these rights. But it is the very essence of government to take away all three. More importantly, it is in government's interest to do so.

Thus, government, because it is the sole agent in society legally entrusted to wield force, is extremely dangerous to liberty. The dilemma faced by the political scientist, therefore, is as follows. a) power is the enemy of liberty; b) but power, as wielded by a human authority, is required to preserve freedom from attacks by society's malefactors: mainly criminals and foreign aggressors. Hence, government is a necessary evil. That government is an evil, however, the framers of the U.S. Constitution never doubted.

It is one of the prices we pay for sin. How to limit this necessary evil called government, while maintaining its legitimate authority, is the problem. James Madison, the great political architect, stated in *Federalist* 51 that in the structure of government "ambition must be made to counteract ambition. The interest of man must be connected with the constitutional rights of the place. It may be a reflection on human nature that such devices should be necessary to control the abuses of government. But what is government but the greatest of all reflections of human nature? If men were angels, no government would be necessary. If angels were to govern men, neither internal nor external controls on government would be necessary."

The framers, in other words, had a Christian under standing of human nature. More accurately, they had a Puritan understanding. No people were more conscious than the Puritans and their descendants of the unalterable reality of man's continuous disobedience to God: "There is no reason to believe the one much honester than the other," wrote John Adams. "They are all of the same clay; their minds and bodies are alike. . . as to usurping others' rights, they are all . . . equally guilty when unlimited in power . . . The people, when they have been unchecked, have been as unjust, tyrannical, brutal, barbarous, and cruel as any king or senate possessed of uncontrolled power. The majority has eternally, without one exception, usurped the rights of the minority." Even democracy, in other words, will not of itself mitigate the problem of sin. For this is a fallen world, and nothing that could be accomplished at Philadelphia would change this truth. As John Adams wrote: "Cold will still freeze, the fire will never cease to burn; disease and vice will continue to disorder and death to terrify mankind."

Whatever they accomplished at Philadelphia, the framers recognized that it would not be a panacea. They had no utopian aspirations, no illusions that they were creating heaven on earth. Salvation, they believed, lay on the other side of the grave. Human nature would be changed there, not here. Other revolutions, such as the French and the Russian, attempted to create a new man, believing that corruptions in man's nature were created by corrupt institutions. Clear away the institutions, the French and the Marxists believed, and man's natural virtue would shine. How wrong they were, and how right America's founders were to seek very limited objectives with their revolution. The American political architects had no illusions that their government would be virtuous. They had no aspirations to purge evil from man's heart, because they knew this to be impossible. The major reason the U.S. Constitution has been so successful is that the aims of the framers were so modest. They sought merely to mitigate the evils that flow from bad govern ment by checking its natural proclivity to plunder wealth and usurp the rights of the people it was established to protect.

The history of constitution-making in America can best be summed up as a litany of "thou shalt nots." Government shall not prohibit the free exercise of religion and expression; government shall not take away people's gnns; government shall not arbitrarily seize property; government shall not enter people's homes without just cause; government shall not deny the ac cused a trial without a jury of his peers. In fact, about all that government is permitted to do, according to the traditional American view of a just social order, is to defend the nation against external and internal threats to the lives, liberties, and property of law-abiding people. The major reason the convention in Philadelphia went so smoothly was that everyone had this understanding of government's very limited role. The debate, then, centered on exactly how to best arrange the institutions of government so that it could carry out these basic functions without threatening the God-given rights of individuals.

The Governor of Virginia, Edmund Randolph, a convention delegate, was the first to propose formally that the Articles of Confederation be scrapped altogether and that a new plan for a union be instituted. Randolph put forward what became known as the Virginia Plan, which was largely the work of James

Madison. The new scheme involved adding executive and judiciary branches to the already existing Congress and then dividing Congress into two legislative bodies. The lower branch would be elected by a popular vote, the upper branch chosen by the lower House from nominees of the state legislatures. The latter provision was changed in committee to have the upper House of Congress selected by the state legislatures on the grounds that it would be unwise to give the lower House so much power over the composition of the Senate. Representation in both houses of Congress would be apportioned according to the population -and thus was a change from the Articles of Confederation in which each state had an equal vote. The Virginia Plan was also known as the Large States Plan, because it shifted the balance of power dramatically toward the large states.

The small states, however, objected. William Patterson of New Jersey presented a proposal-the New Jersey Plan-to keep the basic unicameral structure of the Continental Congress, and to add a judiciary and an executive (with no power to veto) to conduct foreign policy with greater dispatch and singularity of purpose. Congress was clearly incapable of administering military and diplomatic actions with efficiency - as was proven during the Revolutionary War. It can be fairly said that America was able to win the war against Britain despite, not because of, the actions of the Continental Congress. George Washington often made unilateral decisions without consulting Congress; had he not done so, the American cause would have been lost very early. We have seen in our own day the problems that can occur when members of Congress act as 535 Secretaries of State, traveling around the world negotiating with foreign powers, often sending signals that contradict the President's policy. Virtually everyone agreed that an executive was needed to conduct foreign affairs, which is why they called him the Commander in Chief.

The Convention, however, was deadlocked-not over basic political philosophy, but over the structure of the federal power. All agreed that the Articles of Confederation was inadequate to the purposes of sound and stable government, and at the very least needed modification. Support for the new government by both large and small states was required if ever the new constitution was to become a reality. But the conflict between the large and small states over the issue of representation in the Congress seemed irreconcilable. The mood of the Convention became ugly, and the Convention was on the verge of breaking up. On June 28, Benjamin Franklin made his famous speech on the need for each day's session to be opened with prayer. He believed that only God's Spirit could enable the delegates to resolve their differences.

"In the beginning of the contest with Great Britain, when we were sensible of danger," said Franklin, "we had daily prayers in this room for Divine protection. Our prayers, Sir, were heard, and they were graciously answered. All of us who were engaged in the struggle must have observed frequent instances of a superintending Providence in our favor . . . and have we now forgotten this powerful friend? Or do we no longer need His assistance?

"I have lived, Sir, a long time, and the longer I live, the more convincing proofs I see of this truth: 'that God governs the affairs of man.' And if a sparrow cannot fall to the ground without His notice,[1] is it probable that an empire can rise without His aid?

"We have been assured, Sir, in the Sacred Writings that except the Lord build the house, they labor in vain that build it.[2] I firmly believe this. I also believe that, without His concurring aid, we shall succeed in this political building no better than the builders of Babel; we shall be divided by our little, partial local interests; our projects will be confounded; and we ourselves shall become a reproach and a byword down to future ages. And what is worse, mankind may hereafter, from this unfortunate instance, despair of establishing government by human wisdom and leave it to chance, war or conquest.

"I therefore beg leave to move that, henceforth, prayers imploring the assistance of Heaven and its blessings on our deliberation be held in this assembly every morning before we proceed with our business."

After some discussion, Franklin's motion for prayer was rejected - but not because the delegates disagreed with his message. They did not want to present the public with the impression that the Convention was in desperate disarray. Moreover, they did not want to introduce a sectarian controversy over whether the chaplain saying the prayer would be Episcopal, Presbyterian, Congregationalist, Baptist, Methodist, or from some other Protestant sect. In addition, there were no funds in the treasury with which to pay a chaplain. But Franklin's words must have pierced some influential hearts, as local interests began to give way to the welfare of the whole, and disagreements that before seemed major appeared to dissolve into minor dif ferences. An atmosphere of reconciliation appeared to descend over the convention hall. Roger Sherman of Connecticut then introduced his momentous proposal, known as the Connecticut Compromise.

Sherman's solution to the "large-state, small-state conflict" was actually rather simple. The small states would have an equal vote in the Senate. That is, each state would have two senators. But representation in the House of Representatives would be apportioned according to population. The House of Representatives would be close to the people, elected directly every two years. The Senate, however, would be more detached from the momentary urges of the electorate, serving terms of six years. They would also be more statesmen-like, as they would be selected, not by the people directly, but by their state legislatures, which were more capable of identifying leaders of distinction. Upon Franklin's suggestion, the House, as part of the compromise, would have the authority to originate all money bills. The Senate would have the power to either accept or reject such money bills.

There would also be an executive, whose main function was to conduct foreign policy and execute the laws of the land. He would serve four-year terms and be the only public official elected by all the American people. In those days, the logistics of conducting a national election were uncertain, and so the Electoral College was instituted. In theory, the states would choose representatives, "electors," for the special purpose of electing a President. This particular feature never worked very well, in part because the framers never anticipated the rise of the two party system. Though, technically, the President is still chosen by the Electoral College, in practice he is elected by the people. The President was expected to report to Congress periodically on the state of the union. His role in the lawmaking process was mainly advisory. That is, he could recommend but not initiate legislation. He could, however, veto a bill, a veto which, in turn, could be overridden by a two-thirds vote in Congress. After a law was passed, it could then be subject to review by the Supreme Court. Only the Chief Justice is explicitly provided for in the Constitution. The number of associate justices appointed was left up to Congress.

The framers, quite clearly, wanted to make it very difficult for the central government to pass laws affecting domestic life. Domestic legislation was to be left chiefly to the states. The main responsibilities of the federal government were to be national defense, which is why such broad authority in this area was given to the Commander in Chief, and the area of commerce. But even in trade, the federal government's main duty was a negative one: to knock down state laws that inhibited interstate economic activity such as tariffs, "stay laws," and laws that impair the obligation of contracts. The states would also be prohibited from issuing their own money. The federal government would have sole authority over the currency. In other words, the framers intended to create a stable commercial environment to permit the flowering of a *laissez-faire* capitalist system, unimpeded by either local or national government interference. "Thou shalt not covet" and "thou shalt not steal" were biblical principles that also applied to governments.

Perhaps the most important provision in the Constitution was the last one, requiring that only nine states approve the document. The Artides of Confederation stipulated unanimous approval on the part of the states for even an amendment to pass. Had ratification required all 13 states, there could have been no new government. After the details of the Constitution were worked out in committee, a final draft, penned largely by Gouverneur Morris of New York, was presented to the Convention.

Benjamin Franklin was amazed that a frame of government that came about from so many compromises could have been so good: "It will astonish our enemies who are waiting with confidence to hear that our councils are confounded . . . Thus I consent, Sir, to this constitution because I expect no better, and because I am not sure that it is not the best."

Still, the Constitution could only muster 39 signatures of 55 delegates when it was presented on September 17,1787. Many of the delegates had long since departed Philadelphia in disgust. Even revered heroes of the revolution such as Samuel Adams, John Hancock, Patrick Henry, and Richard Henry Lee were among the opponents. Had not America fought a bloody war, almost a decade in duration, to free itself from the evils of central government? To many, this seemed a good point. In fact, if a Gallup Poll had been taken at that time, there is no doubt that the Constitution would have failed to pass. This new government "squints toward monarchy," remarked Hancock.

But the Federalists, those who favored the new government, were well organized. James Madison and Alexander Hamilton immediately launched a massive campaign to educate the nation on the virtues of the Constitution. Samuel Adams' support was eventually won after he was assured that an amendment would be attached stating explicitly that all powers not specifically granted to the federal government would be reserved to the states. In Virginia and New York, however, the chances for ratification appeared remote. Without these two major states, the Constitution was a dead letter. Madison, Hamilton, and New York's John Jay, wrote a series of 85 essays in defense of the Constitution that were published regularly in newspapers throughout the country under the name of *Publiuis*. Though designed principally to influence the contest over ratification in New York, these articles have since been collected and published in many languages. Commonly called *The Federalist Papers,* this collection is considered one of the seminal works of political philosophy. It convinced George Washington who, after reading it, said, "It is clear to my conception that no government before introduced among mankind ever contained so many checks and such efficacious restraints to prevent it from degenerating into any species of oppression."

The anti-Federalists had no such document and no uniform view as to what was wrong with the Constitution. For example, some Southerners opposed the Constitution on the grounds that it was hostile to the institution of slavery. George Mason, however, opposed it for the opposite reason - that its provision for the gradual phasing out of slavery provided too much protection for the abominable tradition, and thus made the new government a moral travesty.

The major apprehension, though, was caused by the absence of a bill of rights. Explicit enumeration of individual rights had been an important feature of free government since *Magna Carta* was signed in 1215, with the English Bill of Rights of 1689, and the bills of rights attached to most state constitutions serving as more recent models. There was no guarantee of such basic rights as a free press, freedom of religion, trial by jury, and no explicit protection against unreasonable searches and seizures. Alexander Hamilton, and other advocates of the Constitution, pointed out that a bill of rights was unnecessary, since the proposed federal government had no authority to do that which was not specifically authorized in the charter. To list specific rights, the Federalists believed, was dangerous because it would imply that rights not listed were not protected.

A number of states were persuaded. But it soon became clear that the necessary nine, including Virginia and New York, would not pass the Constitution until a bill of rights was promised.

The ninth state, New Hampshire, ratified on June 21, 1788. Virginia joined the union on June 25 and New York followed on July 26. North Carolina and Rhode Island, the last hold-outs, were then faced with a choice. Either they could declare themselves independent republics, small, isolated, and of little consequence, such as the Latin American countries; or they could join the union. North Carolina joined on November 21, 1789. Rhode Island, a maverick colony since the days of Roger Williams, held out until May 29, 1790, when it became convinced that the benefits of union outweighed the threat to liberty. Even then, the vote for ratification in Rhode Island was only 34 in favor and 32 opposed. Passage of the U.S. Constitution was a remarkable achievement. A century later, the great British Prime Minister William Gladstone called it "the most wonderful work ever struck off at a given time by the brain and purpose of man." George Washington concluded that "the event is the hand of God."

The most important man in this process was George Washington. He had resolved to take no active part in the debate, believing that it would have been improper for him to do so, given that he was chairman of the Convention. But his sober presence, his noble demeanor, and the fact that everyone knew that he would certainly be the nation's first President were decisive factors in passage. A mere nod from Washington in favor of the new government was enough to convince most people. The sentiments expressed by Luther Martin from Maryland were representative: "The name of Washington is far above my praise! I would to Heaven that on this occasion one more wreath had been added to the number of those which are twined around his amiable brow - that those with which it is already surrounded may flourish with immortal verdure, not wither or fade till time shall be no more, is my fervent prayer!" "Be assured," wrote James Monroe in a letter to Thomas Jefferson, still in France, Washington's "influence carried this government."

* * *

In making his case for rebellion against British rule, John Dickinson, author of "The Declaration of the Causes and Necessity of Taking Up Arms" (July 1775), stated that "those who are taxed without their own consent expressed by themselves or their representatives are *slaves.*" So sensitive were Americans to an encroachment on their liberties that they drew the line against arbitrary British rule over the issue of a tax on tea. But did not the same principle apply to the black plantation worker? The greatest blight on the American achievement was without a doubt toleration of chattel slavery. It violated every principle of liberty and Christianity for which they had fought. The Bible commands: "Loosen the bonds of wickedness,... undo the bands of the yoke, and.. . let the oppressed go free" (Isaiah 58:6).

There was plenty of opposition to the trading of men on the auction block. James Otis, for example, in a famous statement, said that all men are "by the law of nature free born." "Does it follow that 'tis right to enslave a man because he is black? Will short curled hair like wool instead of Christian hair, as it is called by those whose hearts are hard as the nether millstone, help the argument? Can any logical inference in favor of slavery be drawn from a flat nose, a long or short face?" Otis went on to call slavery "the most shocking violation of the law of nature," which "has a direct tendency to diminish the idea of the inestimable value of liberty, and makes every dealer in it a petty tyrant." So corrupting was this heinous tradition, Otis concluded, that "those who every day barter away other men's liberty will soon care little for their own."

Among the most ardent opponents of slavery were ministers, particularly the Puritan and revivalist preachers. Throughout American history, from George Washington's time to Martin Luther King's, churches have played the dominant role in fighting for the civil liberties of under-represented people. Sometimes their efforts have been misdirected, but the Christian impulse in America has always been to reach out and include those who have been excluded from the protections and benefits of civil society. The Reverend Samuel Cooke argued in his Massachusetts election-day sermon in 1770 that, by tolerating this evil, "We, the patrons of liberty, have dishonored the Christian name, and degraded human nature nearly to a level with the beasts that perish." The Baptist preacher John Allen was even more shrill, calling slavery a violation of God's laws: "Blush ye pretended votaries for freedom! ye trifling Patriots! who are making a vain parade of being advocates for the liberties of mankind, who are thus making a mockery of your profession by trampling on the sacred natural rights and privileges of Africans."

In his pamphlet, *A Dialogue Concerning the Slavery of Africans: Shewing It To Be the Duty and Interest of the American Colonies To Eniancipate All the African Slaves,* the preacher and theologian Samuel Hopkins systematically destroyed all the argnments rationalizing slavery. Hopkins, a student of Jonathan Edwards, rejected as absurd the notion that slavery was useful for the purpose of bringing the Gospel to the Negroes, who have "never forfeited their liberty or given anyone the right to enslave and sell them." What sort of "gospel" message is being conveyed when people are enslaved because of the color of their skin? The Declaration of Independence says *"all* men are created equal [emphasis added]," and "they are endowed by their Creator with certain unalienable rights." "Oh, the shocking, the intolerable inconsistence!" said Hopkins.

By the time of the American Revolution, Americans were well aware that toleration of slavery undermined their own struggle for freedom. But recognizing an evil is a far easier task than abolishing it, because once we permit a corruption to enter the social fabric, its tendency is to prey on human weakness, and to fester and grow. Indeed, this is a pretty good description of how sin operates on the human heart.

Slavery in colonial Virginia seemed as natural as the setting sun. The entire tobacco economy revolved around it, and most Virginians by revolutionary times knew no other life. The Bible tells us that to persist in a sin will inevitably harden the human heart to that particular sin. Often we then attempt to rationalize sin as right and good. This is why it is so important to attack it at the beginning-as one would a drug addiction-before it becomes unmanageable, and eventually dominates one's life and character. The tradition of slave-owning was so ingrained in Southern culture that many people who were noble in most other respects were blind to the moral travesty in which they were engaged. George Washington, for example, owned about 300 slaves, and thought little of it until he became directly involved in the struggle against the British for his own freedom. At that point, black slavery to him suddenly became the most graphic illustration of what the loss of liberty can mean for a people.

The entire point of the American Revolution, after all, was to prove to the world that kings and aristocracies were not needed and that people were perfectly capable of ruling themselves. "I clearly foresee," wrote Washington, "that nothing but the rooting out of slavery can perpetuate the existence of our union by consolidating it in a common bond of principle." And shortly before he became President, he told a friend of his own uneasiness in practicing slave ownership: "The unfortunate condition of the persons whose labors I in part employed has been the only unavoidable subject of regret." He acknowledged how his participation in this lamentable tradition must indeed "be displeasing to the justice of the Creator."

But disentangling himself from Virginia's past was problematical. Would it really be humane to suddenly set adrift someone who had been dependent all his life on the plantation owner for every necessity? What might become of the freed slave's family, his children? Suppose they were incapable of supporting themselves? Washington knew quite well that the psychology of slavery was very different from the psychology of freedom. A plantation slave had no need to learn skills of self-reliance, entrepreneurship, and no means of cultivating the competitive instinct so vital for survival.

Washington was much beloved by his black workers. He

fed them well, and encouraged them to marry and build families. He provided their education and made sure they were well instructed in the Gospel. If Washington had permitted his qualms about slave-owning to circulate, panic on a massive scale would have broken out among his slaves over the prospect of being turned off the land. What would they do, and where would they go? It was much easier, in other words, to proclaim noble principles than to actually carry them out.

In addition, half the slaves working on Washington's plantation belonged to the Custis estate; he had no legal authority, therefore, to release them. There had been many marriages between Custis slaves and Washington slaves. To free only his half would tear families apart. So the institutional and humanitarian barriers to Washington releasing his slaves were enormous.

Nevertheless, he was determined to set them free, and laid out a plan to do so involving great personal expense. In order not to disrupt personal and familial ties, Washington resolved not to evict anyone from the property and to pay regular working wages to any former slave who decided to stay. Children would not be released until they were of age, and would continue to receive food, clothing, shelter, and education. In practical terms, Washington became their adopted father. Thus the cost he incurred to cleanse his estate of this shameful blight was truly staggering. Washington died before his program was carried out, but it was carried out. In fact, his estate paid wages, benifits, and pensions to former slave families and their progeny until as late as 1833.

By the time of the Constitutional Convention, slavery, in the eyes of the vast majority of Americans, was a morally bankrupt institution; but its proponents painted vivid pictures of how its elimination would cause the economic collapse of the South. Abolition of slavery, said one Carolinian, would "complete the ruin of many American provinces, as well as the West Indian islands." During the Convention, Charles Pickney and John Rutledge argued that abolition was utopian and impractical. But George Mason of Virginia disagreed: "Every master is born a petty tyrant," he said. "They bring the judgment of Heaven upon a country. As nations cannot be rewarded or punished in the next world, they must be in this. By an inevitable chain of causes and effects, Providence punishes national sins by national calamities."

Many believe that the Civil War was exactly the national calamity of which Mason spoke. If the South as a whole had followed Washington's example and paid the necessary price to forever eliminate from American soil this loathsome evil of pagan origin, 600,000 lives could have been spared; the sad and tragic war between the states probably never would have occurred.3 As the Reverend Stephen Hopkins had warned in his pamphlet on the issue, America is subject to divine justice, and for this national sin God would withdraw His protection and "punish us seven times more."

The Constitution included one measure intended to weaken slavery over time. The importation of slaves would be prohibited after 1808. It was a feeble provision, but if the opponents of slavery had insisted on more, the Constitution would have died in the Southern state legislatures. James Madison often acknowledged that the Convention's failure to deal immediately and completely with slavery was its most serious shortcoming. "The whole Bible is against slavery," he said. But he also understood that in a fallen world all constitutions will be imperfect, and that this constitution was far better than no constitution at all. He was also confident that once the foundations of a free society were established, its benefits could be expanded and others could be enfranchised into the political process over time. Madison knew that freedom had the power of religious conviction behind it, and predicted that once it took root in the minds of the people, it would overwhelm pagan and feudal practices that impeded its progress. Not long after black Americans were freed from human bondage, women began demanding the vote; and their logic for doing so was irrefutable. America was destined not to be a land for the privileged, but a land of opportunity.

* * *

George Washington was elected unanimously to be President of the United States. He had no desire for the office. But everyone agreed, Federalist and anti-Federalist, Southerner and Northerner, that he was the only man suited to lead the new nation. Without his strong presence, the infant union was probably doomed. What was the Constitution, anyway, but a scrap of paper? As Christ had given Peter his commission to establish His church, so Congress commissioned Washington to give legitimacy to the new government. Reluctantly, he accepted the call, but solely out of patriotic obligation. "My movement to the chair of government," he wrote, "will be accompanied by feelings not unlike those of a culprit who is going to the place of his execution." Named the "Father of his Country," he would rear America from infancy to maturity, and impress on the hearts and minds of the people that the Constitution is all but sacred law.

He arrived in New York, the capital, in time to be inaugurated on April 30, 1789. Placing his hand on a Bible, he took the oath of office, and then from the balcony of Federal Hall, before cheering throngs and much fanfare, he made very plain his views on the source of all legitimate authority.

"It would be peculiarly improper to omit, in this official act, my fervent supplication to that Almighty Being, who rules over the universe, who presides in the council of nations, and whose providential aid can supply every human defect, that His benediction may consecrate to the liberties and happiness of the people of the United States . . . Every step by which they have advanced seems to have been distinguished by some providential agency," he said. "We ought to be no less persuaded that the propitious smiles of Heaven can never be expected on a nation that disregards the eternal rules of order and right, which Heaven itself has ordained."

---

3. More died in the Civil War than all other American wars combined.

CHAPTER TWENTY-TWO

THE TRUE THOMAS JEFFERSON

The adoption of the U.S. Constitution in 1788 represented a victory for Protestant and Whig ideals. For almost two centuries Whigs and dissenting Protestants had been partners in the same cause. In fact, the Whig movement in politics was little more than the application of Protestant religious principles to political science. Both had the same conception of government's limited role and often had overlapping membership. That is, Whigs tended to be dissenting Protestants; and dissenting Protestants tended to be Whigs.

America at the end of the 18th century was overwhelmingly Protestant, and of the dissident variety. Though precise figures on church membership are not available, we do have numbers on church bodies. In 1775 there were 668 Congregational churches; 588 Presbyterian; 494 Baptist; 310 Quaker; 159 German Reformed; 150 Lutheran; 65 Methodist; 31 Moravian; 27 Congregational-Separatist; 24 Dunker; and 16 Mennonite churches. The Anglican Church had 495 congregations, making it a decided minority in America at the time of the revolution. About 75 percent of all Americans belonged to churches of Puritan extraction. When dissenting Protestants and Anglicans are combined, we find a religious composition in America that was 98.4 percent Protestant, 1.4 percent Roman Catholic, and three-twentieths of one percent Jewish.

This is important, because the design of a political order at root is a religious issue, contingent on certain assumptions about the origin and nature of man; the kind of God to whom we will be held accountable; how we order our values; our conception of rights and obligations; and how we are to treat our neighbors either in person or through the instrument of the state. Certainly religion is a personal matter; but it has deep social and political implications. Every social order rests on certain religious assumptions, sometimes explicitly and sometimes implicitly.

We don't see many explicit religious or philosophical references in the Constitution, as we do in the Declaration of Independence; but that is because these documents serve different purposes. The Declaration was a general statement of political philosophy, a creed of faith if you will, about the origin of our liberties: "We hold these truths to be self-evident, that all men are created equal, that they are endowed by their Creator with certain unalienable rights . . . " The U.S. Constitution contains no such lofty rhetoric because it is purely functional - a device for the ordering of government and defining its responsibilities. It is a secular document because government in a free society is almost by definition a secular institution. Its purpose is purely mechanical, to enforce laws, provide for the common defense, and serve as a referee in disputes. But the Constitution, as it must, also contains many assumptions, religious in origin, about the nature of man and of human institutions. It is significant that the word "culture" comes from the word "cult," which *Webster's Dictionary* defines as "a system of religious beliefs." Culture is really little more than an expression of a people's religious tradition. This was certainly the case in early America. John Jay in *Federalist* 2 described America as he saw it in 1787:

"With equal pleasure I have as often taken notice that Providence has been pleased to give this one connected country to one united people - a people descended from the same ancestors, speaking the same language, professing the same religion, attached to the same principles of government, very similar in their manners and customs, and who, by their joint counsels, arms, and efforts, fighting side by side throughout a long and bloody war, have nobly established their general liberty and in dependence. This country and this people seem to have been made for each other, and it appears as if it were the design of Providence that an inheritance so proper and convenient for a band of brethren, united to each other by the strongest ties, should never be split into a number of unsocial, jealous, and alien sovereiguties. Similar sentiments have hitherto prevailed among all orders and denominations of men among us. To all general purposes we have uniformly been one people."

Contrary to popular conception, deist beliefs played almost no role in America's founding. Deism is the idea that God does exist and created the universe, but that He is remote from human affairs. Thomas Jefferson wavered between Christian and deistic beliefs, and his views on Christianity are often cited by historians attempting to portray America's founders as humanist rationalists, or at least as theological liberals. But, according to Harvard historian Perry Miller (a fair-minded atheist), "European deism was an exotic plant in America, which never struck roots in American soil." And an English traveler in America made the following observations in 1822-23: "Instances of openly avowed deisni are rare. Persons who hold deistic opinions generally either keep them to themselves, or veil them under the garb of flimsy hypocrisy... In many parts, a man's reputation would be seriously injured if he were to avow himself one," which may have been one reason that Jefferson almost never discussed his own religious views. Timothy Dwight, also writing in 1823, observed that even at this late date European skepticism was almost wholly absent from the American scene: "An universal veneration for the Sabbath, a sacred respect for government, an undoubting belief in Divine revelation, and an unconditional acknowledgement and performance of the common social duties, constituted everywhere a prominent character."

We are fortunate that the American Republic was created at a time when there was such unanimity of opinion on what constitutes good government. The disagreements were over specifics, not fundamentals; means, not ends. There is no longer any such religious or even moral consensus, which is why it would probably be impossible for Americans today to hold a constitutional convention and have any reasonable prospect of producing a charter for government that would not be riddled with internal contradictions and inconsistencies. We can't even agree on the meaning of "religious freedom," as the federal courts have increasingly interpreted the First Amendment to mean "freedom from religion," an idea that is completely counter to what the founders were trying to achieve.

The basic political conflict in American society today is between those who believe God is the ultimate ruler of human affairs and those who think man is the final arbiter of truth. It is no accident that men such as Jerry Falwell and the Catholic Cardinal of New York, John J. O'Connor, are attacked with such irrational virulence by the proponents of so called pluralism, who like to think of themselves as enlightened and rational. Nowhere is this religious or philosophical collision more evident than in the controversy over the relationship between faith and politics, often mislabeled "church and state." The conflict has become so violent precisely because the issue goes straight to the heart of one's belief as to which creed should provide the foundation for the American political order: Judeo-Christian theism, or agnostic civil humanism.

There is no doubt that the majority opinion in America during the late 18th century was that separation of church and state was essential to preserving religious freedom. Americans had just fought a war in large part to free themselves from the shackles of the Anglican Church, which most Americans believed was an apostate church. The Americans saw all men and all human institutions as fallible - an essential Protestant tenet. Hence, for a particular sect to set itself up as the only possible expression of religious truth, and for the state to compel membership, was an abomination of New Testament teaching. Scripture was infallible,

according to the prevailing Protestant view in America during
the founding decades, but institutions and even human understanding of the Scriptures were imperfect, which is why there
were so many Protestant sects. But the fact that there were so
many Christian churches under different names did not bother
most Americans, since most were in agreement on the essential
doctrines of the faith. Americans wanted a government that did
not favor one Christian sect over another. The general feeling
was that competition between the various churches was desirable, tended to breathe fire into the religious life of a nation, and
prevented any one denomination from becoming complacent, comfortable and arrogant, as had the English Church.

The battle for religious freedom in Anglican Virginia between 1776 and 1786 is illustrative. Again, one gets the impression from many histories that disestablishment of the Anglican
Church in Virginia represented a victory for theological liberalism
and was symptomatic of a trend toward religious indifference.
Nothing could be further from the truth. As Jefferson said in his
Autobiography, in Virginia "the majority of our citizens were dissenters," meaning Separatist Protestants and descendants of
Puritanism-Baptists and Congregationalists who were among
the most serious (dogmatic, if you will) about their Christian
beliefs. Indeed, reported Jefferson, "the first republican legislature, which met in 1776, was crowded with petitions to abolish
the spiritual tyranny," by which he meant the Anglican Church.

The "Bill for Establishing Religious Freedom" to disestablish the Anglican Church was penned by Jefferson, proposed by
Madison, and passed the assembly on January 16, 1786. There
was almost no opposition to the bill in the final vote, not because
there was any sentiment in Virginia against Christianity, but because there was steadfast opposition to the legally favored status
of the Anglican Church, which had become a minority sect in
Virginia. According to Jefferson's account, three-quarters of
Virginia's population at the time of the American Revolution was
dissenting Protestant. William Bradford, John Winthrop, Thomas

Hooker, and Jonathan Edwards would have led the dis-establishment movement had they still been alive. Rarely included in most historical accounts of Jefferson's "Bill for Establishing Religious Freedom" is any extensive quotation from the text, because it inconveniently refutes the prevailing thesis that Jefferson intended to move America away from its theistic roots. In fact, his bill justifies itself on Protestant theological principles:

"Whereas Almighty God hath created the mind free; that all attempts to influence it by temporal punishments or burdens, or by civil incapacitations, tend only to beget habits of hypocrisy and meanness, and are a departure from the plan of the Holy Author of our religion, who being Lord both of body and mind, yet chose not to propagate it by coercions on either, as was his Almighty power to do; that impious presumption of legislators and rulers, civil as well as ecclesiastical, who being themselves but fallible and uninspired men, have assumed dominion over the faith of others, setting up their own opinions and modes of thinking as the only true and infallible, and as such endeavoring to impose them on others, hath established and maintained false religions over the greatest part of the world, and through all time; that to compel a man to furnish contributions of money for the propagation of opinions which he disbelieves, is both sinful and tyrannical; that even the forcing of him to support this or that teacher of his own religious persuasion, is depriving him of the comfortable liberty of giving his contributions to the par ticular pastor, whose morals he would make his pattern, and whose powers he feels most persuasive to righteousness."

William Bradford, Thomas Hooker, and George Whitefield would have agreed completely, and probably could not have stated the case better for disestablishment of the Anglican Church.

The Presbyterian minister Caleb Wallace made a similar case: It is, he said, "impossible for the magistrate to adjudge the right of preference among the various sects that profess the Christian faith without erecting the chair of infallibility, which would lead us back to the Church of Rome . . . Neither can it be made to appear that the Gospel needs any such civil aid. We rather conceive that when our Blessed Savior declares His kingdom is not of this world, He renounces all dependence on state power, and as His weapons are spiritual, and were only designed to have influence on the judgment and heart of man, we are persuaded that if mankind were left in the quiet possession of their inalienable rights and privileges, Christianity, as in the days of the Apostles, would continue to prevail and flourish in the greatest purity, by its own native excellence, and under the all disposing Providence of God . . . Therefore, we ask no ecclesiastical establishments for ourselves."

This was the generally held American perspective: liberty of conscience is good because it is good for Christianity. Most believed that in a free society truth, if allowed to flourish, would prevail. To believe otherwise was to lack faith in the power of God's Word and His saving grace. So freedom of conscience was hardly an Enlightenment or humanist notion; it is a Christian principle applied to politics-though a principle, sadly, that many Christians through the ages have failed to grasp.

No issue in American politics today is prone to more egregious distortion than the entire controversy over separation of church and state. The religion clause of the First Amendment has been interpreted by the courts in recent decades to ban religious expression in the public schools - from prayer to the posting of the Ten Commandments - as an assault on the liberties of nonbelievers. How the posting of the Ten Commandments, or how publicly expressing thanks to our Creator for all He has given us threatens the liberties of anyone, no one has explained satisfactorily. But one would have to have a very warped perspective on American history to believe the Founding Fathers intended or foresaw the federal government being used to bludgeon Christianity.

The religion clause of the First Amendment states: "Con-

gress shall make no law respecting an establishment of religion or prohibiting the free exercise thereof." The clear intent of the First Amendment was to protect a religious people from government, not to protect government from a religious people. The entire Constitution, in fact, is about placing restraints on the federal government, which is only empowered to do a few very specific tasks, none of which involves interfering in the religious lives of the people of the several states. "Congress shall make no law . . ."is the operative phrase. Nothing is said here about the states. Indeed, Massachusetts, New Hampshire, and Connecticut all had officially recognized religious establishments, supported by tax revenue, for more than a half century after the First Amendment was passed. In fact, it was the established churches that were among the most vociferous proponents of the religion clause because they were worried about federal interference in the religious practices of the states. Although it was James Madison who first introduced the amendment, it was the version proposed by Fisher Ames, a Congregationalist from Massachusetts, that was adopted. The Ames version was more explicit than Madison's in protecting state religious establishments from federal interference. He was a staunch defender of the Congregational establishment, which was the official church of Massachusetts.

It should be stressed here that one should never favor any state establishing any church (even if it is one's own church) because this is not a proper government function. A state-supported church structure is a contradiction of a basic Protestant tenet, and is especially anathema to a central principle of Congregationalism that each church was to be a voluntary assembly of "saints"-which is yet more evidence of how even the best ideas and institutions become corrupted under human stewardship. But the fact remains: the First Amendment does not prohibit religious establishments in the states. It only forbids a national religious establishment, as is suggested by the fact that the First Amendment was not applied to the states until 1940. Defenders of liberty should not be excessively alarmed, however, because the religious establishments that existed in America at the start of the 19th century were very mild.

Each town in Massachusetts, for example, was authorized under the state constitution "to make suitable provision," at its own expense, "for the institution of the public worship of God, and for the support and maintenance of public Protestant teachers of piety, religion, and morality." But, under the Massachusetts constitution each citizen could designate the church of his preference to which his tax money could be sent. If no church was indicated, his tax-the equivalent of a tithe-would support the Congregational Church. Almost no one, except a few malcontents, thought this idea terribly oppressive, since most residents of Massachusetts were Protestants and tithing to one church or another. Holders of public office in Massachusetts also had to take an oath that they "believe in the Christian religion and have a firm persuasion of the truth," which certainly would not have excluded many Americans at the time. In fact, 10 of 13 states officially sanctioned a particular religious perspective long after passage of the Constitution, and most states had religious requirements for public office, such as an elected official had to be a Protestant, a Trinitarian, or a believer in God.

To vote in New Hampshire one had to be not only a Christian, but a Protestant, a requirement that was not eliminated for more than a century after the signing of the Declaration of Independence. According to a study on religion and the First Amendment by M. Stanton Evans, only Christians could hold office in Maryland until 1826. Only Protestant Christians could hold office in North Carolina until 1835. In New Jersey, Catholics were explicitly excluded from holding office until 1844. Even Vermont, one of the most theologically liberal states, required holders of public office to take the following oath: "I do believe in one God, the Creator and Governor of the universe, the Rewarder of the good and Punisher of the wicked. And I do acknowledge the Scriptures of the Old and New Testaments to be given by divine inspiration and own and profess the Protestant religion."

These laws, though archaic from a modern perspective, merely reflected widely held sentiment during the founding of the American nation. In a Moslem country we would expect to find a code of laws that stem from an Islamic tradition.

Certainly, religious tests are wrong, because they can be twisted by men in power to suit their own political aims, as indeed such religious tests were used for perverse ends by the English Church and its allies in the British government. Nevertheless, the U.S. Constitution does not prevent the several states from imposing religious tests for public officials; it only bans religious tests for those holding national office.

The Constitution also does not forbid the federal government from promoting religion in a general way, as the Continental Congress had done in 1780 when it authorized, among other measures, the printing of a Bible, so long as it was orthodox. The First Amendment was not supposed to contradict the Northwest Ordinance, first passed in 1787 and reenacted in 1789, which set aside federal lands and funds for the building of schools in order to promote "religion, morality and knowledge," such things "being necessary to good government and the happiness of mankind."

Justice Joseph Story was more specific. Appointed to the Supreme Court in 1811 by the father of the Constitution, James Madison, Story is considered one of the foremost authorities on the Constitution and the intent of its framers. In his multivolume classic of American law, *Commentai.ies on the Constitution of the United States,* Story wrote: "The real object of the First Amendment was not to countenance, much less advance, Mohammedanism, or Judaism, or infidelity, by prostrating Christianity; but to exclude all rivalry among Christian sects, and to prevent any national ecclesiastical establishment which should give to a hierarchy the exclusive patronage of the national government. It thus cut off the means of religious persecution (the vice and pest of former ages), and the subversion of the rights of conscience in matters of religion which had been trampled upon almost from the days of the Apostles to the present age. . ."

What could not occur under the American system was the establishment of, say, the Baptist Church as the official faith of the nation. An important objective of the religion clause was to avert disunity among the states, which would have occurred if the national government had favored a particular denomination over all others. The First Amendment was designed to avoid sectarian conflict over control of the government. But it was clear, in the view of Justice Story and virtualy everyone else at the time, that the federal government could be a friend to Christianity in general, and would be expected to be so since Americans were overwhelmingly Christian.

A government "of the people" ought to reflect the values of the people it is to govern, which is why one of the initial acts of the first House of Representatives was to elect a chaplain, the Reverend William Linn. Indeed, the Reverend Linn was paid an annual salary of $500 out of federal funds. James Madison, who originally proposed the First Amendment, sat on the committee recommending that Congress needed a chaplain. Also passed, the day after the First Amendment was adopted, was a national day of "Prayer and Thanksgiving," a holiday we still celebrate. Madison, as President, issued at least four "Thanksgiving Day" proclamations, sample excerpts of which follow: "The Senate and the House of Representatives of the United States have by a joint resolution signified that a day may be observed by the people of the United States with religious solemnity as a day of thanksgiving and of devout acknowledgements of Almighty God for His great goodness manifested in restoring to them the blessings of peace.

"No people ought to feel greater obligations to celebrate the goodness of the Great Disposer of events and of the destiny of nations than the people of the United States. His kind providence originally conducted them to one of the best portions of the dwelling place allotted for the great family of the human race. He protected and cherished them under all the difficulties and trials to which they were exposed in their early days. Under His fostering care their habits, their sentiments, and their pur suits prepared them for a transition in due time to a state of independence and self-government.

"And to the same Divine Author of every good and perfect gift we are indebted for all those privileges and advantages, religious as well as civil, which are so richly enjoyed in this favored land. . ."

Thus James Madison's understanding of the religion clause, which he proposed, in no way whatsoever prevented the federal government from having a general religious perspective. Madison would probably agree with Justice Story, who wrote in his *Commentaries* that "the general if not universal sentiment in America was that Christianity ought to receive encouragement from the state so far as it was not incompatible with the private rights of conscience and the freedom of religious worship. An attempt to level all religions, and to make a matter of state policy to hold all in utter indifference, would have created universal disapprobation, if not universal indignation." The framers clearly believed that religious faith influences, and should influence, the political order.

One should consider liberty to be in grave danger if an American political leader were to announce that he had no religious convictions, or that he drew his morality from some source other than the Bible and the Judeo-Christian tradition. To which god would he then be paying tribute? The answer would have an important bearing on the future of our political system. The Christian faith is, and should be, concerned mainly with the state of the heart, mind, and soul. Ultimately, the kingdom of Christ and the kingdoms of the world are in conflict, as Charles Colson has pointed out so brilliantly in his book, *Kingdoms in Conflict*. But as long as Christians must live in this world, they cannot help but bring their faith to bear on political questions-a fact that the Supreme Court does not seem to understand. Indeed, it seems obvious that the world would be far freer and more humane if Christians were more active than they currently are in the political realm.

There is little point in going extensively into the tedious
and convoluted reasoning behind the Supreme Court's ongoing
project to expunge all references to God from the public domain.
The various cases have been dealt with voluminously in other
books. But it is interesting that the Court says virtually nothing
about the history of the religion clause in handing down its decisions regarding it. The modern Court hangs its entire interpretation on a phrase - "building a wall of separation between
church and state"-contained in a letter by Thomas Jefferson
addressed to the Danbury Connecticut Baptist Association on
January 1, 1802. Jefferson wrote:

"Believing with you that religion is a matter which is solely
between man and God, that he owes account to none other for
his faith or his worship, that the legislative powers of government reaches actions only, and not opinions, I contemplate with
sovereign reverence that an act of the whole American people
which declared that their legislature should make no law
respecting an establishment of religion, or prohibiting the free
exercise thereof,' thus *building a wall of separation between church
and state* [emphasis added]."

Jefferson here was clearly talking about the "whole
American people," meaning the federal government could not
impose a national church, as Jefferson explained later in a letter
to a Presbyterian minister: "Certainly, no power to prescribe any
religious exercise or to assume authority and religious discipline
has been delegated to the general government. It must then rest
with the states as far as it can be in any human authority."

Jefferson did not believe the central government had the
authority to knock down state religious establishments; nor did he
think the central government should be neutral on the question
of religion. In fact, as President he used federal money to build
churches and establish missions for the purpose of bringing the
Gospel to the Indians. What the federal government was prohibited from doing, in Jefferson's view, was prescribing a particular set of religious rites or promoting a particular sect at the

expense of others.

According to Robert L. Cord's *Separation of Church and State,* one of the most thoroughly researched books on this issue, Jefferson would have been aghast if he had thought the First Amendment could be used to undermine the Christian faith, or even if the religion clause could be used to bar the federal government from favoring the Christian religion in a general way over, say, Mohammedanism, atheism, or some other creed completely at odds with America's founding principles. In 1803, according to Cord, Jefferson asked the Senate to ratify a treaty with the Kaskaskia Indians which stipulated the following: "And whereas, the greater part of the said tribe have been baptized and received into the Catholic Church to which they are much attached, the United States will give annually for seven years one hundred dollars towards the support of a priest of that religion, who will engage to perform for the said tribe the duties of his office and also to instruct as many of their children as possible in the rudiments of literature. And the United States will further give the sum of three hundred dollars to assist the said tribe in the erection of a church."

The Catholic Church, Cord points out, was recognized by Jefferson as the legitimate beneficiary of this legislation because it was Catholics who happened to be most involved in educating and ministering to this particular tribe. The bill was passed into law on November 25, 1803. Thus, in Jefferson's view, not only could the federal government, under the Constitution, advance the cause of religion generally; it could do so, as circumstances warranted, by using a particular denomination as its agent, even so unpopular a one as the Catholic Church. Similar projects to educate and convert the Indians were also passed into law with respect to other tribes under the Jefferson presidency. Moreover, Jefferson never expressed opposition to a law passed on June 1, 1796, by the Fourth Congress (prior to his presidency) "regulating the grants of land. . . for the Society of the United Brethren [a church], for the propagating of the Gospel among the Heathen," the point of which was to provide federal resources to this church for the purpose of proselytizing. Indeed, Cord points out, many Presidents, including George Washington, James Monroe, James Madison, John Quincy Adams, Martin van Buren, and Andrew Jackson, also built churches of various denominations with federal money through treaty agreements with the aim of bringing the Gospel to the Indians.

According to J. M. O'Neill, in his book *Religion and Education Under the Constitution,* "By 1896, Congress was appropriating annually over $500,000 in support of sectarian Indian education carried on by religious organizations." The Seventh Congress passed legislation making churches tax exempt, a tradition that continues today, but which is under attack by People for the American Way, the American Civil Liberties Union, and other anti-religious lobbies. President Jefferson, quite clearly, did not believe giving tax exempt status to churches was a violation of the First Amendment, since he signed the provision into law.

Jefferson is frequently cited here because his views are often erroneously used to support complete government neutrality on religious matters-an impossible task given the fact that government is an institution administered by men who presumably think. Also, the Jefferson position, properly understood, is correct. But it is amusing, if not tragic, that the prevailing misinterpretation of the religion clause is wholly based on a distorted analysis of the intentions of a man who was not even present when the First Amendment was proposed, debated, and passed. He was the U.S. Minister to Paris at the time. Moreover, even if Jefferson were present, and even if his views were hostile to Christianity (which is not the case), he would still represent the opinion of only one man. What Jefferson thought of the First Amendment is actually irrelevant from the standpoint of interpreting the law, which he had no hand in shaping. It is extremely frustrating to write histoiy today because so much effort must go toward correcting the countless distortions that have been inserted into accounts of our heritage by militant secularists who twist facts to suit their narrow anti-religious political agendas.

Because of the popular portrait of Jefferson as a radical secularist and enemy of religion, Christians are sometimes inclined to completely dismiss Jefferson. This is a serious mistake. A parenthetical phrase taken out of context in a letter he wrote to Baptist ministers in Danbury, Connecticut, has been used to distort the true Jefferson. Ignored, for example, are Jefferson's Regulations for the University of Virginia which he founded. Written on October 4, 1824, his rules state: "Should the religious sects of this State, or any of them, according to the invitation held out to them, establish within, or adjacent to, the precincts of the University, schools for instruction in the religion of their sect, the students of the University will be free, *and expected to attend religious worship at the establishment of their respective sects,* in the morning, and in time to meet their school in the University at its stated hour" (emphasis added).

Furthermore, Jefferson's rules stipulate: "The students of such religious schools, if they attend any school or University, shall be considered as students of the University, subject to the same regulations, and entitled to the same rights and privileges." Whether or not Jefferson himself was a Christian is open to question. The evidence suggests that he wavered between deism and the New Testament faith. But there is no doubt that he believed religious ideas essential to education and the development of character. "The relations which exist between man and his Maker, and the duties resulting from those relations, are the most interesting and important to every human being, and most incumbent on his study and investigation," he wrote in an October 7, 1822, memorandum clarifying the University's regulations. He, therefore, recommended the establishment of a professional school of "Theology and Ecclesiastical History." He also believed that "profane swearing," meaning deriding that which is "sacred and holy," if not immediately corrected, was grounds for dismissal from the university - which incidentally was financed by tax revenue. If

Jefferson's mind was shaped by the Enlightenment, it was the sober Christian Enlightenment of Locke, Montesquieu, and Blackstone, not the bitter and God-hating doctrines of Rousseau, Diderot, and D'Alembert.

We have seen how Jefferson's and Madison's efforts to disestablish the Anglican Church in Virginia have been egregiously distorted to support strict separation between faith and politics. Usually omitted from the legislative histories penned by radical secularists is Madison's "Bill for Punishing Disturbers of Religious Worship and Sabbath Breakers" - especially interesting because it was presented the same day (October 31, 1785) as Madison's and Jefferson's "Bill for Establishing Religious Freedom." The law providing for the punishment of Sabbath breakers included the following language: "If any person on Sunday shall himself be found laboring at his own or any other trade or calling, or shall employ the apprentices, servants or slaves in labor, or other business, except it be in the ordinary household offices of daily necessity, or other work of necessity or charity, he shall forfeit the sum of ten shillings for every such offense, deeming every apprentice, servant, or slave so employed, and every day he shall be so employed as constituting a distinct offense." Jefferson wrote many of the bills introduced by Madison, and probably drafted this one as well.

Even those alarmed today by the general moral laxity and deterioration of religious life of the nation would probably consider a law punishing Sabbath breakers as symptomatic of fundamentalist zealotry, and placing at peril the civil liberties of all Americans. Madison's proposal, which passed in 1789, went well beyond the usual request by Christians today that they be permitted equal time and equal access to public facilities. If Jefferson did not actually write the Madison bill, which he probably did, there is no evidence that he objected to it, or that he found it in any way contradictory to his view of religious freedom.

Also on the same day that Jefferson and Madison introduced their bill for religious freedom in Virginia, Madison introduced another bill, again probably written by Jefferson, "For Appointing Days of Public Fasting and Thanksgiving," which called for "forfeiting fifty pounds for every failure, not having a reasonable excuse," if such a day was not observed by the local churches. Thus it seems clear that Jefferson's and Madison's views on religious freedom would not involve the Supreme Court mandating that the Ten Commandments be torn off the bulletin boards of public schools; nor require that there be any restrictions on prayer whatsoever. These founding fathers would consider the firing of a teacher for holding a voluntary Bible study for her students after hours in the privacy of her own home - as recently occurred near my home in Fairfax County, Virginia-to be the height of moral confusion.

CHAPTER TWENTY-THREE

WHERE THE LORD IS A STRANGER, SO IS LIBERTY

Men such as Jefferson and Madison would recoil in horror if they could see how their words, ideas, and actions have been so misrepresented to inhibit rather than expand religious freedom; that while the words of the Constitution seem to be intact, they bear little resemblance to the ever-expanding government now in existence. The First Amendment was designed to restrict governmental power, not religious expression. Indeed, if these men could see the enormous expansion of federal power during the post New Deal Age, they might have concluded that the anti-Federalists had a point: specifically, that centralization of authority presented a grave threat to individual liberty and that the Articles of Confederation, even with all its faults, may have been sufficient.

The major problem with the strict separation of church and state position becomes more apparent as the state grows so big and assumes so large a role that the practice of one's religious faith becomes impossible-indeed, illegal-because the private sphere has disappeared. This is the case in the Soviet Union. The Kremlin uses the exact same "separation of church and state" argnment that Justices William Brennan, Thurgood Marshall, and Harry Blackman use in an attempt to completely obliterate the religious life of a nation. Article 124 of the Soviet Constitution states: "In order to ensure to citizens freedom of conscience, the church in the U.S.S.R. is separated from the state, and the school from the church. Freedom of religious worship and freedom of anti-religious propaganda is recognized for all citizens."

This position is identical to that of the American Civil Liberties Union, People for the American Way, and the National Education Association. "It's fine for people to practice their Christian faith so long as they do so in the private sphere," they say. But this becomes difficult and even hazardous when everything is owned and controlled by the state. The Warsaw government also used the separation of church and state argument to justify the removal of all crucifixes from the public schools in Poland. The strict "wall of separation" position then would not be so alarming if the public sector in America were not so pervasive.

Not surprisingly, radical secularists also tend to be statists, believing that government should control education, raise children, run the economy, make it difficult for religious institutions to operate, and impose a secular value-system on a Judeo-Christian people. They know that in a truly free society such causes as abortion on demand, affirmative action for homosexuals, and the expunging of all religious references from text books could not flourish. Like the Soviets, radical secularists make every attempt to avoid a frontal assault on Christianity, which would be unpopular, and they attack it instead on procedural grounds and under the guise of such acceptable notions as "pluralism" and "liberty of conscience." The practical effect of the prevailing interpretation of the First Amendment's religion clause is that the secularization of America has become the law of the land.

All laws are religious in origin. The conception of rights one subscribes to is contingent on the authority to whom one appeals and is, therefore, a religious decision. In a conflict between faiths, we will inevitably see a dispute over what constitutes a right. Jefferson's view, for example, that government should protect the people's right to pursue happiness is very different from the modern conception that government is to guarantee happiness. The right to own private property is incompatible with the state's right to seize it and use it for its own purposes.

Under the doctrine of pure pluralism - to which many secularists say they subscribe-all lifestyles are permitted. Thus, in the end, cannibalism, human sacrifice, group suicide, the Manson Family, polygamy, and kiddie porn would have to be allowed. "Who are we to say what is right and what is wrong?" is the common refrain. Clearly, society cannot long survive if this principle is pushed to its logical conclusion and everyone is free to write his own laws. Thus, we subscribe to pluralism within certain limits. We allow a wide range of behavior, even though we don't always approve of it. But we do not permit all behavior. We do not even allow all so-called "victimless" behavior - such as prostitution, drug addiction, drunkenness, and the like.[1] The reason we don't is that our laws presuppose certain truths. Pure freedom of conscience, then, can never really be tolerated. Government neutrality on matters of religion and morals is a modern myth. We can never escape the question: Whose faith, whose values, whose God undergirds the civil laws of a nation?

A society based on Christian principles provides for pluralism, but with enough restrictions to prevent civilization from degenerating into chaos. The important Christian principle incorporated into the American political order is that God did not create the state in His image, He created man in His image. Nor is man created in the image of the state. It is the individual, not the state, not even society as a whole, that is of primary importance to God, according to the Bible. "Behold, the nations are like a drop from a bucket, and are regarded as a speck of dust on the scales," says the Prophet Isaiah (v.40:15). "All the nations are as nothing before Him, they are regarded by Him as less than nothing and meaningless" (v.40:17). It is the individual, not the state, that is God's main concern.

Paul says in his letter to the Romans (13:4) that government's purpose is to bring "wrath upon the one who practices evil," meaning criminals, foreign invaders and those who present a threat to liberty. This is in fact the only government function condoned by God in the entire New Testament. The major source of conflict throughout history is the tendency of the state to take on the responsibilities of the church, defining dogma, compelling people to submit to authorities with whom they do not agree, and generally penetrating the domain of conscience. Government's responsibilities must always be limited, strictly defined, leaving as little as possible up to the discretion of those in power. This is the intent of our Constitution.

The early churches, significantly, were autonomous, held together by a common faith, but carried out their respective religious duties in various ways. Paul wrote in a different style to the church at Rome than he did to the church of Corinth, because their customs and ways of thinking were different. The early church represented the concept of federalism in action. Christ's church was a voluntary union, a "mystical" body, not held together by man-made constraints. It is a loose confederation of believers who agree to submit to the same authority, Jesus Christ, whose rules often collide with Caesar's.

Important to notice is that Paul's letter to the Romans restricts the state to punishing "wrongdoers" and not wrong thinkers. That is, the government can punish the wrong thinker only if his thoughts drive him to break the law by committing some abominable act. For government to extend its authority beyond its law and order function is extremely dangerous, even when done in the name of Christianity. The punishment of heretics under the Spanish Inquisition was carried out by the state, not the church, and occurred after the state had centralized and consolidated its power, placing the church under its control. The Anglican Church in England was under control of the king and Parliament, and the result was the horrendous persecution of dissenting Christian sects, social disturbance, and civil war.

---

1. We now know that such behavior is not really victimless at all.

Because the God of the Bible is transcendent, man has the freedom of the world, to sin or obey, to serve or rebel against God. But who can turn his back on the state when the Internal Revenue Service knocks on his door? The God of the New Testament exercises oversight, speaks to individuals through Scripture and conscience. But it is strictly up to man to obey. The God of Scripture is very definitely present in human relations; but He coerces no one: "Where two or three have gathered together in My name, there I am in their midst," says Jesus, suggesting the absence of a coercive institutional structure (Matt. 18:20).

Contrast Christ's regime with that of the state. The state is insecure, always suspicious of individual autonomy. It relentlessly seeks to restrict the area of choice. Christ has no such in securities. The state is always unsure of itself because its existence is wholly dependent on man. Without man, there is no state. God, however, is dependent on no one. All creation is dependent on Him. He has no need to crush dissent. He gave man the freedom to choose, His way or man's way, good or evil, death or eternal life. He rules far more with the carrot than the stick. He provides the map, but it is up to man to read it and follow. His regime, properly understood, is a libertarian regime.

In this respect, Jefferson and Madison probably erred by introducing a bill for the punishment of Sabbath breakers, which became Virginia law in 1786. This example serves only to dispel the myth that these men were strict separationists. Whether or not one keeps the Sabbath is a matter of conscience, under the guidance of family, peers, and teachers-who can influence enormously the conduct and thinking of individuals, and who have plenty of means at their disposal to deter unacceptable behavior. Similarly, most Americans today would not have wanted to live in Massachusetts, Connecticut, or New Hampshire under the Congregational Church establishment. These examples function only to illustrate that the framers intended to restrict *federal* and not state authority on religious matters. Jefferson was correct in his effort to disestablish the Anglican Church in Virginia on the grounds that people ought to be free to support and attend the denomination of their choosing- or not to attend at all. Church attendance should not be a government concern, but is a matter between man and Maker.

But Christians today are forced to support, with their tax money, the establishment of another religious faith that stands opposed to everything they believe. The new state church has taken the form of the public school, which is messianic in nature and preaches relentlessly the doctrine that the human intellect and will is the supreme moral authority. Meanwhile, the other major faith in America, Christianity, is outlawed from a major segment of American society, and is under heavy pressure even in the "private sphere," which is becoming less and less private. To tax Christians to support a doctrine that they believe false and evil was called tyranny in George Washington's day.

This principle, it seems, leads inexorably to the position that the federal government has no business involving itself in education. Education cannot avoid transmitting values, beliefs, or religious creeds, whether that creed is Christian or civil humanist in content. For a school to present history, literature, and science outside the context of a certain world-view is impossible. Federal involvement in education, in effect, is no different from establishing a particular church in that it dangerously permits the central government to trespass into the area of mind and conscience.

The conventional wisdom today is that education is a responsibility of the federal government. But this is not the Judeo-Christian view. Moses told his people: "And you shall teach them [God's laws]diligently to your sons and shall talk of them when you sit in your house and when you walk by the way and when you lie down and when you rise up" (Deut. 6:7). Moses said nothing about government's duty to teach Israel's children. Teaching falls principally under the domain of parents. Indeed, this is exactly how education was conducted in the colonies and early America.

Long before public education was formally introduced on

a national scale by Horace Mann and others in the 19th century, Thomas Jefferson commissioned a study, conducted by his friend DuPont de Nemours, on American education in 1800, and discovered a literacy rate of better than 99 percent. Jefferson's report stated: "Not more than four in a thousand are unable to write legibly - even neatly . . . In America, a great number of people read the Bible, and all the people read the newspaper. The fathers read aloud to their children while breakfast is being prepared - a task which occupies the mothers for three-quarters of an hour every morning. And as the newspapers of the United States are filled with all sorts of narratives - comments on matters political, physical, philanthropic; information on agricul ture, the arts, travel, navigation; and also extracts from the best books in America and Europe-they disseminated enormous amounts of information, some of which is helpful to young people, especially when they arrive at an age when the father resigns his place as reader in favor of the child who can best succeed him.

"It is because of this kind of education that the Americans of the United States, without having more great men than other countries, have ihe advantage of having a larger proportion of moderately well-informed men."

At the turn of the century, in other words, Americans did very well without the National Education Association or the U.S. Department of Education, and were in fact far better educated. Tocqueville reported in 1830 in even more glowing terms that "there has never been under the sun a people as enlightened as the population of the United States." Anyone who reads Madison, Hamilton, and Jay in *The Federalist Papers,* or the Lincoln-Douglas debates, will be struck immediately by the depth of ignorance and superficiality to which 20th-century political discourse has plummeted. Though there are other factors contributing to the demise of American learning, federal involvement certainly hasn't helped. Education, at the time of Jefferson, was provided in the home, or by the community under parental oversight. Moreover, if the national government were not involved in education there would be far less controversy over the issue of prayer in the public schools.

Jarring clashes between church and state occur only when the state enters areas where it has no business being. Civil wars break out when government performs duties reserved to church, family, and community-community defined here as people we know personally and with whom we voluntarily associate, not some nebulous idea of a "national community" or the United Nations' "world community." These distinctions are essential. Education cannot escape the teaching of a particular orthodoxy. Orthodoxy is the domain of church, family, and community-not that of a remote Department of Education, Supreme Court, or Congress. State-enforced orthodoxy is extremely dangerous to liberty, even when the state is enforcing pluralism - since pluralism, meaning the phony sort of pluralism as imagined by modern secularists, can never really exist where individuals are free to form their own associations with like-minded people. Jefferson understood this point exactly when he wrote to those Baptist ministers in Danbury, Connecticut, that the First Amendment built "a wall of separation between church and state." Jefferson's intent was to ease the fears of the Baptists who worried that the federal government might attempt to interfere with their religious communities. The point of the letter was to illustrate how the U.S. Constitution, and the religion clause in particular, was supposed to handcuff the central government-not parents, pastors, and teachers.

America has veered sharply from the course charted by such men as William Bradford, John Winthrop, Thomas Hooker, Jonathan Edwards, George Whitefield, Samuel Adams, James Otis, James Madison, Thomas Jefferson, and George Washington. Even the intellectual centers of secular humanism have noticed that America has lost its moral bearings. "What ever happened to ethics?" was a question posed on the cover of *Time* magazine (May 25, 1987), which was alarmed by the number of scandals taking place in all quarters of American public life.

But in the absence of the transcendent God of the Bible, the substitute is not a universal code of conduct, but a myriad of regulations, rules, and laws which we are supposed to think will keep public order. To curb campaign abuses, for example, Congress passes election reform laws, as if this in itself will solve the problem. New rules are proposed to prevent people from working for a foreign government for 10 years after government service. A new law forbids any Pentagon official from taking a job with a defense contractor for two years after leaving government. Congress has an ethics committee, which has become chiefly a vehicle for moral posturing and administering political litmus tests, instead of serving as a watchdog to protect the public from congressional excesses. The Justice Department has an "Ethics Director." The American Hospital Association now hires ethical consultants to help doctors make decisions.

But the result of all this is not the restoration of firm moral standards, or any rekindling of the notion that the life of an individual amounts to anything more than a bundle of urges, sensations, and appetites. Instead, we get a patchwork of burdensome rules and nosy government regulators, whose moral authority is based on nothing, and whose very existence en courages the impression that it is government's responsibility to monitor every decision made by an individual, peer into his soul, and ascertain motives. Traditionally, this has been God's job, not the Security Exchange Commission's. To give this task to a government agency, to some committee, or to an "ethical consultant" is to abdicate responsibility for one's actions, and gives the impression that anything is all right so long as one is not caught (or so long as it's "legal") which is probably one reason we rarely see contrition on the part of public people who are caught in wrongdoing. They believe that to be "discovered" cheating the stockholder, or cheating on one's wife, is merely "unfortunate," and not as potentially having eternal consequences for one's soul.

Others, meanwhile, are put in jail for violating laws they've never heard of, and never could have guessed - perhaps for not keeping adequate tax records for the IRS, or for failing to fill out properly some government form, which was probably produced by an "ethics director." Democratic Congressman Richard Gephardt has proposed making it a violation of the law to close a factory on the grounds that it's hard on the employees. Go out of business and get a couple of years in jail, seems to be the Gephardt idea. Heaven help us if he ever becomes President.

One reason the U.S. Constitution is so brief is that the framers never envisioned a society in which the only people capable of determining whether laws have been broken are lawyers. The colonists believed firmly that common sense, not legal technocrats, ought to determine guilt or innocence, which is why they were so adamant about the right to trial by a jury of one's peers. The concept of the transcendent or "Higher Law" no longer plays a role in American legal theory. The Higher Law principle, so central to the thinking of Jefferson and the American colonists, and upon which the entire history of British and American constitutional law is based, is no longer studied by the overwhelming majority of today's law students. The result is increasing ambiguity in society over what constitutes right and wrong. Under such conditions, freedom cannot long survive.

Even Will and Ariel Durant, both ardent apologists for the secular humanist perspective on history, in their massive work, *The Story of Civilization,* conclude: "Moveover, we shall find it no easy task to mold a natural ethic strong enough to maintain moral restraint and social order without the support of supernatural consolations, hopes and fears." Actually, it is impossible, as the Durants admit: "There is not a significant example in history, before our time, of a society successfully maintaining a moral life without the aid of religion." Their observations are made more powerful by the fact that *The Humanist* magazine presented the Durants with the Humanist Pioneer Award in February 1977.

With the erosion of a nation's religious life, we inevitably find a dissipation of the will. Americans have lost sight of the fact that a price must be paid for freedom. The preservation of liberty sometimes involves personal sacrifice. Americans in the past have believed that there are certain values more precious than life itself, and one of those is freedom.

Ancient Greece ultimately collapsed because the Greek philosophy never provided individuals a rationale for making sacrifices in defense of principle. The perpetuation of the state, or even of the society, was not, in the final analysis, reason enough to lay down one's life. Athens, instead of building up its defenses in preparation for a Macedonian invasion, spent its resources on debauched festivals and games to entertain the public. Aristotle, through logic, arrived at the concept of the "unmoved mover" (God), the causer of all things who Himself is uncaused. But Aristotle's prime mover was impersonal, was not involved in the lives of the people, and provided no motivation for the individual to make sacrifices for his friend, family, or nation. His god offered no hope for eternal life, no notion of rewards and punishments in accordance to one's conduct on earth, no promise of protection, and no sense that God cared one way or another about one's choices in life. Aristotle's metaphysics provided no real answers to the problem of death and was, in the end, unsatisfying.

As a result, James Reichley argues in his book, the average Athenian felt a sense of isolation, rootlessness, and that he was living a life without purpose. Internal demoralization began to set in, an outlook that was embodied in the Greek tragedies. "Alas, poor men, their destiny," Aeschylus wrote. "When all goes well a shadow will overthrow it. If it be unkind, one stroke of a wet sponge wipes the picture out; and that is by far the most unhappy picture of all." In the end, the Greek perspective was one of despair, and the culturally inferior Macedonians were able to overrun Greece in the fourth century B.C.

Ancient Greece imploded into a spiritual abyss before it was defeated militarily, and from this many parallels can be drawn with the West today. The free world is threatened now, not because of lack of resources, but from a spiritual and moral void, which is always accompanied by a corrosion of the will. With religious expression now outlawed from large portions of American public life - in the name of a very distorted civil libertarian creed-can it be long before America goes the way of Greece and Rome? Tocqueville had this to say of those who attack faith in God in the name of pluralism: "When such men as these attack religious beliefs, they obey the dictates of their passions, not their interests. Despotism may be able to do without faith, but freedom cannot. Religion is much more needed in the republic they advocate than in the monarchy they attack, and in democratic republics most of all. How could society escape destruction if, when political ties are relaxed, moral ties are not tightened?" Tocqueville, although he made this observation more than a century ago, could just as easily have been talking to tbe Supreme Court or Norman Lear's People for the American Way. Asked Tocqueville: "What will happen to a people master of itself if it is not subject to God?"

The great task ahead must be to return to first principles, principles upon which America's founders were in overwhelming agreement. For they were firmly convinced that liberty was essential to happiness and prosperity in this world; that constitutional government was essential to liberty; that the preservation of both was contingent on Christian morality informing both voters and leaders; and that Christian morality could not long stand without firm faith in Christ. As Tocqueville wrote: "Liberty regards religion as its companion in all its battles and triumphs, as the cradle of its infancy and the divine source of its claims," which in itself was but an echo of Paul's warning to the Galatians: "It was for freedom that Christ set us free; therefore keep standing firm and do not be subject again to a yoke of slavery" (v.5:1).

SELECTED BIBLIOGRAPHY

Included here is a compilation of major sources. For works that contributed substantial information and analysis shaping the perspective of this author, special mention is given. Also indicated where appropriate, are the specific chapters in *Faith & Freedom* that draw on the titles listed below.

Adams, John. *The Political Writings of John Adams.* Edited by George A. Peek. Indianapolis: 1954.

Ahlstrom, Sidney A. *A Religious History of the American People.* New Haven, Conn.: 1972.

Andrist, Ralph K., ed. *George Washington: A Biography in His Own Words.* 2 vols. New York: 1972. Useful for Chapters 15,18, and 19.

Aristotle. *Politics.* Many editions. 330 B.C. Drawn on for Chapter 20, illustrating the difference between the American and the Greek understanding of a just social order.

Ashley, Maurice Percy. *The English Civil War: A Concise History.* London: 1974.

—. *The Glorious Revolution of 1688.* London: 1966. Provides quotations and narrative information for Chapter 12.

—. *The Greatness of Oliver Cromwell.* London: 1957. A sympathetic portrait of this enigmatic English leader, drawn on for Chapter 11.

Atkinson, James. *Martin Luther and the Birth of Protestantism.* London: 1968.

Bailyn, Bernard. *The Ideological Origins of the American Revolution.* Cambridge, Mass.:1967. A standard interpretive study, which provides material and insights for Cha~ ters 21 and 22.

—. *New England Merchants in the Seventeenth Century.* Cambridge, Mass.: 1955. Provides supporting data and insights into the Puritan work ethic for Chapter 9.

—. ed. *Pamphlets of The American Revolution, 1750-i 776.* Cambridge, Mass.: 1965. A superb collection of the popular political literature of the American Revolution, indispensable for understanding the issues that moved Americans of that time.

Baldwin, Alice M. *The New England Clergy and the American Revolution.* New York: 1928. Investigates the substantial role of the so-called "black regiment" of Protestant clergy in the American War for Independence.

Bancroft, George. *History of the United States.* 10 vols. Boston: 1838. A classic, and untalnted by modern prejudice.

Bass, Archer B. *Protestantism in the United States.* New York: 1929. Provides material supporting the thesis of this book.

Becker, Carl. *The Declaration of Independence.* New York: 1942. A standard Whig interpretation, providing insights for Chapters 1 and 18.

Booloff, Max. *Thomas Jefferson and American Democracy.* London: 1965.

Bonner, Gerald. *St. Augustine of Hippo: Life and Controversies.* London: 1970. A balanced portrait, useful for Chapter 3.

Boorstin, Daniel J. *The Americans: The Colonial Experience.* New York: 1958. One of the best interpretive accounts of the cultural, religious, and geographical forces shaping the early American mind, drawn on for Chapters 10 on Virginia and 13 on Pennsylvania.

—. *The Lost World of Thomas Jefferson.* Boston: 1960.

Bowan, Catherine Drinker. *Miracle at Philadelphia: The Story of the Constitutional Convention, May to September 1787.* Boston: 1966. A fascinating and dramatic narrative, providing dennis for Chapter 21.

Bradford, M. E. *A Better Guide than Reason: Studies in the American Revolution.* La Salle, III.: 1979.

—. *A Worthy Company: Brief Lives of the Framers of the United States Constitution.* Marlborough, N.H.: 1982. A well-written and handy reference, providing materlal for Chapters 15 and 21.

Bradford, William. 'Of Plymouth Plantation." From the original manuscript. Boston: 190L A firsthand account of the Mayflower voyage and settlement at Plymouth, and the primary source for Chapter 5.

Bridenhaugh, Carl. *Mitre and Sceptre: Transatlantic Faiths, Ideas, Personalities and Politics, 1689-1775.*

New York: 1962. An indispensable work on the American struggle *to* prevent England from imposing an Anglican bishop on the colonies.

Bronner, Edwin B. *William Penn's "Holy Experiment',: The Founding of Pennsylvania 1681-1701.* New York: 1962. Provides colorlal material on the Quakers' problems in running a government for Chapter 13.

Brown, Peter R. L. *Augustine of Hippo.* Berkeley, Ca.: 1967. Indispensable for Chapter 3.

Brydon, George M. *Virginia's Mother Church and the Political Conditions Under Which it Grew.* 2 vols. Richmond, V~: 1947-52. Provides important material and insights for Chapter 10.

Buchan, John. *Oliver Cromwell.* London: 1934. A balanced portrait, providing quotations and narrative history for Chapter 11.

Bunyan, John. *Pilgrim's Progress.* Many editions. 1678.

Burke, Edmund. *Reflections on the Revolution in France.* Many editions. 1789. A classic of poiltical philosophy, shaping the thesis of Chapter 20.

—. *Speech on Reconciliation with the Colonies.* Introduction by Jeffrey Hart. Chicago: 1964.

Bushman, Richard L., ed. *The Great Awakening: Documents on the Revival of Religion. 1740-1745.* New York: 1970. Contains useful primary source material drawn on in Chapter 14.

Calder, Angus. *Revolutionary Empire: The Rise of the English-Speaking Empires fom the Fifteenth Century to the 1780s.* New York: 1981. A sweeping narrative of British imperial expansion.

Chabannes, Jacques. *Saint Augustine.* New York: 1962. A standard biography of this troubled saint, providing material for Chapter 3.

Chadwick, Henry. *The Early Church.* London: 1967.

Chadwick, Owen. *The Reformation.* London: 1968.

Chapman, Hester W. *Four Fine Gentlemen.* Lincoln, Neb.: 1977. Contains an excellent short biography of the Earl of Shaftesbury.

Clarke, Rev. S. J. *The Life of James 11.*2 vols. London: 1816.

Cochrane, Charles Morris. *Christianity and Classical Culture.* London: 1939. An important source for Chapter 2.

Cord, Robert L. *Separation of Church and State.* New York: 1982. An excellent study on the true meaning of the religion clause of the First Amendment, providing important material for Chapter 22.

Corwin, Edward S. *The "Higher Law" Background of American Constitutional Law.* Ithaca, New York: 1957. An indispensable study on the origins of American constitutional thought.

Craag, Gerald R. *The Church and the Age of Reason, 1648-1789.* New York: 1960. A good overview of the spiritual and intellectual life of the period, helpliil for Chapter 12.

—. *Puritanism in the Period of Persecution, 1660-1688.* Cambridge, Mass.: 1957. Provides material for Chapter 12.

Cranston, Maurice W. *John Locke: A Biography.* London: 1957. Drawn on for the portrait of Locke in Chapter 12.

Craven, Wesley F. *The Dissolution of the Virginia Company: The Failure of a Colonial Experiment.* Gloucester, Mass.: 1932. Provides valuable material and narrative for Chapter 10.

Davies, Godfrey. *The Restoration of Charles IL* London: 1955. An important work on this peculiar period in Engiish history.

Deane, Herbert A. *The Political and Social Ideas of St. Augustine.* New York: 1963. Provides supporting material for the thesis of Chapter 3.

Dillon, Francis. *The Pilgrims.* Garden City, N.Y.: 1975.

Edwards, Jonathan. *Thoughts on the Revival of Religion in New England.* New York: 1740. A primary source for Chapter 14.

Eidsmoe, John. *Christianity and the Constitution.* Grand Rapids, Mich.: 1987.

—. *God* and *Cacsar.* Westchester, Ill.: 1984.

Firth, Charles H. *Oliver Cromwell and the Rule of the Puritans in England.* London: 1901. An important source for Chapter 11.

Flexner, James Thomas. *George Washington.* 4 vols. Boston: 1965-72. A major source for the portrait of Washington in Chapters 15, 18, and 19.

Fralin, Benjamin. *The Autobiography of Benjamin Franklin.* Many editions. 1791.

Frend, W. H. C. *The Donatist Church: A Movement of Protest in Roman North Africa.* Oxford: 1971. Provides background and details for Chapter 3 on this dissenting Christian movement which was so loathed by St. Augustine.

Gibbon, Edward. *The History of the Decline and Fall of the Roman Empire.* Many editions. 1776-88.

Goldberg, George. *Church, State and the Constitution: The Religion Clause Upside Down.* Washington, D.C.: 1984. A brief, but excellent, account of how modern court rulings have not merely distorted, but reversed the original intent of the First Amendment.

Grant, Robert M. *Augustus* to *Constontine: The Thrust of the Christian Movement Into the Roman World.* New York: 1970. A good overview ofthe period for Chapter 2.

—. *Early Christianity and Society.* New York: 1977.

Haley, K H. D. *The First Earl of Shaftesbury.* Oxford: 1968.

Hall, Thomas Cummings. *The Religious Background of American Culture.* Boston: 1930. An important study of the pervasive inlluence of Puritan ideas on American life and thought. Contributes evidence for the thesis of Chapter 4, which is that the theology of John Wyclitfe laid the foundation for America's culture of dissent.

Hall, Verna N., ed. *The Christian History of the American Revolution.* San Francisoo: 1976.

—. ed. 2 vols. *The Christian History of the Constitution of the United States of America.* San Francisco: 1962 and 1966. An enormously useful compilation of original documents and much ignored historical accounts, of which this book makes extensive use.

Haller, W. *Liberty and Reformation in the Puritan Revolution.* New York: ~55. Provides material buttressing the overall thesis of this book.

Hamilton, Alexander, James Madison, and John Jay. "The Federalist Papers." Many editions: 1787. Drawn on extensively throughout this volume to illustrate the purpose of the federal government.

Harrison, Everett F. *The Apostolic Church.* Grand Rapids, Mich.: 1985.

Heimert, Alan. *Religion and the American Mind: From the Great Awakening to the Revolution.* Cambridge, Mass.: 1966. Expands on Alice Baldwin's work on the role of the "black regiment" in the American Revolution.

Hill, Christopher. *Milton and the English Revolution.* New York: 1961. Provides quotations and supporting material for Chapter U.

—. *Reformation to Industrial Revolution.* New York: 1967. A readable economic history, useful for Chapter 9.

—. *Society and Puritanism.* New York: 1964.

Hilton, R. H. *The Decline of Serfdom in Medieval England.* London: 1970. Hunt, Gaillard. *James Madison and Religious Liberty.* Washington, D.C.: 1902. Provides important material for Chapter 22.

Jefferson, Thomas. *Autobiography.* Introduction by Dumas Malone. New York: 1959.

—. *The Portable Thomas Jefferson.* Edited by Merrill D. Peterson. New York: 1975 Contains Jefferson's "Notes on the State of Virginia" and his other basic writings.

Johnson, Paul. *A History of the English People.* New York: 1972. Supplies unflattering details for a portrait of King James I in Chapter 5, as well as needed specifics for Chapter 11 on the Puritan Revolution.

—. *A History of Christianity.* New York: 1976. Contains graphic descriptions of early Christian martyrs useful for Chapter 2. Supplies details on how Augustine, Bishop of Hippo, helped provide the intellectual justification for uniting church and state, the aubiect of Chapter 3. A fascinating general narrative of Christianity through the ages.

Johnson, William J. *George Washington, the Christian.* Nashville, Tean.: 1919. Provides details on the much neglected aspects of George Washington's spiritual life, drawn on in these pages.

Jones, A. H. M. *Constantine and the Conversion of Europe.* London: 1948.

Jones, J.R. *The First Whigs: The Politics of the Exclusion Crisis, 1678.1683.* London:1961.

Kirk, Russell. *The Roots of American Order.* l"a Salle, 111.: 1974. An interesting polemic, stressing the virtue of tradition over messianic ideology, generally critical of the Puritan "City on a Hill" vision of the Bible society.

Lacy, Dan. *The Meaning of the American Revolution.* New York: 1964. A solid narrative of events leading up to the break from England and the formation of a new union, with special attention given to economic factors.

LaHaye, Tim. *Faith of Our Founding Fathers.* Breotwood, Tenn.: 1987. A very useful survey of the religious convictions of the framers.

Locke, John. An *Essay Concerning Human Understanding.* Many editions. 1690.

—. *The Reasonableness of Christianity.* Many editions. 1695.

—. *Two Treatises of Civil Government.* Many editions. 1690.

Madison, James. *The Complete Madison: His Basic Writings.* Edited by Saul K Padover. New York: 1953.

—. *Reports of the Debates in the Federal Convention.* Many editions. 1787.

Mair, Paul L. *First Christians: Pentecost and the Spread of Christianity.* New York: 1976.

Malone, Domas. *Jefferson: The Virginian.* Boston: 1948.

—. *Jefferson and The Ordeal of Lii'erty.* Boston: 1962.

Marshall, Peter, and David Manuel. *The Light and the Glory.* Old Tappan, N.J.: 1977. A polemical, but thoroughly researched, work arguing that the hand of God may have directed events leading to the creation of the United States. A source of quotations and useful detail supporting the thesis of this book.

Marty, Martin E. *Pilgrims in Their Own Land: 500 Years of Religion in America.* New York. 1984. A very readable survey of American Christianity.

—.*Religion, Awakening and Revolution.* Wilmington, N.C.: 1977.

—.*The Righteous Empire: The Protestant Experience in America.* New York: 1970.

Mather, Cotton. *Magnalia Christi Americana.* 2 vols. Edited by Kenneth B. Murdock. Cambridge, Mass.: 1977.

May, Henry F. *The Enlightenment in America.* New York: 1976. Provides analysis and particulars on how Protestant and Whig ideas merged to form a distinct American political ideology, drawn on in Chapters 14 and 16.

McDonald, Forrest. *A Constitutional History of the United States.* New York: 1982.

—. *E Pluribus Unum: The Formation of the American Republic 1776-1790.* Boston: 1965.

—. *Novus Ordo Seclorum: The Intellectual Origins of the Constitution.* Lawrence, KanSas: 1985. A landmark study on the ideas that had currency, as well as explaining exactly what occurred at the Constitutional Convention in Philadelphia in 1787 and the subsequent contest for ratification.

McNeill, J. T. *The History and Character of Calvinism.* Oxford: 1954.

Mead, Sidney E. *The Lively Experiment: The Shaping of Christianity in America.* New York: 1963. Provides quotations and supporting detail for Chapters 10 and 22.

Miller, John. *Popery and the Politics of England, 1660-1688.* New York: 1973. An excellent study on religion as the driving force in English politics during the Restoration peried.

Miller, Perry. *Errand into the Wilderness* Cambridge, Mass.: 1956. A slim classic on the Puritans, which proved very helpfil in developing the thesis of Chapter 7 on Thomas Hooker's contribution to democracy in America.

—. *The New England Mind.* 2 vols. New York: 1939.

—. *Jonathan Edwaros.* Cleveland, Oh.: 1959. A thorough, but not entirely sympathetic, study of the mind of America's greatest theologian. Miller's book inspired a resurgence of recent scholarly interest in Edwards.

Miller, Perry, and Alan Heimert, eds. *The Great Awakening.* Indianapolis: 1967.

Momighano, A. D. *The Conflict Between Paganism and Christianity in the Fourth Century.* Oxford: 1963.

Montesquiea, Baron de. *The Spirit of the Laws.* Many editions. 1748.

Morgan, Edmund S. *The Puritan Dilemma.* Boston: 1958.

Morison, Samuel Eliot. *Harvard College in the Seventeenth Century.* 2 vols. Canabridge, Mass.: 1936.

—. *The Oxford History of the American People.* Vols. 1 and 2. New York: 1965. An important factual source on America's early history throughout these pages.

—. *Builders of the Bay Colony.* Boston: 1964. A basic source for Chaptens 6 through 8.

Morley, Felix. *The Power in the People.* New York: 1949. A well-written polemical history making the case for limited government.

Neuhaus, Richard John. *The Naked Public Square.* Grand Rapids, Mich.: 1984. Points out the dangens in obliterating religion of the public life of a nation.

Newnon, Arthur Percival. *The Colonizing Activities of the English Puritans.* New Haven, Corm: 1914. One of the best works on the subject.

Niebuhr, H. R. *The Kingdom of God in America.* New York: 1937.

Nock, Albert Jay. *Jefferson.* New York: 1960.

Noll, Mark A. *Christians in the American Revolution.* Washington, D.C.: 1977.

Ogg, David. *England in the Reign of Charles IL* 2 vols. Oxford: 1934. Provides important narrative information for Chapter 12.

Paine, Thomas. *Common Sense.* Many editions. 1776.

Paolucci, Henry, Sd. *The Political Writings of St. Augustine.* Chicago: 1965.

Parker, T. M. *The English Reformation to 1558.* New York: 1966.

Paul, Rebert S. *The Lord Protector: Religion and Politics in the Life of Oliver Cromwell.* London: 1955.

Perowne, Stewart. *The End of the Roman World.* London: 1966.

Perry, Ralph Barton. *Puritanism and Democracy.* New York: 1944. A sprawling, learned work which was instrumental in shaping this book's thesis on the link between Puritanism and constitutional democracy, and provided many of the particulars illustrating the workings of the Puritan mind cited in Chapters 5 and 6.

Plato. *The Republic.* Many editions. 850 B.C. Drawn on for the sections in Chapter 20 on the difference between the American and Plato's republic.

Plum, Harry Grant. *Restoration Puritanism: A Study of the Growth of English Liberty.* Chapel Hill, N.C.: 1943.

Pollock, John, *George Whitefield and the Great Awakening.* Garden City, N.Y.: 1972. Provides colorfid details on this great evangelist's nnnistry throughout the United States for Chapter 14.

Pound, Roscoe. *The Development of Constitutional Guarantees of Liberty.* New Haven, Conn.: 1957. Provides vital background for any study of the development of American constitutional ideas.

Prall, Stuart E. *The Bloodless Revolution: England, 1688.* Madison, Wisc.: 1985. Provides narrative information and insight into the meaning of events for Chapter 12.

Reichley, James N *Religion in American Public Life.* Washington, D.C.: 1985. Provides material for Chapter 23 supporting the thesis that ancient Greece, the archetype of the civil humanist polity, ultimately fell apart because of the absence of a spiritual bond.

Rosenberg, Nathan, and L. E. Birdsell, Jr. *How The West Grew Rich: The Economic Transformation of the Industrial World.* New York: 1986. Contributes important in-sights and material for Chapter 9 on how Protestant thoology reinforced the capitaiist impulse.

Rossiter, Clinton, *The Grand Convention.* New York: 1966. One of the most relied upon studies of the Constitutional Convention.

—.*Seedtime of the Republic: The Origin of the American Tradition of Political Liberty.* New York: 1953.

Rothbard, Murray N. *Conceived in Liberty.* Vol.1. New Rechelle, N.Y.: 1975.

Rushdoony, Reusas John. *Christianity and the State.* Vallecito, Ca.: 1986. A valuable little book, demonstrating why Christianity is one of the greatest restraining iniluences on government expansion.

—. *The Messianic Character of American Education.* Nutley, N.J.: 1963. Charts the growth of public education in America and its flinction as a government tool of indoctrination into the secular humanist world-view.

Rutman, Darrett B. *Winthrop's Boston.* Williamsburg, Va.: 1965.

Sanders, Thomas G. *Protestant Concepts of Church and State.* New York: 1964.

Schaefer, Francis A. *A Christian Manifesto.* Winchester, Ill.: 1981.

Scott, Otto J. *Robespierre: The Voice of Virtue.* New York: 1974.

Simpson, Alan. *Puritanism in Old and New England.* Chicago: 1955. A largely negative portrait of the Puritan movement.

Singer, C. Greg. *A Theological Interpretation of American History.* Nutley, N.J.: 1969. A study of the role of theology, and specifically Scripture, in shaping the American political and cultural tradition.

Smith, Adam. *An Inquiry into the Natum and Causes of the Wealth of Nations.* Many editions. 1776.

Smith, John H. *Constantine The Great.* London: 197L A mostly favorable portrait of this pivotal Roman emperor, drawn on for Chapter 2.

Smith, M. A. *The Church Under Siege.* Downers Grove, III.: 1976. A useflil account of Christianity during the Dark Ages.

Smith, Page. *A New Age Now Begins: A People's History of *he American Revolution.* 2 vols. New York: 1976. A large, but very readable, narrative history of the American Revolution that supplied details and useflil quotations for Chapters 16 through 19.

Stacy, John. *John Wycliffe and Reform.* London: 1964. Supplies quotations and particulars for Chapter 4.

Starkey, Marion Lona. *The Congregational Way.* Garden City, N.Y.: 1966. A well written narrative of the influence of Congregationalist Christians on American life, drawn on for Chapters 6 through 8.

Stokes, Anson Phelps. *Church and State in the United States.* 3 vols. New York: 1950. Sweet, William W. *Religion in Colonial America.* New York: 1942.

Sydnor, Charles S. *American Revolutionaries in the Making*. New York: 1952. Provides usefiil themes for Chapter 10's assessment of why Virginia produced so many of America's most prominent political leaders during the founding decades.

Tawney, R. H. *Religion and the Rise of Capitalism*. New York: 1926.

Thornton, John W., ed. *The Pulpit and The American Revolution*. Boston: 1860. Contains important sermons of the Revolutionary War period, drawn on for Chapters 16, 17, 18, and 19.

Tocqueville, Alexis de. *Democracy in America*. Many editions. 1835.
　　A classic of political and sociological reporting and analysis, quoted extensively throughout this work:

Tracy, Patricia J. *Jonathan Edwards, Pastor: Religion and Society in Eighteenth Century Northampton*. New York: 1979.

Trevelyan, G.M. *England in the Age of Wycliffe*. London: 1946.

—. *The English Revolution, 1688-1689*. London: 1938. Provides a Wnig interpretation of events, useftil for Chapter 12.

Tindall, George Brown. *America: A Narrative History*. New York: 1984.
　　Very helpftil as a reference for important events.

Tyson, Joseph B. *A Study of Early Chrtstianity*. New York: 1973.

Ver Steeg, Clarence L. *The Formative Years, 16074763*. New York: 1964.
　　An intelligent analysis of the cultural, economic, and religious forces shaping colonial America.

Walsh, Michael, S. J. *The Triumph of the Meek: Why Early Christianity Succeeded*. New York: 1986.

Weber, Max. *The Protestant Ethic and the Spirit of Capitalism: The Relationship Religion and the Economic and Social Life in Modern Culture*. Germany: 1904; reprinted., New York: 1958. A classic study on the psychological conditions that laid the foundation for the emergence of capitaiist society. Weber's thesis forms the core of Chapter 9.

Weiss, J. *Earliest Christianity*. London: 1959.

Wertenhaker, Thomas J. *The Shaping of Colonial Virginia*. New York: 1958.

Western, J. R. *Monarchy and Revolution: The English State in the 1680s*. Totowa, N.J.: 1972. A thorough study of the events and intellectual changes leading to the English Revolution of 1688, providing material and insights for Chapter 12.

Whitehead, John. *The Second American Revolution*. Elgin, 111.: 1982.
　　An excellent polemic arguing for America's return to the original intent of the Constitution, providing material for the section in Chapter 1 on the origin of America's common law tradition.

Wilbur, William H. *The Making of George Washington*. DeLand, Fla.: 1970.

Wills, Garry. *Inventing America: Jefferson's Declaration of Independence*. New York: 1979. Grievously flawed in its analysis of this period in American history, but supplies some useful details.

Wilson, Jr., Vincent. *The Book of Great American Documents*. Brookville, Md.: 1982. An important primary source.

Winslow, Ola Elizabeth. *Jonathan Edwards, 1703-1758*. New York: 1961.
　　The Pulitzer Prize winning biography of the great Puritan divine, providing material for Chapter 14.

Winthrop, John. *History of New England, 1630-1649.2* vols. Edited by James Savage. New York: 1972.
　　A primary source for Chapters 6, 7, and 8.

Wood, Gordon S. *The Creation of the American Republic, 17764787*. Chapel Hill, N.C.:1969. Examines the evolution of an American philosophy of government during the founding period.

Wood, H. G. *Christianity and Civilization*. New York: 1973.

Woodward, W. E. *George Washington: The Image and the Man*. New York: 1926.

Workman, H. B. *John Wyclif A Study of the English Medieval Church*. 2 vols. Oxford:1926. The dellaitive biography drawn on substantially for Chapter 4.

Wright, Esmond. *Fabric of Freedom, 1763.1800*. New York: 1961.
　　A study by a British author of the emergence of American nationalism under the stress of war, useful for Chapter 19.

Wright, Louis B. *First Gentlemen of Virginia*. San Marino, Ca.: 1940.

INDEX